Psychoanalysis in Hong Kong

How is it possible that a phenomenon like psychoanalysis, which has dominated the cultural and intellectual life of the last century in Europe and North and South America, has seemingly had little to no resonance in Hong Kong? This book attempts to explain this phenomenon. Addressing the subject from an East to West approach, this book proposes an experience of displacement, as it is argued that the opportunity for psychoanalysis today is not just to be exported to the East, but rather to be reinvented after an encounter with a radically different culture. This encounter allows the Western practitioner to question their experience and highlights the assumptions of Western thought and knowledge. Following this, what remains of psychoanalysis as we know it? How can psychoanalysis be rethought and re-formed today in a format independent of different theoretical orientations and schools?

The book addresses key issues such as:

- Is there psychoanalysis in Hong Kong?
- How does one do research on psychoanalysis in Hong Kong?
- Why was the Freudian unconscious not discovered in China?
- How can we describe the core of psychoanalysis, and how can this description be understood in different cultural contexts?
- Can psychoanalytic research be led by adopting a quantitative or statistical methodology?

Founded on the belief that psychoanalysis should be reinvented in light of its encounter with non-Western cultures, this book highlights an opportunity to undertake this as an intellectual, cultural, and artistic challenge. It will enrich researchers' and students' understanding of psychoanalysis and inform broader views of psychoanalysis in non-Western contexts. Practicing psychoanalysts, students of psychoanalysis and those seeking to understand psychoanalysis in different cultural contexts will be particularly interested readers.

Diego Busiol is a certified clinical psychologist and psychoanalyst with a private practice in Hong Kong, and a research fellow at the Department of Applied Social Sciences, City University of Hong Kong.

Routledge Studies in Asian Behavioural Sciences
Series Editor: T. Wing Lo, City University of Hong Kong

Archaeology of Psychotherapy in Korea
A study of Korean therapeutic work and professional growth
Haeyoung Jeong

Hidden Youth and the Virtual World
The process of social censure and empowerment
Gloria Hongyee Chan

Psychoanalysis in Hong Kong
The absent, the present, and the reinvented
Diego Busiol

Psychoanalysis in Hong Kong
The absent, the present, and the reinvented

Diego Busiol

LONDON AND NEW YORK

First published 2017
by Routledge
2 Park Square, Milton Park, Abingdon, Oxon OX14 4RN

and by Routledge
711 Third Avenue, New York, NY 10017

First issued in paperback 2018

Routledge is an imprint of the Taylor & Francis Group, an informa business

© 2017 Diego Busiol

The right of Diego Busiol to be identified as author of this work has been asserted by him in accordance with sections 77 and 78 of the Copyright, Designs and Patents Act 1988.

All rights reserved. No part of this book may be reprinted or reproduced or utilised in any form or by any electronic, mechanical, or other means, now known or hereafter invented, including photocopying and recording, or in any information storage or retrieval system, without permission in writing from the publishers.

Trademark notice: Product or corporate names may be trademarks or registered trademarks, and are used only for identification and explanation without intent to infringe.

British Library Cataloguing in Publication Data
A catalog record for this book is available from the British Library

Library of Congress Cataloguing in Publication Data
Names: Busiol, Diego, author.
Title: Psychoanalysis in Hong Kong : the absent, the present, and the reinvented / Diego Busiol.
Description: Abingdon, Oxon; New York, NY : Routledge, 2017. | Includes bibliographical references and index.
Identifiers: LCCN 2016011809 | ISBN 9781138909656 (hardback)
Subjects: LCSH: Psychoanalysis–China–Hong Kong. | Counseling psychology–China–Hong Kong. | Cultural psychiatry–China–Hong Kong.
Classification: LCC RC451.H85 B87 2017 | DDC 616.89/17–dc23
LC record available at https://lccn.loc.gov/2016011809

ISBN 13: 978-1-138-60458-2 (pbk)
ISBN 13: 978-1-138-90965-6 (hbk)

Typeset in Galliard
by Out of House Publishing

Contents

Acknowledgments   vii

Introduction   1

1 **Two apparently distant worlds: psychoanalysis and Hong Kong**   7

   How psychoanalysis was born in Europe   7
   Psychoanalysis in the Chinese context   11
   Hong Kong: history, culture, and society   14
   Past and current situation of counseling in Hong Kong   18
   Basis of Chinese thought and how theories are understood   33

2 **How to do research on psychoanalysis in Hong Kong**   45

   Psychoanalysis and psychotherapy   45
   The analytic attitude: a different listening disposition   50
   What is counseling?   61
   What are the major criticalities against psychoanalysis?   66

3 **The research study**   76

   Introduction   76
   The study   77
   Combining Approaches scale   80
   Psychoanalysis (PACWS) and counseling (CACWS) scales   81
   Psychoanalysis Use/Non-Use scale (PUNU) and Conflicts with Hong Kong Chinese Culture scale (CHKCC)   89
   Predictors: multiple regression analysis   93
   The three components of psychoanalytic listening   98

4 **Is there psychoanalysis in Hong Kong?**   106

   Absence of psychoanalytic theory from Hong Kong   106
   Overview of the listening orientation   110

What factors affect the reception of psychoanalysis? 125
*What factors affect psychoanalytic and counseling dimensions in
    Hong Kong? 128*
*Psychoanalysis: groundbreaking for the West but not
    for the Chinese? 136*
*Different reception of psychoanalysis between Hong Kong, mainland
    China, and Taiwan 138*

5   Why the (Freudian) unconscious was not discovered in China: other and desire in Hong Kong — 147

The Freudian unconscious 147
Individualism and collectivism 148
The subject: highway to the Other 153
Opening 157
Curiosity 161
Psychoanalysis beyond Western discourse and Chinese thought 164

Glossary — 166
References — 173
Index — 190

Acknowledgments

First of all, I would like to thank Prof. LO T. Wing 盧鐵榮 for giving me the opportunity to come to Hong Kong and for supervising this study. I particularly appreciated his wisdom on how to develop this research. Dr. WU, Keung Fai Joseph 胡強輝 was always there to answer my questions about statistics with invaluable kindness and endless patience. From Italy, Dr. Gabriele Lodari has continuously helped me refine my research questions and advance the development of the theory. A number of friends and colleagues in Hong Kong greatly helped me to improve chapters of this book, and I am infinitely grateful for their time and the precious comments they gave me: Prof. Geoffrey Blowers, Prof. Michael Holosko, FANG Luxi 方露茜, Prof. Lawrence Gerstein, Dr. CHEN Hui Fang 陳慧芳, Laura Giavitto, Dr. HUANG Hsuan-Ying 黃宣穎, Dr. FU Wai 符瑋, ZHENG Zhijun 鄭至君, and ZHANG Peichao 張沛超. Finally, I am thankful to all those persons who have taught me without being aware of it: they have been my greatest source of inspiration.

This book is partially based on three previously published articles: "Help-seeking behaviour and attitudes toward counselling: a qualitative study among Hong Kong Chinese university students," *British Journal of Guidance & Counselling*, 44(4), 382–401, "Factors affecting the understanding and use of psychoanalysis in Hong Kong, Mainland China, and Taiwan," *Journal of the American Psychoanalytic Association*, 63(3), 411–435, and "The development of a listening scale," *Research on Social Work Practice* (2016 online ahead of print).

Introduction

My encounter with psychoanalysis occurred at a relatively young age and shaped a significant direction to my life in the following years. At that time, and despite my technical background, I took Clinical Psychology at university (in Italy and Germany). Similarly, a few years after my Master's degree, I started a four-year postgraduate training in psychoanalysis, and set up my practice. One of the most formative experiences, however, was the psychoanalytic association I was part of: Tracce Freudiane. Here I started my formation as analyst. It is here where I attended the first psychoanalytic seminars, and it is here where at some point I published my first articles and delivered my first speeches at conferences.

My interest in psychoanalysis has also led me to work for several years in mental health, mostly in community residences for adult chronic patients and mental health hospitals, and normally with the professional qualification of "social worker," "counselor," or "psychologist," but [unofficially] always as a psychoanalyst in training, meaning someone who tries to listen psychoanalytically to people and the places, the institutions around him. Working in such different environments has also been a great opportunity to become more familiar with the multidisciplinary fields of psychology, social work, psychotherapy, psychiatry, and, of course, psychoanalysis.

Traveling outside of Europe (mainly in non-Western countries), I realized how important it is to encounter a different culture for recognizing one's own culture. We may find our way of thinking "natural" until we encounter a different discourse. Then we have an opportunity to understand that the way we think is rooted in some culture as well, and thus what we think and see is grounded on some assumptions. This perspective is also important for the development of psychoanalytic theory. For example, traveling in Southeast Asia, I became gradually dissatisfied with the explanations offered by some psychoanalysts concerning transsexualism and psychosis; I felt their approach in some cases to be overly dogmatic and universalistic. Instead my observations in such different cultural contexts revealed a wider range of possible theoretical elaborations, and by contrast showed the inconsistencies, limits, and contradictions of "classic" interpretations. It became clear to me that an operation of cultural *relocation* would be needed, so in 2010 I ventured to

Hong Kong. Since then, I have been conducting my research at a university. In Hong Kong, I decided to reside in Mongkok, one of the most densely populated areas in the world, an area which is an expression of the very local culture, and which unsurprisingly has very few Western residents. At university in Hong Kong, quite contrary to my previous experiences in Europe, I found much freedom to experiment, because in Chinese culture, the theory does not suffocate the practice. In fact, Chinese culture has never developed any dogma, preferring a practical attitude to life.

On my arrival here I realized that the great majority of people were totally unaware of psychoanalysis. When I told others that I was a psychoanalyst, most people simply could not understand. Even the name Sigmund Freud, or the term "unconscious," was not familiar to them; apparently, the only term (although minimally related to psychoanalysis) that seemed to give my interlocutors a vague idea of my profession was "counseling."

Talking about psychoanalysis in Hong Kong reminded me of the word-guessing game Taboo, where one has to have others guess the name on a card, without using the word itself or a few additional words. Indeed, how could we describe what psychoanalysis is without using the word psychoanalysis, or related terms like unconscious, Freud, or Oedipus? And on the other hand, how is it possible that a phenomenon like psychoanalysis, which has dominated the cultural and intellectual life of the last century in both Europe and North and South America, is so largely unknown in this part of the world? How is it possible that the revolutionary discovery of the unconscious has had apparently no resonance in Hong Kong?

Some asked me why I was doing research on psychoanalysis in Hong Kong when psychoanalysis is apparently missing here. I would say it is exactly because (only) psychoanalysis is missing that suggests that there is something worth investigating: Is Chinese thought indifferent to psychoanalysis? Is psychoanalysis too distant from Chinese culture? Is it just because of a lack of training opportunities? Or instead, are some characteristics of psychoanalysis already embedded in the Chinese culture?

Hong Kong can become a case study for renewing psychoanalysis; for example, how can we describe the core of psychoanalysis? Can we come to a description of it that can also be understood in a different cultural milieu like this one? If we are able to do so, then it means that psychoanalysis is really different from other counseling approaches. Finally, even though psychoanalytic theory is not expressly cited, can we retrace any aspects of psychoanalysis in Hong Kong and in the way local professionals operate?

Despite psychoanalysis being seemingly largely unknown in Hong Kong, since the first year of my arrival I have tried to see if it could raise some interest. Initially, I had the chance to join a small psychoanalytic reading group composed of four people. We met weekly for six months and then we delivered a conference (see Freund, 2012). The conference received attention from several participants, and thus new study groups about psychoanalysis with new participants, mostly local people, were subsequently organized.

I was rather surprised to see that psychoanalysis could attract so much interest; however, this initial interest for the study of psychoanalytic theory does not necessarily prelude an interest for the understanding or developing of psychoanalysis.

Nowadays, a few Western psychoanalysts come to China to teach psychoanalysis; in most cases they come for a few days, or a few weeks. Although they visit China (some quite regularly), it is difficult to gain a deeper understanding of Chinese culture while still residing elsewhere. I believe their contribution is essential to the development of psychoanalysis here; however, I preferred to move to Hong Kong and experience this culture from the inside. Thus, my perspective is very different; rather than asking how to export psychoanalysis to China? I asked: how can Chinese culture help us to rethink the theories and the practices of psychoanalysis? Psychoanalysis within Chinese contexts is still at an early stage, and original contributions from Chinese psychoanalysts are still limited, and yet to develop. On the other hand, most of the Western literature generally assumes an anthropological or a sinological perspective: from West to East. To me, such a position is theoretically and practically not very interesting. Instead, I think that the encounter with Chinese culture can serve to examine the "unthought" of the Western discourse, its limitations and assumptions, as well as its strengths. Psychoanalysis (which indeed was born precisely as a critique to the prevailing Western discourse) after Freud has been increasingly absorbed by the mainstream, and has lost part of its critical stance towards society; nowadays it is often considered just as a "psychotherapy" among others.

I believe psychoanalysis should be reinvented, particularly in the light of an encounter with a culture grounded on premises totally different from Western cultures, as Chinese culture is. For too long, psychoanalysis has been under attack from many fronts, both in the West and in the East, and it needs to come to a new reformulation. Even the unconscious is being more and more misunderstood and its importance questioned. Psychoanalysis can start in Hong Kong if we are able to understand why its language is not understood, and why psychoanalysis still makes no difference here. Why has psychoanalysis lost its rousing power, and what of the original Freudian invention is lost? Why is the originality of psychoanalysis not understood? And finally, how can psychoanalysis also become essential here in Hong Kong? There remains an opportunity to take this as an intellectual, cultural, and artistic challenge.

Unique features of the text

Existing literature has generally taken a historical perspective on the reception of psychoanalytic theory in China, and this kind of research has usually been carried out by researchers with interests in psychoanalytic theory but who have limited clinical experience as psychoanalysts. Conversely, when clinicians have conducted research on psychoanalysis in a Chinese context, they have mainly focused on how to export psychoanalysis to China, how to teach it effectively to the Chinese, or how to apply it in a Chinese context. Instead, this study was designed and carried out by a researcher who is also a clinician trained in psychoanalysis practicing in Hong Kong. Thus, it was not simply an exploration between psychoanalysis and Chinese culture but a study on psychoanalysis from within a Chinese cultural context.

Further, previous research mostly focused on *psychoanalytic theory* rather than on *psychoanalysis* as a practice. Indeed, it is easy to conclude that there is no psychoanalytic theory in China; however, this study started with a different working hypothesis. It was not taken for granted that a psychoanalytic attitude was totally absent. Instead, the study investigated whether a disposition toward a psychoanalytic attitude existed, or not, among a sample of Hong Kong counseling professionals. This psychoanalytic attitude or disposition has been described in terms of the unique listening that underscores the psychoanalytic method. This is probably the first time a definition and operationalization of psychoanalytic listening was used in this empirical way. It is interesting that, after Freud, only a limited number of psychoanalysts expressly theorized the concept of listening in psychoanalysis. This study is unique because, starting from conceptualizing psychoanalytic listening, it aims at providing a definition of psychoanalysis regardless of different theoretical orientations and schools.

This study has implications that go beyond the focus of psychoanalysis in Hong Kong. First, it has led to a reconceptualization and redefinition of psychoanalysis not just as a "talking cure" but as a "listening cure." *Indeed, one may say that "talking cure" is already a Western interpretation, but no talking can lead to any change if, first of all, a different listening is not activated.* Only after such a theoretical shift was it possible to conduct this cross-cultural research.

Furthermore, it is seemingly impossible to combine psychoanalysis with the use of quantitative statistics. Traditionally, psychoanalysts have overlooked statistics as a method of investigation. Indeed, the psychoanalytic method is rather removed from the assumptions of statistics, and these two methods pursue different goals. However, the statistical methodology adopted has possibly required an even more accurate theoretical background. The construction of a questionnaire is a great exercise because it compels one to conceptualize and operationalize general ideas into precise sentences, and leads one to reformulate and refine again and again the salient research questions on the questionnaire. Building a questionnaire for cross-cultural research that aimed to assess a psychoanalytic dimension, in a place where psychoanalytic theory is largely unknown, was truly a challenge within a challenge. Indeed, the formulation and wording of the items allowed an initial process of revision of the common assumptions about psychoanalysis, what is normally taken for granted. Further, it required a process of continuous reflection about culture in general, about Hong Kong Chinese culture specifically, and about counseling methods, techniques, and theory. Additionally, items needed to be formulated in ways that translated a psychoanalytic attitude without explicitly referring to psychoanalysis (i.e. respondents did not know that the focus of research was specifically on psychoanalysis, but they were told that it was generally about what they used to deliver counseling). Finally, it required a continuous work of translation, which was not just linguistic translation, but more so through a cultural contextual lens, i.e. how to build a tool, in Chinese, for assessing the dimensions of a practice that is not well known or practiced in Hong Kong. In short, it has been an experience of displacement, which required the ability to move simultaneously along two directions: *from west to east, and from east to west.*

The statistical approach used compelled a continuous confrontation with the literature review and interpretation of results. The data obtained allowed for the unmasking and overcoming of stereotypes about, for example, the nature of the (Hong Kong) Chinese culture and its supposed disposition against psychoanalysis. Much of the current literature on Chinese culture is misleading. As this study shows, there is some interest and openness toward psychoanalysis in Hong Kong, although its reception and understanding is strongly mediated by cultural factors and will largely depend on the future availability of training opportunities, personal analysis, and clinical supervision.

Although this was by nature an exploratory research investigation, construction of the questionnaire itself was altogether significant. Factor analysis led to obtaining a clear and simple factor structure in all cases. The internal reliability of the scales was adequate, according to the standards recommended in the literature, and in some cases was very good. Importantly, the correlation between the subscales was generally as expected, meaning that the theory behind the model was largely supported by the results. Then, regression analysis provided some precious empirical hints for the interpretation of results. Altogether, the results debunked the myth that psychoanalytic research cannot be understood by adopting a quantitative/statistical methodology.

Finally, I want to comment on a few aspects that the reader should consider. First, I am European, Italian to be precise. My professional training and my personal psychoanalysis have led me to be familiar with Freud and Lacan more than others. I might say that this is where I come from. In my research I have tried to include different perspectives and psychoanalytic orientations; however, my understanding of psychoanalysis reflects my personal experience and may not be comprehensive of any theoretical approach. Second, I am writing from Hong Kong, which is a unique city with its own features, very different from both mainland China and Taiwan. Hong Kong is a good blend of tradition and modernity, and my understanding of "Chinese culture" is largely based (or biased) on the "Hong Kong Chinese culture." Thus, I do not expect my analyses to apply to other Chinese contexts or to be representative of "Chinese culture" in general (if an ideal-type version of Chinese culture exists), although some generalizations in the text may happen. Similarly, an attentive reader will not overlook the cultural, financial, and social differences between Hong Kong, mainland China, and Taiwan, and s/he will not simply consider Hong Kong as one of the Chinese cities. Instead, as I have tried to highlight several times here, there are a few important (historical, geographical, political) characteristics that make it a unique place. Third, the core of my research journey is a quantitative study that I conducted among Hong Kong counseling professionals; however, this book is much more than just a report of this study. In this book I present a lot more observations and reflections about Hong Kong Chinese culture and psychoanalysis that arose as part of my life and work experience here. Not all ideas and observations became hypotheses or have been directly tested; however, they all contributed to developing the research questions and the hypotheses of the study. I therefore considered it important to include them here. Similarly, the findings have implications that are not limited to psychoanalysis in Hong Kong or China, but are open to reconsidering the theory and practice of psychoanalysis in various contexts. This is to say that the experience is not transmissible and not communicable, whereas instead a story can be told. This is the story of my research journey, and the theory presented in this book is a consequence of this story.

1 Two apparently distant worlds
Psychoanalysis and Hong Kong

At a first perception, psychoanalysis, and only psychoanalysis, is largely unknown in Hong Kong. Both in society and in the clinical context, psychoanalysis has had almost no impact here. This is even more striking when considering that: (1) the great majority of other psychotherapeutic orientations have been received and are normally practiced; (2) Hong Kong was for a long time a colony of Great Britain, and has been (and still is) greatly exposed to Western cultures; and (3) in Taiwan and mainland China, psychoanalysis has traditionally raised some interest, and recently it is increasingly drawing the attention of both clinicians and intellectuals. The questions underpinning this chapter may be summarized as: Is Hong Kong resistant or indifferent to psychoanalysis? Are there any particular characteristics of the Hong Kong culture that hinder the reception of psychoanalysis?

The articulation of such questions requires first of all, retracing the history of psychoanalysis from its birth. Today, there is very little agreement on what psychoanalysis is, even among psychoanalysts. This chapter will explore the context in which psychoanalysis emerged in Europe, and then how it later spread to different countries and cultures, and what this meant for its growth, development, and use. This brief retrospective of psychoanalysis will describe a psychoanalytic attitude and examine the core of what psychoanalysis is, and what psychoanalysis is not. Not only will this help to refine the research questions, it will also help to critically reanalyze some issues emerging from cross-cultural studies, for example, indigenization.

How psychoanalysis was born in Europe

Psychoanalysis was invented in Austria by Sigmund Freud, a neurologist who soon realized the inefficacy of the medical paradigm for treating neuroses and developed a new method for reading the symptoms and in general all the expressions of what he named the unconscious. Thus psychoanalysis was born within a precise cultural, social, and historical context. It is a product of its time (a combination of scientific assumptions and a tragic European view of life, Hansen, 2002), but it also had an enormous influence upon it as well (Eizirik, 1997). In fact, beyond its clinical application, psychoanalysis has represented a strong and profound critique to the dominant discourse* in society.[1] Together with Darwinism and Marxism it has radically changed ways of thinking. It pointed out the limits of the Western discourse and its principle of free will. From the beginning, Freud underlined the crisis of the philosophical subject who was not whole and the master of his faculties as the positivist philosophers used to believe, but rather divided in itself ("The ego is not master in its own house"). This different conception of the subject is one of the main differences between psychoanalysis and other psychotherapies. One of the principal contributions of Freud, the unconscious, has disappeared in most of today's psychotherapies, or has been reconceptualized in cognitive or medical terms.

The crisis: some notes on how psychoanalysis emerged in Europe

Psychoanalysis arose in a situation of deep philosophical, societal, and individual *crisis*, and developed as one of the main instruments for assuming, thinking, and investigating such crisis. Society was in turmoil, at every level, and the past paradigm was no longer able to provide the answers that society needed. The crisis was unavoidable, and psychoanalysis became one of the elective instruments for investigating it and potentially turning the individual crisis into opportunities for advancement. However, this crisis reflected an intrinsic and structural crisis of the *subject*; it was not simply the effect of a temporary condition. With the theorization of the unconscious, psychoanalysis was finally able to provide a new theoretical framework for understanding a broad range of phenomena in different fields of humanities, science, arts, and languages. Finally, it was possible to subvert the positivist paradigm. However, can we retrace in Hong Kong the same premises that opened the way to psychoanalysis in Europe over a hundred years ago? Are we at any point of paradigm change? And how, then, is the *crisis* understood in Hong Kong?

The rise of psychoanalysis in Europe is very much in line with what Kuhn (1962) says about the structure of scientific revolutions in Western cultures, where a new paradigm comes and subverts the old one, when the old one is no longer satisfying. However, it is possible that this alternation of paradigms is not as universal; Chinese culture is not foreign to science, particularly today, but it may be distant from the kind of *revolutions* described by Kuhn, as moments of deep rupture and subversion of the ongoing thinking (Huff, 1993; Needham, 1956; Sivin, 1982). For instance, Chinese culture is known for being the oldest culture on Earth, with a high degree of stability and continuity of traditions and conservatism. Thus *it may be that the "subversive" and critical power of psychoanalysis is not particularly appealing to Chinese culture, at least not today in Hong Kong.*

Invention and diffusion of psychoanalysis

Sigmund Freud gave birth to psychoanalysis with his revolutionary "Analysis of dreams" in 1900. After him, there has been a proliferation of different approaches that today we conventionally consider under the umbrella of psychotherapies. Although Freud stated that psychoanalysis was not just an art of therapy, psychoanalysis is probably most known for its application in the clinical setting.

No psychotherapy has aroused such contradictory reactions, on both a social and political level, as psychoanalysis did. This is probably a sign that psychoanalysis has always been something very different, something more than just one form of psychotherapy among others. Indeed, in some countries, psychoanalysis has had a big following, for certain periods being literally in fashion; in other countries, particularly under dictatorships, psychoanalysis was banned by governments, which considered it potentially dangerous to their cause. Looking at the history, it is easy to see that psychoanalysis has always found fertile ground in democratic countries, whereas it has always been banished in totalitarian regimes. In general, psychoanalysis acted as a form of resistance and critic to the mainstream. Indeed, the reasons why dictatorships (which are always very attentive to keep control over society, mainly by limiting free speech) consider psychoanalysis a risk should not be overlooked. It may be because the goal of psychoanalysis is not just restoring the person to a predetermined order; it may be because psychoanalysis does not simply aim at fixing the conflicts of a person with his/her environment; it may be because psychoanalysis aims at developing a person's critical thinking; because psychoanalysis aims at enhancing individual differences that come from unconscious desires rather than adaptation to the mass and social conformity. Psychoanalysis, more than any other psychotherapy, could tell us something about a society, its underlying ideals, the attitude of its people, the relations between the individual and the society, and the dominant discourse. Potentially, this is a question that goes beyond just the field of counseling and can open up opportunities for broader speculations.

The history of psychoanalysis is inevitably tied to the Western discourse, and to different paradigms underlying Western societies. The Western discourse, which originates from Plato and Aristotelian logic, is logocentric, based on reasoning and the laws of causation. The Western discourse is gnostic and ideological and aims at identifying the fundamentals, the principles, and the universals. It is substantialist, in that it proceeds by concepts, ideas, and "things." It represents death, and in fact things are thought to have an origin and an end. The Western discourse considers speech* nothing more than a medium of communication: this is the essence of *discourse*, which is closed in itself. Another consequence of being a discourse is that it is more inclined to produce answers, slogans, and statements rather than questions that could possibly show its paradoxes and inconsistencies. The experience of psychoanalysis goes in the opposite direction, showing that the unconscious cannot simply conform to the mainstream discourse. For this reason, there cannot be anything like a "psychoanalytic discourse." Psychoanalysis begins at the margins of the Western discourse, partially as a critique to it (Verdiglione, 1986, 1992).

The diffusion of psychoanalysis around the world was not casual, nor merely geographical, but cultural and linguistic; it has traveled particular routes and is tied to specific cultural and historical conditions. Translation of psychoanalysis into other languages and cultures, its transformations into other form of psychotherapies, and even its rejection tell us much about changes in societies, values, and dominating discourses. In some countries, psychoanalysis has had a profound influence over intellectual life, while in others its remains almost unknown after more than a hundred years. For instance, it has had certain success in Great Britain, where Freud spent the last years of his life. It has had a certain fortune in France too, while it encountered more obstacles in Italy, first because of fascism and later because of the opposition of the Church. One of the first countries to acknowledge psychoanalysis, Russia, was also one of the first to forbid its practice, since it was not functional to support the construction of the "new man" of communism. To the same end, in Germany, where a "Jewish" scientist (as Freud was) could not have any right of citizenship, it arrived only after a certain delay. Several scholars exported psychoanalysis to the United States when they had to migrate there because of the persecution they suffered in Europe (many of the first psychoanalysts were also Jewish). In the States, psychoanalysis "underwent a transformation that was also consistent with the American value system. [...] American psychoanalysis emphasized adaptation to one's environment (i.e. ego psychology; Hartmann) far more than the tragic dimensions of living that were originally underscored by Freud" (Hansen, 2002, p. 319). Though it undoubtedly had a certain success, it also ended up different from the Freudian version. The goals of analysis and its spirit changed in accordance with the American way of life. Some suggest that attention to theory also diminished, and new ideas developed from some particular thinkers, rather than a scientific discourse, so that today instead of a real and fruitful pluralism, we have a plurality of orthodoxies (Cooper, 2008).

Nowadays we assist the diffusion of the Western discourse in non-Western countries, in what is called *Westernization*. Is Hong Kong Westernized? What is the dominant discourse in Hong Kong? Westernization means significant changes in people's lifestyles, desires, expectations, and, not surprisingly, also new social problems and psychological symptoms. Even though these theories arose in very different environments, different times, and are grounded in very different premises, they are now being adopted and applied in the context of Hong Kong. Interestingly, some schools grew more than others, while apparently psychoanalysis did not develop at all. How is this possible? It is possible that psychoanalysis does not represent anything new to Chinese culture? Psychoanalysis represented a turning point in Western culture, a break with the traditional thought; but it may be the case that it is not as relevant to Hong Kong. It may be that psychoanalysis is too distant from the local culture. Or instead, it may be the case that some characteristics of psychoanalysis are already embedded in the local culture, under a different name. Following this, one question is: does the practice of the local counselors show any similarities and contiguity to a psychoanalytic attitude? Exploring the discourse sustaining the practice of counseling in Hong Kong, how counseling is intended, and how theories are assimilated, this study aims to understand the causes of this general indifference toward psychoanalysis.

Another important factor which determines the diffusion of psychoanalysis is of course the language. We can see that different schools proliferate more in some countries than others; psychoanalysis has spread differently in the Anglo-Saxon world than in Latin and South American countries. This is probably due to the different role of speech given by philosophical tradition, and by the cultural attitude of these countries. This also should be taken into account, particularly when considering such a different linguistic system as Chinese. However, the diffusion of psychoanalysis in the Chinese world is a very interesting case; apparently it is able to raise some interest in mainland China and Taiwan, whereas it is absent in Hong Kong. It is not possible to simply speak of a generic Chinese culture that would be opposed to psychoanalysis; the phenomenon is likely more complex.

Psychoanalysis in the Chinese context

Between 1920 and 1949 there was a wide reception of psychoanalytic ideas in China (Blowers, 1997; Larson, 2009). Just as in Europe or America, Freud's work was acknowledged mainly outside academic circles, which were dominated instead by behavioral theories. Most of the leading intellectuals used and discussed psychoanalytic concepts in their works (Zhang, 2003), and some of Freud's works were translated into Chinese (Zhang, 1992). Eminent writers like Lu Xun (among others) took inspiration from psychoanalysis (Huang, 2015). It was during the thirties that China had its first psychoanalyst, Dr. Bingham Dai, a psychiatrist of Chinese origin who received his training from Stack Sullivan in New York and from Leon Saul in Chicago before returning to China to work at the Peking Union Medical College from 1935 to 1939 (Blowers, 2003; Varvin & Gerlach, 2014). Psychoanalysis was becoming popular in China, likely more as an instrument for pointing out the weaknesses of society than as a therapy.

Reception of psychoanalysis was initially distorted because of some misunderstanding of its theoretical basis: the very concept of "psyche" does not belong to Chinese culture (Graziani, 2007; Qian, Smith, Chen, & Xia, 2002; Sun, 1991), and as such is difficult to render. Concepts like "symbol" or "censorship" were considered "mystery of the mystery" (Blowers, 1997) and on top of this, some early translations of Freud's works came from other languages, such as English or Japanese, which contributed to creating some confusion (Zhang, 1992). Some intellectuals like Zhang Dongsung have tried to introduce psychoanalysis to China, perceiving that psychoanalysis could serve to build a new and developing society. Unfortunately, in such efforts to adapt psychoanalysis to Chinese society and its culture, they distorted the former, proposing sublimation (which is originally a defense mechanism) as a way of social reform, or claiming that the goal of psychoanalysis was "to eliminate the human desire" (Blowers, 1997). In any case, with the founding of the People's Republic of China in 1949, psychoanalysis was no longer useful for political causes, and as such was criticized as an element of bourgeois ideology and was summarily rejected for many years. As observed by Zhang (1992, p. 155):

> the implications of psychoanalytic ideas and assumptions of ideas about individuality and society have induced the government to view Freudian psychoanalysis as a threat to the socialist structure. Freud has been put on trial time and again, during almost all major official political campaigns against the infiltration of Western ideology into China.

As happened in the Soviet Union, psychoanalysis in China was criticized, with Pavlovian experimental psychology being adopted as the official doctrine:

> While rejecting "bourgeois" emphasis on subjectivity and personality, the 1930–40s essays and talks of Mao Zedong stressed the importance of human will, and in the 1950s, psychology was one discipline charged with theorizing this focus. Revolutionary Chinese psychology valorized the Leninist notions of reflection and recognition, both of which demanded a keen awareness of position, and also consciousness as opposed to the unconscious, social contextualization as opposed to the isolated interior mind, and jingshen (often translated as "spirit") as opposed to the sexual.
> (Larson, 2009, pp. 5–6)

Only after the intellectual reopening in the 1980s did psychoanalysis begin its revival (Zhang, 2003). According to Larson, during the 1980s, "a 'Freud fever' broke out again, with some replay of ideas and interpretations that had been popular in the 1920s" (p. 33). Huang (2015) observes that this "fever" was transient. However, it is during these years that the first Western psychoanalysts went to China. In 1988 the first Chinese–German Symposium for Psychotherapy was held in Kunming, and in 1990 and 1994, similar international conferences were replicated in Qingdao and Hangzhou. From 1997 to 1999, the group organized more intense training, which was delivered twice a year, in different cities of China (Xu, Qiu, Chen, & Xiao, 2014). Between 2000 and 2010, similar training was offered at the Shanghai Mental Health Center. From 2006, a three- to four-year training program has been implemented in Beijing and Wuhan by the Norwegian Psychoanalytic Society. The program is delivered twice a year (similar to the previous Sino-German course) and includes lectures, and group and individual supervision. Finally, here, from 2008, the China American Psychoanalytic Alliance (CAPA) started a two-year program in psychoanalytic psychotherapy, where most of the training, as well as the personal analysis, is conducted using Skype, in addition to intense face-to-face training conducted yearly in China (Varvin & Gerlach, 2014; Kirsner & Snyder, 2009).

The situation in Taiwan is more complex (Rascovsky, 2006); for several years, psychoanalysis has been present in some university departments of literature and philosophy, and not only among therapists or psychiatrists. According to Liu (2013a), in the last four decades, psychoanalysis has been drawing the attention of intellectuals in Taiwan, and some of the classic works of Freud have been translated into Chinese, mainly by medical students or young psychiatrists; however, the main problem was setting up proper training, so that many candidate psychoanalysts went to London, Paris, or the USA in order to pursue a proper formation and their own analysis. According to Liu (in Thomson-Salo, 2013), in Taiwan, psychoanalysis benefits from at least two conditions: on the one hand, psychoanalysis and psychotherapy are seen as linked with medicine, because something tangible can be financially subsidized by the government; on the other hand, Buddhism and Daoism may predispose people to endure suffering in a difficult phase in an analysis. The development of psychoanalysis among professionals has also been possible thanks to various psychoanalysts who visit Taiwan; today, a diversity of psychoanalytic approaches like Kleinian and Bionian concepts about primitive processes, and French psychoanalysis has been received; Jungians are also active in Taiwan with a training program. Finally, it is possible to say that psychoanalysis in Taiwan has emerged as the most elite among all kinds of psychotherapies, and the psychoanalytic movement – mostly led by psychiatrists – has remained small, but it has built up a few institutes or centers that have regular activities. In addition, psychoanalysis can be found in major universities like the National Taiwan University or the National Chiao Tung University, where certain psychoanalysis (Lacan, Zizek) is applied to literature, gender studies, philosophy, social studies, and cultural studies and where the clinic gains a broader meaning than the therapeutic technique. Psychoanalysis assumes a societal relevance, and enters departments such as the Department of Foreign Languages and Literature, or the Institute for Social Research and Cultural Studies (most professors in these departments received their Ph.D. abroad). This is not an isolated case, and it is similar to the situation in Europe or America; in many Western universities, psychoanalysis finds more appreciation in departments of humanities in general (philosophy, literature, arts, and media) than under psychology specifically, where the mainstream is represented by cognitive and behavioral sciences.

To conclude, Hong Kong represents an unknown. Surprisingly, here the word "psychoanalysis" means little to most people. Both in society and in the clinical context, psychoanalysis has had little impact there. Contrary to China and Taiwan, there is not even a single psychoanalytic association. Nobody who claims to be a psychotherapist professes himself as a psychoanalyst. Some university programs make some reference to psychoanalysis, as a brief theoretical introduction; some of the students do not know who Freud is. Although some therapists have been trained abroad in psychoanalysis, they seem to operate quite differently upon their return, as if they have to adapt to the local context. Chan and Lee (1995) conducted a survey among psychologists in Hong Kong, which reported that the most commonly endorsed orientation was behavioral/cognitive, followed by existential/humanistic. Two years later, Cheung (1997) confirmed that psychoanalysis was not very popular in Hong Kong; although most professionals did claim to have a general understanding of psychoanalysis, and some could even make use of some psychoanalytical concepts in their practice, practically none of them had a strong foundation in psychoanalysis and operated purely as psychoanalysts. In many cases there might be some interest in some psychoanalytical concepts or in the psychoanalytic technique, but then psychoanalysis was at best practiced in association with other orientations/techniques. Paradoxically, given the earlier exposure of Hong Kong to the West, one should expect to find the highest interest toward psychoanalysis here, yet this is not the case. It is difficult to understand whether there is no psychoanalysis because there is no demand for it, or whether, on the contrary, there is no demand because psychoanalysis is unknown to individuals.

Hong Kong: history, culture, and society

In less than a century Hong Kong transformed from a fishing village with a deep-water harbor to a post-industrial, world-class financial hub. While mainland China was undergoing the Cultural Revolution (1966–1976), Hong Kong was a British colony (from 1841–1997) and its annual economic growth rate was 7 percent, the fifth highest rate in the world. Since 1997, Hong Kong has been a Special Administrative Region of the People's Republic of China. It has a population of more than seven million people and is one of the most densely populated cities in the world, with many high-rise buildings; not surprisingly, it is also famous for exorbitant prices and small residential units. Hong Kong is a cosmopolitan city. Today, Hong Kong's economy is regarded internationally as one of the top free-market economic venues in the world (Heritage Foundation, 2014).

Being a trilingual (Cantonese, English, and Mandarin) and bi-literate (Chinese and English) society, it is commonly described as "a place where East and West meet." However, Hong Kong's pluri-cultural identity cannot be defined unambiguously (Busiol, 2012a); instead, it seems to be very extreme. In the late 1960s, the city was described as "superficially Westernized but deeply Chinese" (Agassi & Jarvie, 1969, p. 152), and today this is possibly even more evident. Likely, Hong Kong is *more Westernized than the West* (at least compared to Italy or Europe), and *more Chinese than mainland China*. It is Westernized (or most likely *Americanized*, see Watters, 2010) in the way it ideally assumes and exacerbates all the values founding the Western discourse: technique and technology, capitalism, happiness, results, efficiency, a fast-paced life (Wang, 2007). At the same time, it remains very traditional because it did not experience the Cultural Revolution and has maintained very traditional Chinese values, structure of social relationships, family organization, attitude to speaking, and relations between genders. Tsang (2004) suggests that Hongkongers "*remain quintessentially Chinese* and yet share a way of life, core values and an outlook that resemble at least as much, if not more, that of the average New Yorker or Londoner, rather than that of their compatriots in China" (p. ix). It has been described as "the city that never sleeps" (Cagape, 2007); in such a fast-paced environment, there are many pressures on individuals, such as long working hours, lack of private and public space, and rapidly escalating property prices (Yuen, Leung, & Chan, 2014). Despite the fact that majority of Hong Kong citizens do not feel content with their quality of life, materialistic and familial values still trump post-materialistic ones. This historic emphasis on longstanding materialistic and familial values has been used to explain the lack of democratic, environmental, and spiritual movements in Hong Kong (Sing, 2009). However, in recent years, in conjunction with the handover to China in 1997, the transition to a post-industrial economy and the consequent increase in social inequality and job insecurity, a value change in Hong Kong (albeit slow) has been observed, particularly among the new generations. Several indicators report a shift from basic-needs issues to values of self-expression and political participation, a greater concern for quality of life and issues such as environmental protection, education, and health services (for a review, see Ma, 2011). Hong Kong aspires to be a regional education hub, and in its eight universities (of which four are ranked among the top hundred in the world), English is the only teaching medium. These universities are mostly known for hosting many of the world's best programs in finance, accounting, banking, law, tourism management, and science and technology; again, this orientation reflects the money-oriented and practical nature of Hong Kong.

Immigration in Hong Kong

Throughout history, Hong Kong has been mainly a transit point and a major hub for business and has never been the site of exceptionally prolific and varied artistic activity. For various reasons, its people developed a rather practical attitude toward life and showed little interest in more intangible expressions of culture. This background may also help us to understand why psychoanalysis was not well received here.

From its inception, Hong Kong has been a society of immigrants, particularly from Guandong province in the south of China. Initially, the very first settlers who came to Hong Kong were not wealthy Chinese of respectable background but more likely the "scum" of Chinese society (Lau & Kuan, 1988). Later, Hong Kong became a city of refugees as well. Some

750,000 people entered Hong Kong between 1937 and 1941 to escape the Sino Japanese War (Young, 1992); then, massive flows of illegal immigrants occurred repeatedly in 1949–1952, 1958–1962, 1967–1973 and 1979–1980. They were in search of refuge for political reasons (i.e. anti-communist Kuomintang officials in 1949), capitalists, or simply people "pushed" by specific developments in China (Ma & Cartier, 2003; Ku, 2004). Thus, immigrants to Hong Kong had a very distinctive socio-cultural profile, different from that of China.

When an elite started to emerge in Hong Kong, this was made up of contractors, merchants, government servants, compradores, and missionaries. Oftentimes, members of the Hong Kong elite came from humble origins, meaning that this was a land of opportunity. However, in contrast to mainland China, elite status in Hong Kong "was not based on cultural accomplishment (for example, distinction in Confucian learning), moral excellence, or political achievements, but, most importantly, on economic success" (Lau & Kuan, 1988, p. 36). Confucian values continued to influence Hong Kong society, but these were mainly maintained more by social customs and family socialization than by any institutional underpinnings. Kwan and Ng (1999) observed that during the 1960s, 1970s and 1980s, in Hong Kong expenditure on tertiary education was dismal when compared with Taiwan, Singapore, and South Korea. Ting and Chiu (2000) observed that, in this context, "education served more as a means for social success than for moral development. These trends began to change in the early 1990s when the decolonization process gained momentum" (p. 23).

Most likely, these first immigrants to Hong Kong had very concrete exigencies of survival (i.e. immigrants had to rely on themselves in adjusting to the new environment), so that their values were different from their counterparts in mainland China. Some suggested that materialism (concern for economic security and basic needs above social ideals) and "utilitarianistic familism" (the tendency to place one's familial interests above the interests of society, or other individuals and groups) ran rampant in the economically based Hong Kong, and were not counterbalanced by "spiritual" and moral values so pervasive in traditional China; thus, the Hong Kong elites were often described as having a shaky moral status and no sense of cultural or moral mission (Lau & Kuan, 1988). On the other hand, these structural and developmental conditions converged to foster other features, such as a utilitarian familism as the dominant cultural code of the Chinese in Hong Kong, a suspicious attitude toward outsiders and distrust of them, and limited involvement with co-workers, neighbors, and friends, and low social involvement with others (Liu, 1984).

Chinese vs Hong Kong identity

For more than a century, the majority of the people living in Hong Kong were born elsewhere. According to Price and Ho (2012, p. 5):

the Hong Kong populace resembled streams with many currents rather than a single pool; it was a collection of essentially transient Chinese people from a variety of Han ethnic subgroups who moved frequently in and out of the territory according to timeless reasons including family responsibilities, political persecution, festivals and changed business circumstances.

Until the Second World War, in the British imaginary all Chinese were viewed as a single, broad, and undifferentiated Chinese "race." During the 1950s and the 1960s, no Hong Kong identity had yet developed among the people residing in the city (Ku, 2004). However, the border closure in the early 1960s and British assimilation of extant refugee populations started to create the Hong Kong identity on a foundation of mainlander "otherness."

A more distinctive sense of local identity had emerged by the 1970s. In 1971 the notion of the "Hong Kong belonger" was introduced in local immigration law; this was the first attempt (by the British government) to define the rights to reside in terms of a positive identity category. However, this created a group (in the everyday term, the "Hong Kong people") that was politically and culturally different from both Chinese residents and British. Gradually, by the 1970s, immigrants were represented as a burden and a threat to the existing order. Thus, Hong Kong people and Hong Kong identity were constructed as a group of "us" sharing similar history and aspirations, different from the generalized "other" represented by "mainlanders" (Ku, 2004).

Today, Hongkongers hardly recognize themselves as being part of China, although the feeling of being ethnically Chinese remains relatively strong. It seems that identification with mainland China and to what it represents is no longer possible. The University of Hong Kong conducts an annual survey to assess the people's ethnic identity. Results from 2014 show that Hong Kong people's feelings are strongest as "Hongkongers," followed by "Asians," "members of the Chinese race," "global citizens," "Chinese," and finally, "citizens of the PRC." Particularly, the proportion of people identifying themselves as "Hongkongers" outnumbers that of "citizens of the PRC" by 24 percentage points and that of "Chinese" in a broad sense by 34 points, a gap that is at its highest since the compilation of these indices (Public Opinion Program, the University of Hong Kong, 2014).

Hong Kong people's adherence to their particular cultural identity is also reflected in its languages. Cantonese is their mother tongue, followed by English, with Mandarin being only the third option. After it was returned to the sovereignty of the People's Republic of China by the British in July 1997, the Hong Kong Government announced a trilingual policy with the intention of training a new trilingual generation of students being able to speak Cantonese, Mandarin, and English fluently. This imposition of learning Mandarin created concerns among the population of Hong Kong. In an interesting study, Lai (2001) correlated the language spoken by people from the middle and working classes with their sense of identity, and concluded that "if Putonghua [Mandarin] is used as a means to hasten national unity, the respondents in this survey, mainly the middle-class group, tend to reject the idea" (Lai, 2001, p. 129). Finally, he noted that since language is power, as long as Hong Kong people still believe that they are superior to the mainland Chinese, it is not likely that Mandarin will replace any of the roles that Cantonese and English are playing in society without much government imposition.

Past and current situation of counseling in Hong Kong

In Hong Kong the word "psychoanalysis" is not very well known to the majority of people, whereas the term "counseling" is widely recognized. What is the meaning of "counseling," and how is it translated in Mandarin, and in Cantonese? A brief linguistic analysis can give us some hints about the premises founding the discourse that sustains and shapes the practice of counseling in Hong Kong. In Italian and in English, counseling has quite a broad definition, referring to general advice, counsel, deliberations, and thoughts. It comes from the Latin *consilium*, meaning "plan, opinion." A counselor, or a consultant, can be any professional giving advice in any field, for example in law. It is someone "who knows," who has a knowledge, and from whose position should be able to provide precise answers and advice. Interestingly, for mainland China, Hong Kong, and Taiwan three different translations of counseling are used:

- Zī xún 咨询 / 諮詢 (simplified/traditional Chinese): Mainly used in mainland China, it refers to the idea of "asking, posing questions" to some expert. It may refer to different kinds of consultations, not only within the psychological field.
- Fu dou 辅导 / 輔導: Commonly used in Hong Kong, it expresses the attitude of "giving guidelines, advice." It also implies a disciplined master, someone who can indicate the way; in a broader context, a counselor for example, can be interpreted by this definition as an educational counselor in an academic context. In mainland China, this term often indicates "guidance" toward one's political behavior, particularly in universities in more remote cities.
- Zī shāng 咨商 / 諮商: Used in Taiwan, it refers more generally to a discussion, for example to a business discussion. Unlike the first two terms, this definition seems to imply a more equal relation, in which no one is the master.

With regard to Hong Kong, the term chosen expresses even more clearly what the outcomes of the process should be, and who should provide them. Counseling is not just the process of asking questions; in Hong Kong counseling becomes precisely producing advice, giving guidelines, instructions, and answers (Lin, 2001).

Despite the emergence of counseling in Hong Kong during the 1960s, it is still underdeveloped, possibly because of a lack of public understanding of its importance (Leung, 1999; Yuen et al., 2014). A recent study on the public perception and understanding of counselors and counseling in Hong Kong revealed that the majority of citizens did not know a counselor, had not experienced counseling, and were not willing to do so (Yu, Fu, Zhao, & Davey, 2010). Further, the general public was simply unaware of what counseling psychology was, what counseling psychologists do, and what exactly the distinction is among the overlapping fields of psychological, counseling, and social service disciplines. Many people simply find it hard to understand that professionals may use only speech in their work, and that they would not prescribe any additional treatment: it is something very distant from the practical attitude of Hong Kong. Previous studies in Hong Kong have shown that general feelings associated with help-seeking were shame, uneasiness of showing one's own weaknesses, fear of being labeled and losing face, and worries about the helper's trustworthiness (Rudowicz & Au, 2001), or being afraid to disturb others (Mok, Kennedy, Moore, Shan, & Leung, 2008).

Counseling is normally associated with school counseling, career counseling, and community counseling, and is delivered primarily by social workers, then clinical psychologists, counselors, or psychiatrists, and at times even by teachers (Leung, Chan, & Leahy, 2007). In Hong Kong, there is a shortage of psychiatrists, especially in the public mental health sector (Ng & Li, 2010; Wong, 2013), and currently there are only about 300 psychiatrists serving a population of over 7 million people (WHO, 2011), whereas the Social Workers Registration Board accounts for more than 18,000 members. In short, social workers represent the majority of those actively counseling vulnerable clients in Hong Kong. This is because counseling was first formally introduced as one of the responsibilities of social workers (Hong Kong Council of Social Service, 1979). Thus, normally in Hong Kong, most people identify "counselors" as what we term "psychotherapists" and, more specifically, they deem "counselors" to be "social workers." Further, counselors work in various settings such as schools, universities, healthcare agencies, family and youth centers, rehabilitation agencies, service centers for the elderly, and private practice. In such settings, counselors provide services to clients who present with a wide spectrum of needs, ranging from acute problems to chronic ones.

When compared to other counselors from the US, Korea, Japan, and the Philippines, Hong Kong counselors suffer a higher level of burnout (feeling exhausted, overstressed, and tired most of the time) due to the nature and demands of counseling work (Puig, Yoon, Callueng, An, & Lee 2014). Finally, here, it is interesting that a large number of counselors and many organizations offering counseling in Hong Kong are founded on Christianity.

Perhaps, according to Leung et al. (2007, p. 60):

> due to their early entrance into Hong Kong's mental health arena, social workers have generally been regarded as the professional group best equipped to provide counseling to the general population. [...] However, counseling skills and psychological interventions may not be the major strengths of social workers because their training at the undergraduate level has to encompass a broad array of social service and system issues.

Training opportunities in counseling are quite scarce. Only in the past few years has there been a significant change in this trend, and the counseling profession in Hong Kong still remains undeveloped. Many professionals offering and teaching counseling have multicultural and cross-cultural experience because they were trained in different parts of the world, including the United States, Canada, Europe, and Australia (Leung et al., 2007). It is understandable that these first professionals have "imported" the theories and the knowledge they have acquired during their training. Since we are speaking mainly of English-speaking countries, the mainstreams, in particular in the academic world, such theories were first of all behavioral therapy, Cognitive Psychology, Person-Centered (Rogerian) Therapy, Narrative Therapy, Positive Psychology and Brief Therapy. It is unsurprising, then, that these orientations, and those derived from them, are now the most known and practiced in Hong Kong.

Variables hindering the development of counseling in Hong Kong

When I first arrived in Hong Kong and realized that talking to a counselor was seldom an option for people, I tried to understand what factors could affect this pattern, and what alternative strategies for receiving support Hong Kong people adopted. Results from several studies have shown that Chinese students in Hong Kong, China, Taiwan, and North America underutilize professional psychological and counseling services, even given a certain awareness of needing formal help (e.g. Busiol, 2016; Chang, 2008; Chang, Tong, Shi, & Zeng, 2005). Asian Americans are reported to have less favorable help-seeking attitudes, lower levels of stigma tolerance, greater mental health stigma and greater self-concealment than European Americans (Masuda & Boone, 2011). Chinese international students in the UK reported significantly less interpersonal openness than that reported by British home students (Tang, Reilly, & Dickson, 2012). Chinese culture also emerges as a major factor in explaining the differences in mental health consultation among Chinese immigrants in Canada, Canadian-born Chinese, and White Canadians (Chen, Kazanjian, & Wong, 2009). Generally speaking, a lower adherence to Asian values is often associated with a more positive help-seeking attitude (Shea & Yeh, 2008). A study from Boey (1999) among Chinese university students shows that they generally prefer managing problems alone, and if help is absolutely required, they might ask friends. Generally, however, support from professionals is not sought, even when it would be beneficial. Other studies on community samples demonstrated that only 5 percent of respondents sought formal help (Kung, 2003).

From my initial research in the field and an extensive literature review, several cultural and social issues emerged that may limit the development of various forms of counseling emerged. These are presented below. Other factors, which may be particularly critical for the reception of psychoanalysis (among counseling professionals), will be presented in the Chapter 2.

Attitude toward speech

Historically, Chinese culture has developed a very different attitude toward speech than has the Greek-Christian tradition. Furthermore, the power-status of Chinese words is much more modest in contrast to Western traditions such as the Judeo-Christian and the Islamic, all of which place strong emphasis on the "Word" as message from the divinity, located in some kind of sacred text. Greek thought arose around the notion of *logos*, which throughout time referred to: word, speech, account, reasoned discourse, the principle of order and knowledge. The ancient Greeks also celebrated rhetoric and speech as the way for gaining knowledge and accessing the truth. For Christianity the word is the principle of life itself, as the word was used to found the universe. The gospel by John begins with the well-known statement: "In the beginning was the Word, and the Word was with God, and the Word was God."

In China things have been different. In general, Chinese thinkers who have reflected on language were primarily interested in the pragmatic aspects of the relation between language and those who use it, rather than the semantic aspect of its relation with reality. In other words, language matters on account of its regulatory function rather than the descriptive function favored by the Aristotelian tradition. Instead of questioning whether a proposition is true or false, Chinese thinkers ask what effect a certain belief would be able to exercise, or what moral and social implications may result from a given proposition. The use of the word tends to be rather utilitarian, instrumental; it serves for communicating and exchanging information, and not for the pleasure of speaking.

Confucianism emphasized societal structure and relations among individuals. If in the West the word was founding the world, on the contrary, Confucius* in the *Analects* (*Lunyu* 論語) reduced the word to a tool for communicating (15.41 – 辭達而已矣), and recommended using it sparingly (Slingerland, 2003):

【十九章】【一節】子曰、予欲無言。子貢曰、子如不言、則小子何述焉。
【三節】子曰、天何言哉、四時行焉、百物生焉、天何言哉。

> 17.19 The Master sighed, "Would that I did not have to speak!"
>
> Zigong said, "If the Master did not speak, then how would we little ones receive guidance from you?"
>
> The Master replied, "What does Heaven ever say? Yet the four seasons are put in motion by it, and the myriad creatures receive their life from it. What does Heaven ever say?"

Confucius was not interested in discussion or conversation. He scolded his students when they kept trying to refute him. Confucius argued that it was exactly their interest in the word (*ning*) that would prevent them from "understanding" (Slingerland, 2003). The word is not what opens us up to new word, instead, it becomes something to avoid:

> 【第四章】【一節】或曰、雍也仁、而不佞。【二節】子曰、焉用佞、禦人以口給、屢憎於人、不知其仁、焉用佞。
>
> 5.5 Someone said, "Zhonggong is Good but not eloquent (*ning* 佞)" The Master said, "Of what use is eloquence? If you go about responding to everyone with a clever tongue you will often incur resentment. I do not know whether or not Zhonggong is good, but of what use is eloquence?"

Not only is speaking useless, but it even becomes something that depreciates the person:

> 【第三章】子曰、巧言令色、鮮矣仁。
>
> 1.3 A clever tongue and fine appearance are rarely signs of Goodness

Only the Maoists approached the question of the word, though in a rather shallow way, but their school was defeated by Daoism and Confucianism, which, as we see, had quite opposite attitudes. Confucius expressly banned eloquence from the qualities that define the goodness of a person.

> 【廿七章】子曰、剛、毅、木、訥、近仁。
>
> 13.27 Resolute, decisive, straightforward, and reticent – these qualities are close to Goodness.
>
> 【廿四章】子曰、君子欲訥於言、而敏於行。
>
> 4.24 The gentleman wishes to be slow to speak, but quick to act.

The motto of Hong Kong could thus be "fewer words and more action." Indeed, Hong Kong Chinese culture emphasizes being able to solve one's own problems alone (Cheung, 2001; Leong, 1986) and places little value on talking. Hongkongers are generally more prone to action and not as open to speech that might not be followed by an immediate action.

Literature shows that Chinese tend to focus more on finding solutions rather than on talking about problems (Chong & Liu, 2002). This is in contrast to Westerners, who are apparently more concerned with understanding and analyzing problems, searching for the truth, and understanding why and what options one should undertake (Hall & Ames, 1998). The Western discourse relies much on logic and argumentation, as the core of a reflective and analytical dimension. The Chinese attitude seems to differ in that it gives little room for complex speculations or any search for hidden meaning.

Even today, a general distrust toward speech emerges, particularly in Hong Kong; conversing is not perceived as beneficial or necessary, but as something potentially harmful because it can disrupt social harmony, putting the person (and those close to him/her) in an awkward position. As the wellbeing of the group is so important (and the concern of being judged is high), the use of the word tends to be rather sparing, utilitarian, and instrumental. This does not mean that Hong Kong people are not talkative; they are, and they can also be quite loud, even when speaking in public. However, I would say that in most cases, communication is initiated to exchange or obtain information rather than being a completely casual conversation for the pleasure of talking. Many share the belief that speaking does not lead to any change. These exchanges are normally quite short, and it is uncommon in this context to engage in some form of conversation with a stranger for no purpose. Thus, talking often becomes a medium for addressing a request or posing a question to others, rather than for starting a conversation or expressing one's own thought or idea. This is particularly true among people who feel insecure, fear criticism or have low self-esteem and self-confidence, as asking questions of others may be a strategy for limiting one's own exposure and instead controlling others. Communication must therefore be effective; everything that is said is said for a reason, and more remains unsaid (Gu, 2003). In this sense, it would be difficult to imagine here something like a free-association process, the analytic invitation to relate "what comes to mind." Even professionals may find it hard to believe that a practice based only on speech (a non-directive practice) could ever be effective. This may partially explain why Chinese societies have for a long time been indifferent to counseling theories in general, and to psychoanalysis in particular. Because speaking is often understood as a matter of communicating or exchanging knowledge, rather than a process of self-discovery, counseling is likely understood as a short-term, directive, and focused process in Hong Kong, and it is normally limited to a few sessions only (Busiol, 2016).

Relational concern

Hong Kong Chinese culture is a Confucian-based culture, which is quite normative and regulative toward social interactions. While the Greek and Christian traditions emphasized speech and logos, on the contrary, Confucianism and Chinese tradition emphasized societal structure and relations among individuals. In Chinese culture, the relationship comes first, before speech. The hierarchy is given in advance, defined by the social status of the speakers, and not by the truth of their word (Hall & Ames, 1998). As the group is so important, talking is often a medium for comparing and adapting to others (Zou et al, 2008), for addressing a request, or for gossip, rather than for starting a talk. The Confucian conformity might drift to conformism. In such a cohesive society, relational aspects are fundamental. The Chinese are less inclined to seek support from others if they perceive that it will become a threat to their "face," meaning their public self-image. Such a tendency to worry about another person's opinions also leads them to avoid direct communication, therefore making them meet others' expectations in order to obtain social acceptance, maintain relational harmony, and avoid social sanctions (Hwang & Han, 2010). For this reason, the Chinese might prefer quick counseling techniques, which do not require them to become too involved in a relationship with a stranger, as the counselor initially is. Chinese communication has been described as insider-oriented communication (Gao, Ting-Toomey, & Gudykunst, 1996), meaning that the Chinese tend to speak more openly with people they know or they have been introduced to ("insiders"), but they rarely speak to people they do not know ("outsiders") (Gao & Ting-Toomey, 1998). Dynamic relations among individuals are emphasized (Zhou, 2008). Hong Kong Chinese culture belongs to the so-called collectivistic or interdependent cultures, where attention to the needs of the relevant others is higher than that in independent cultures of Europe or North America.

Trust is an essential part of social relationships, and is a good predictor of help-seeking behavior (Jones & George, 1998). Most people would probably subscribe to this, irrespective of cultural background. However, in Hong Kong, concern about trust seems to be much more central and much more influential in regard to help-seeking behavior than in Western societies. Chinese society has been defined as a "low-trust" society (Fang & Faure, 2010; Ke & Zhang, 2003), meaning that trust is high within the family but low outside it. Following Liu and Rau (2012), interdependent cultures build trust based on intimate relationships, while independent cultures establish trust on the basis of rules and regulations. Western clients may, for example, think that professional counselors have to adhere to a code of conduct, so that their confidentiality and privacy are secured by a set of rules and regulations. In contrast, for the Chinese, trust grows with the relationship, and so it requires more time. Trust is an issue in Chinese culture, and it affects several aspects of society; for example, it determines the quality of *Guanxi* (personal connection), and greatly influences how business is carried out (Chen & Chen, 2004). More so in Hong Kong than in Western countries, it is necessary to build a solid relationship before any confidentiality is possible; without complete trust it is not possible to open up to others. Trust in Hong Kong not only refers to privacy/confidentiality issues but also signifies having someone to listen non-judgmentally. For these reasons, Hong Kong Chinese might prefer quick counseling techniques which do not require them to become too involved with a stranger.

Relational dynamics, social desirability, and interconnectedness all influence what can and cannot be expressed, and therefore affect people's coping strategies. Indeed, the relevance of the social network in the help-seeking process of Chinese people cannot be more clearly stressed.

Western vs Chinese roots of counseling

Psychoanalysis and the majority of Western counseling theories originated from, and in part still rely on, the concept of *catharsis* (Powell, 2007). Catharsis indicates a purification and purgation of emotions that occur when they are expressed, physically or verbally, rather than repressed. The majority of Europeans and Americans today probably share the idea that emotions should find expression, and that this will help one to feel better (Bushman, 2002). For example, people may feel the need to talk to express their emotions for emotional relief. The term catharsis comes from the Greek κάθαρσις, and was originally used by Aristotle in the Poetics to describe the effects of tragedy on the spectator (particularly, the purgation of fear). Since then, the term has become popular in theories of drama and in the humanities in general (Scheff, 2007). As Western cultures are described as a "culture of guilt," whereas Chinese culture is a "culture of shame" (Bedford & Hwang, 2003), the idea of catharsis seems to match better with Western cultures, since feelings of guilt demand the need to be recognized, expressed, atoned for, and forgiven, while feelings of shame cause no desire for the source of the embarrassment to be recognized. Instead, in the Chinese culture one would likely wish to hide the source of shame, and thus it cannot be processed through catharsis. Indeed, it might be that Chinese culture has never produced anything similar to catharsis, and has favored instead different mechanisms. For example, Ho's (1996) studies on filial piety have indicated that the social structure of the Chinese allows an affect–role dissociation that may serve as a defense mechanism to fulfill obligations with emotional detachment. It is often reported that in Chinese culture, teachings focus on the repression rather than the expression of feelings and emotional vulnerability (Parker, Gladstone, & Chee, 2001). Somatization has been described as the presentation of somatic symptoms in place of personal or social problems (Kleinman, 1980). Somatization among Chinese patients has often been interpreted as a consequence of repression (Kleinman & Good, 1985) or suppression (Hsu, 1949). Repression can be understood as the outcome of the conflict between one's desires and ideas and one's internalized norms and sense of morality; in this case, unacceptable or unpleasant thoughts are likely to be repressed by consciousness. Instead, suppression may be intended as the outcome of the conflict between one's desire and ideas and external rules and social norms; in this case, the conflict is less compelling and restraint from certain actions may not necessarily require the content of representations to be excluded from consciousness. In accordance with

Freud's theory, we may think of repression as a universal mechanism, while suppression may be particularly applicable to cultures of external control and situation-centered behavior like Chinese culture. Interestingly, Hsu (1949) describes suppression as a mechanism of socialization. Understandably, suppression does not match the idea of catharsis well. Tseng (2004) observed that Westerners might consider some of the defense mechanisms that are frequently used by the Chinese as "immature," although these mechanisms can be "adaptive" in a Chinese society. Yu (2006) found that among a sample of Hong Kong undergraduates, "participants were more inclined to the neurotic and immature defense styles, and were more likely to use such defenses as somatization, dissociation and autistic fantasy" (p. 170). In contrast, he observed that among Westerners "humor, anticipation and rationalization" are ranked highest on average. Finally, he found denial clearly higher among Hong Kong Chinese than among the Western counterpart (Yu, 2006). Thus, the very concept of catharsis may be relatively new to the Hong Kong culture.

Open expression of emotions

Maybe a strategy for living peaceably in one of the most densely populated places on Earth is to limit the expression (and the self-awareness) of one's own emotions. Unsurprisingly, Hong Kong Chinese culture does not emphasize expression of overt emotions, as this could undermine social harmony; emotions are not neglected, but they are generally devalued, at least on a conscious level (Soto, Perez, Kim, Lee, & Minnick, 2011); further, when compared to Western cultures, for instance, we find that expression of emotions occurs with minimal signs and gestures in Hong Kong, so that one has to become well trained to be able to read and appreciate this different way of expressing. As a consequence, to Western eyes, the Hong Kong Chinese may seem less experienced in dealing with emotions, more awkward when trying to express feelings, less able to even admit or name their own feelings and desires.

Some might even argue that because Hong Kong is a city, whereas mainland China and Taiwan are countries (where people can relocate from one place to another and reinvent themselves, as is the case of the Chinese "factory girls," for instance), the social pressure in Hong Kong remains higher. In fact, Hong Kong has been described as "a commercial society operated on the principle of self-interest and materialistic pursuit" (Ting & Chiu, 2000, p. 31), in which the majority of people's concerns are about money and career, with emotions likely considered as a consequence of the former two and thus deserving less attention. However, Chinese society is changing rapidly, and in modern Hong Kong, the younger generations seem to behave very differently than those described in the literature twenty or more years ago. For instance, if one thinks about the extreme popularity of social networks like Facebook or WhatsApp in Hong Kong (Cheung, Chiu, & Lee, 2011), and how young people make use of it for sharing thoughts and feelings, it is difficult to conclude that they repress or deny emotions. More likely, Chinese people tend to open up and share thoughts and feelings given some conditions and in different media, in different ways, not necessarily face-to-face.

Help-seeking behaviors

When support from social networks is lacking (for example when a person is suddenly without his/her social context due to immigration), many Chinese people may find it more difficult to proactively go out to seek help, make explicit requests, or demand assistance from strangers. Two issues are thought to explain this attitude: (1) some Chinese may find it more difficult to directly express their feelings and needs because Chinese culture emphasizes listening more than speaking; people may experience difficulty and uneasiness in making a direct request, as they have not been taught to do so; and (2) Chinese people prefer to approach those who belong to their social network for a matter of trust; they prefer to approach those with whom they have already established a trustful relationship with, rather than those who are external to their circle and have no relation with them.

For the principle of reciprocity everyone should take care of someone and have someone to take care of him/herself (Chan & Young, 2012). Caretaking becomes mutual, and much is accepted and almost normative and well known to individuals. As such, it becomes an unspoken understanding. Thus, offering help may be a strategy for establishing and reinforcing that norm of reciprocity in which the other will also give his/her support, when needed. This may explain why the Chinese may be less active in seeking help for themselves compared to Western cultures; however, it does not mean that they are less willing to receive help. People in Hong Kong may be eager to offer their help to others in need, but find it difficult to ask for it themselves. However, they may expect help within a relationship; someone else is expected to notice their uneasiness and offer help. As a consequence, they might try to find help, support, and resources only within their social network, and they may not feel comfortable considering resources from outsiders; this attitude might greatly limit the range of their help-seeking behavior (Tata & Leong, 1994), particularly when support from the social network might be lacking.

It may also be that the very definition of "help-seeking behavior" is culturally biased, and that the definitions of "help" and "behavior" are not as universal as commonly thought; particularly, such a definition seems to imply that a demand for help should always be expressed or addressed (the very etymology of seeking also refers to "visit, inquire, pursue"). Furthermore, behavior already refers to something observable, such as actions. But in some cultures help-seeking may be better expressed by mean of bodily complaints rather than explicit mention of emotional disturbance or inner conflict. This might, for example, be an indirect request for help that simply does not fit the Western category of "help-seeking behavior." A few studies (e.g. Busiol,

2016; Maxwell & Siu, 2008) have indicated that the Hong Kong Chinese show a greater proclivity for using avoidant strategies (indicating or asking by indirect means, leaving others with the responsibility of understanding and interpreting the message) or emotion-focused coping (e.g. "cry by myself," "get upset"), both of which are generally labeled as "passive" coping in the Western literature. Stewart and colleagues (2002) also showed that Hong Kong Chinese do show more somatic symptoms, but they are not necessarily concomitant with denial or unawareness of the nature of the problem; this suggests that avoidant coping could be a coping strategy of Hong Kong, rather than suppression. This also suggests that people may want to try to ignore the problem or think about something else entirely. Tam and Lam (2005) compared 750 local-born youth and 243 migrant adolescents from mainland China and found that migrants reported lower use of withdrawal/ passive coping and a lower incidence of delinquent behavior. Interestingly, they also found that the longer the migrants had stayed in Hong Kong, the higher their use of withdrawal/passive coping. Finally, here, use of avoidant strategies also marks the difference in support-seeking processes between Chinese and Westerners (Cheng, Lo, & Chio, 2010). Selmer (2002) found that, more so than Americans and Germans, Hong Kong people generally attempt to minimize anxieties through physical or verbal withdrawal from the situation or by avoiding the problem. At the same time, he found them to be less likely than Americans and French people to face the problem and change the situation. All these embedded cultural factors may determine if and how a demand is formulated, to whom it is addressed, what help is expected, and how long the counseling may last.

Integration and eclecticism

Previous research showed that counselors in Hong Kong tend to mix different approaches and techniques and consider this a normal part of their professional practice. Chan and Lee (1995) interviewed 49 psychologists in Hong Kong, and found that the majority (62 percent) endorsed more than one orientation. When psychologists were asked to indicate their theoretical orientations, the total reached 198 percent, because the majority of respondents reported more than one choice. For example, 42 counselors out of 49 endorsed a behavioral/cognitive orientation, but half of them (26) also endorsed another orientation; 12 percent of the counselors were said to adopt behavioral/cognitive together with psychodynamic/analytical approaches, while 1 percent used social/community and systemic/strategic approaches. Furthermore, the literature shows that the Chinese normally combine or transform existing counseling theories, but very seldom do they give birth to completely new theories.

In Europe, debate between various schools of thought within a particular orientation is rather fierce, and professionals tend to distinguish themselves as belonging distinctly to their orientation. As a psychoanalyst, I was more naturally inclined to agree with Lemmens, de Ridder, and van Lieshout (1994, pp. 250–251) that

> client-centered psychotherapy, behavioral therapy and psychoanalysis are incompatible, and even incommensurable. These therapies are built on different foundations; they differ in human perception, values and work method. Thus, they can never be classified in a single system. Their fundamental differences are apparent from, for example, the different aims which the therapy attempts to realize. Self-development and self-realization appear to belong to a very different order than self-efficacy and the ability to cope.

I was therefore very surprised by the opposite attitude found in Hong Kong; mixing different theories together seems to be the standard in Hong Kong, and is not a cause for concern.

In my experience, an a priori adherence to a school of thought could sometimes lead to some sort of dogmatism and sectarianism. On the one hand, I perceive the pragmatic attitude of the Chinese as potentially less prejudicial against different approaches and thus opening to psychoanalysis; on the other hand, this inclination toward eclecticism confines theorization to something marginal, and this could particularly limit the understanding and the practice of psychoanalysis.

Psychoanalysis: integration and eclecticism

Freud himself was not sympathetic toward eclecticism, as he claimed that there had to be one correct explanation, and not many. Theoretical divergences with colleagues and pupils have oftentimes led to separation. For example, examining the correspondence between Freud and Breuer, Bouveresse (1995) describes Breuer's attitude as one of "unproductive skepticism" compared with Freud's "creative dogmatism." Although Freud has recognized that in practice one is sometime required to mix the gold of the analysis with the copper of psychotherapy, from the *Studies on Hysteria* to the end of his days, he advocated the integrity of psychoanalytic theory against any eclectic (partial) revision of it: "Though the structure of psycho-analysis is unfinished, it nevertheless presents, even to-day, a unity from which elements cannot be broken off at the caprice of whoever comes along: but these eclectics seem to disregard this" (Freud, 1933, p. 138). To be clear, the eclectics are people who accept the validity of some portions of analysis, but who reject other portions of it (i.e. sexuality, unconscious, symbolism), depending on personal sympathies.

Thus, psychoanalysts might see integration/eclecticism as leading to wild-psychoanalysis and thus prefer to avoid it. Psychoanalysis itself was born and has often prospered by the encounter with various disciplines such as literature, philosophy, linguistics, history; however, Freud did not combine different disciplines together into a collective reality as if they were just complementary. Instead, he referred to other disciplines as a source of inspiration for adding something more to what was already known, and then coming to a new theorization and not a "synthesis." So doing, he continuously noted the difference between psychoanalysis and other disciplines, particularly psychiatry and psychology. Freud did not acritically assemble various disciplines (as in eclecticism), nor did he suggest that psychoanalysis could ever become a complete system of thought (as in integration; *to integrate*, etymologically means to make one, meaning one system) or part of one, just like, for example, a philosophical system is; instead, he stated clearly that psychoanalysis is not a *Weltanschauung*, a vision of the world.

It is important to understand the origin of this eclectic attitude, as it might affect the understanding and use in Hong Kong: is eclecticism strong because counseling is a relatively new practice here, or because local counselors lack experience, or is it something rooted deeper in the culture? A comparison with other contexts might help us to reach a better understanding. Particularly, does the eclectic attitude of counselors in Hong Kong represent an exception, or is eclecticism currently a major orientation also in Europe, North America, and other Asian countries?

Integration and eclecticism across cultures

In South Korea, social workers were shown to be more eclectic (85 percent reporting more than one salient orientation, or no salient orientation) than psychiatrists (37 percent), psychologists (61 percent), and counselors (55 percent) (Bae, Joo, & Orlinsky, 2003). In the USA, Norcross, Karpiak, and Santoro (2005) examined the demographic characteristics and theoretical orientations of the members of the American Psychological Association in the last 40 years. They found that in 2003, among the 694 respondents, eclecticism/integration was the modal orientation (29 percent), with cognitive therapy a close second (28 percent), followed by psychodynamic (15 percent) and behavioral (10 percent). Further, examining the data from 1960 to 2003, they found that the psychodynamic orientation has declined from an initial 35 percent to the present 15 percent; by contrast, cognitive therapy has reported the most consistent growth over the years; finally, eclecticism/integration has consistently emerged as the modal orientation, between 27 percent and 36 percent. Although their study did not distinguish between integration and eclecticism, it showed that in the US, psychologists, more so than counselors, tend to adopt a single-school orientation. Marquis, Hudson, and Tursi, (2010) surveyed 416 American counselors and found that 76 percent of them counsel with an integrative approach, whereas only 14 percent reported an eclectic approach, and only 10 percent a single-school approach. In addition, counselors in this study reported negative evaluations of eclecticism ten times as frequently as they did against integration; this means that counselors valued having a coherent conceptual framework and considered the lack of a theory-driven approach as in eclecticism a serious limitation. Another study among North American practitioners confirmed that they prefer the term integration over eclecticism because integration implies a more systematic use of concepts and techniques from different approaches (Lambert, Garfield, & Bergin, 2004). Norcross, Karpiak, and Lister (2005) found that among a sample of 187 clinical psychologists, half previously adhered to a specific theoretical orientation; further, they found that the majority of respondents (59 percent) preferred the term integrative to eclectic (20 percent).

A survey in 21 European countries showed that several therapeutic approaches are practiced in Europe (Zerbetto & Tantam, 2001); however, only four modalities are practiced in the large majority (from 78 percent to 90 percent) of countries: psychodynamic, systemic family, gestalt, and cognitive behavioral. Among a sample of Italian psychotherapists (Cesa-Bianchi, Rezzonico, & Strepparava, 1997) it was found that 60 percent adhered to a single approach, whereas the remaining 40 percent reported using two or more theoretical orientations. Interestingly enough, among this sample those with a psychoanalytic formation were reported to be more likely adherent to their school. Another research study among Italian psychotherapists working in the public sector showed that those who reported more than one salient orientation were more frequently inclined to an integrative approach rather than a merely technical eclecticism (Bettini, Strepparava, & Rezzonico, 1998). Hollanders and McLeod (1999) reported that among their sample of 309 British practitioners (counselors, psychologists and psychotherapists), only 49 percent explicitly described themselves as eclectic/integrative; however, when asked about their practice, a large number of them reported multiple orientations and/or approaches, revealing some form of eclecticism (to a total of 87 percent of the sample). Among those who reported a pure-form single orientation, psychoanalysis ranked first. Interestingly enough, the researchers described a tendency among some respondents to shift from one single orientation toward a more eclectic/integrative approach, but not the other way round. Specifically, they observed this trend among more experienced practitioners, as in response to clients' needs, or as an opportunity to use a more innovative approach, or for the therapist's own satisfaction. This mean that practitioners are not eclectic in nature and some might adopt more techniques if they experience limitations with their main approach. A survey among 161 Portuguese therapists (Vasco, Garcia-Marques, & Dryden, 1992) revealed that only 13 percent of them identified as eclectic, although almost all of them mentioned referring to a few theoretical approaches in their practice. The authors suggested that Portuguese psychotherapists might want to avoid the term eclectic as it meant that one did not have a firm commitment about the nature of psychotherapy. Further, results did not show any relation between the demographics of the counselors, years of working experience, and eclecticism; in addition, data show that the breadth of Portuguese eclecticism is very limited, since the most frequent combinations are of rather similar and related theories. A research study among 179 Spanish therapists (mainly psychologists and secondarily psychiatrists and social workers) showed that 62 percent of the respondents adopted one main orientation (largely psychodynamic/analytic) and the remaining two or more. Further, results showed that among that 38 percent who indicated more than one approach, integration largely prevailed over eclecticism (Coscollá et al., 2006).

Stoltenberg and Delworth (1987) have proposed a three-stage model of the development of therapeutic orientation. First, novice therapists are inflexible and focus only on one approach; second, they become able to consider other models, but are unsure of when to pursue a particular orientation; and, third, they may adopt a main orientation but also enjoy dialogue with other approaches. However, Buckman (2006, p. 8) observed that

> despite the large numbers of clinical psychologists professing to work eclectically or integratively, many clinical psychologists find themselves drawn more strongly towards certain orientations than others, and anecdotally can often become rigid and dogmatic in their adherence to the principles of one model and exclusion of alternatives.

Finally, it can be said that in Europe, more so than in North America, professionals seem to adhere to a single-school theoretical orientation; this may reflect different degrees of pragmatism. Further, in both geographic areas psychotherapists tend not to identify themselves as eclectics, as in most cases this is perceived as a lack of professionalism; instead, they prefer to refer to integration. Among Western professionals, eclecticism appears to be higher among social workers and counselors than psychologists and psychiatrists. Similarly, counseling professionals who work for the public sector are more likely to be eclectic than those working in private practice, as they may prefer standardized approaches for short-term results. Eclecticism is in most cases caused by dissatisfaction with a single orientation; this suggests that eclecticism is not embedded in the culture, and in fact a consistent number of eclectic therapists initially started with a single approach. In addition, eclecticism is relatively new, as it mainly arose starting from the 1960s. Finally, those with a higher adherence to psychoanalysis generally reported the lowest inclination toward eclecticism.

Thus, it is important to further examine the trends among Hong Kong professionals. For instance, how many of them adopt a single orientation? And among the others, do they practice theoretical integration or technical eclecticism? On what grounds do they combine various theories? Does it reflect a cultural disposition or simply a lack of professionalism? Is eclecticism more so than integration a factor limiting the understanding of psychoanalysis in Hong Kong?

Basis of Chinese thought and how theories are understood

The fact that counseling professionals in Hong Kong mix two or more theoretical approaches together, rather than adopting one elective theory or method and specializing in that, may be due to various factors.

The large majority of counseling theories originated in Europe or America. Thus, Hong Kong counseling professionals may have a particular position toward these "Western theories"; for instance, all these theories might be perceived as being at the same time foreign to the local context (so that no single approach is considered as being completely effective) yet sharing a common background (because of their common origin, these theories might be understood as not being in opposition to each other). This attitude might enhance an inclination toward mixing several approaches, regardless of the theoretical differences among these theories and the contexts in which they originated. After all, peripheries are often more syncretic than centers where theories originated. Something similar happens in Western countries where, for example, Europeans and Americans with little knowledge of Asian cultures may tend to perceive very different practices like yoga, feng shui, and sushi as necessarily related because (to them) they come from an undifferentiated geographical area, and they are thus all "oriental" to them. Further, some approaches may be very well received (e.g. humanism), although they originally developed in a context apparently very distant from this. Thus, it is not completely clear what influences the understanding of various approaches, and what determines their success or rejection.

The history of the reception of psychoanalysis across cultures and societies shows that even in countries like Argentina (today one of the countries with the highest number of practicing psychoanalysts in the world), before the emergence of a psychoanalytic culture, psychoanalysis did not immediately *replace* other disciplines but was added to them. On the one hand, this eclecticism was understood as the resistance that society and other professionals put up against psychoanalysis; on the other hand, the combination of psychoanalysis with other accepted disciplines contributed to its popularization and legitimation. Not only that, but the counterpoint to this initial eclecticism is that when psychoanalysis became popular and established in society, then it quickly turned to orthodoxy and bureaucracy, with psychoanalytic institutions which imposed standards of training and practice (Plotkin, 1997).

The way the Chinese tend to receive foreign theories may also explain why there have been no innovative theories in the world developed by Chinese theorists. First, Yang and Ye (2014) maintain that "Chinese theoretical psychology is 'congenitally deficient' and has always been burdened by a 'loss of originality'[...] Chinese psychologists mainly introduced and absorbed psychology from other countries" (p. 817), meaning that, at least in psychology, they tended to import theories rather than developing their own. Second, they observe that theoretical psychology developed more slowly than experimental psychology, suggesting that the Chinese may not place a high value or priority on theories. Third, Yang and Ye agree that most Chinese scholars have a tendency to repeat or elaborate only the theories of their predecessors rather than having their own original ideas or creating something new. Finally, they observe that the Chinese do not normally place their faith in a particular theory (or, we could say, in the theorization), but tend to adopt different approaches quite easily.

This tendency to mix different approaches may also reflect a more consolidated and cultural specific tendency in Hong Kong and China to *combine* practices, theories, and knowledge in different fields and aspects of life. Some peculiarities of Chinese thought may unconsciously orient counselors toward one approach or another. For this reason, it may be worth investigating the basis of Chinese thought, in order to get a broader picture of the factors that possibly influenced the development of counseling in Hong Kong. For example, throughout history, we have seen how China assimilated and sometimes rejected disciplines from outside. This is the case with Christianity, for example, which did not arouse significant interest in China in spite of the efforts of Western missionaries during the sixteenth century (see Jullien, 2004; Kim, 2004). Also exemplary is the case of how Marxism has been assimilated in China (Geeraerts & Jing, 2001). So, why does it matter? Such an attitude may be reflective of a more established tendency, likely grounded in the Hong Kong Chinese culture. Then, what does it imply for counseling? What are the specific characteristics of Chinese thinking that might be relevant for the reception of counseling and psychoanalysis? What other examples can we find in history that might give us hints on how disciplines are received and understood? And how does Chinese thinking proceed?

Syncretism?

To Western eyes, the Chinese attitude toward counseling and beyond may seem syncretic and not well grounded in theory. However, it may be helpful to analyze the attitude that Chinese and European cultures have toward religions, for example, as this sheds light on the different attitudes that they also have toward counseling theories. European and American cultures normally have monotheistic religions, which are mutually exclusive: one person can have one religion (and one God) at a time. This was not the case in China, where Confucianism, Daoism, and Buddhism were (and still are) not mutually exclusive. In particular, there was a time in history (briefly, when Confucianism was considered a religion) when "The Unity of the Three Teachings" was named *sanjiao heyi*. Even today, both in Hong Kong and in mainland China, we can find several temples that combine elements from different cults and even folk beliefs. This might represent an authentic puzzlement for a Western person, who instead would normally be inclined to ask whether the temple is *either* Daoist *or* Buddhist. If this attitude already reveals a different attitude toward sacrality, it also shows a different logic at work. Brook (1993) suggests that "we should not leap too quickly to embrace the concept of syncretism for the Chinese case, although it may appear to fit nicely" (p. 34). Rather than syncretism he prefers the term *condominium* for describing the coexistence of Buddhism, Daoism, and Confucianism together: "the term condominium connotes that the Three Teachings lived together in late-imperial China with a considerable degree of harmony: *equal in principle, equally available to worshippers, and free to associate and interact in a multitude of ways*" (p. 15, italics added). The term condominium seems particularly appropriate, as it refers to a building in which individuals own some parts of the complex and share some others; at the same time its etymology refers to "joint rule or sovereignty." More specifically, he observes that the Chinese "were *eclectic* in their borrowings of gestures and language, *ecumenical* in their toleration of other teachings, but *inclusivist* in their belief that Confucianism stood as the highest representation of truth" (p. 36, italics added).

This attitude toward religion, or counseling, may reflect a peculiarity of Chinese thought more established than the definition of syncretism seems to suggest. The term syncretism is misleading, as it seems to imply some mistake. Syncretism seems to allude to a temporary condition that sooner or later should be overcome (after appropriate training, for example). However, the Chinese attitude may not be simply syncretic in the negative sense that Westerners normally perceive, as the goal is apparently not a *reconciliation* of different beliefs; in fact, contrary to Western thought that is traditionally more concerned with theory, Chinese thought is more oriented toward practice.

Disposition toward theory and practice

These rather different attitudes toward theory and practice reflect an important cultural difference. Since the debates over the relationships between *episteme** and *techne*, Western thought has emphasized the centrality of theory. Conversely, historians like Bodde (1991) and Sivin (1973) report that brilliant Chinese intellectuals and astronomers left behind only sets of commentaries, letters to friends, and writings that generally lack organization and theoretical acuteness, and that they did not organize their observations into general theories. Further, Needham (1969) observed that from the first century BC until the fifteen century the Chinese were much more efficient than Western societies in applying natural knowledge to practical human needs; however, this superiority was of a practical and technological nature, not one of theoretical understanding (Huff, 1993).

As theory is so important in the Western thinking tradition, a fully theoretical reconciliation of distant approaches is simply not possible, or at best is understood as a syncretism. Instead, because in Chinese tradition observations did not converge into a theory, there was likely no need to solve any contradictions. In Western tradition, a strong theory should not only be able to integrate existing observations and data, it should also predict/explain newly observed phenomena without undermining its theoretical grounds.

Thus, in Western tradition, a *theoretical integration* is normally understood as a first option and *technical eclecticism* is considered a weaker model. The former implies that different elements converge (make one) into one theory where every component is *subordinate* to a main part, so that the theory has internal coherence, whereas the latter suggests that different approaches can coexist together even if they may conflict, and they can be equally important. This different attitude toward having a coherent theory of the world has had very concrete consequences. It is likely not by chance that the monotheistic Western discourse (one God, one belief), has stressed so much having a coherent theory to guide practice; however, this emphasis on theory has in some cases led to some extreme, what we might call *dogmatism, sectarianism, integralism,* or even *fundamentalism*. Conversely, we hardly find these extremes in Chinese cultures.

Different logics

In Western philosophy, things are defined on the basis of Aristotelian logic, based on the law of identity (A = A), the principle of the excluded third, or the principle of the excluded middle (all statements are either true or false: *tertium non datur* in Latin, meaning that no third possibility is given), *and the law of non-contradiction* (no statement can be both true and false; thus A ≠ not A). Instead, Chinese thought is grounded in three very different principles: the principle of change (reality is a process, in constant flux), the principle of contradiction (reality is not precise but full of contradictions), and the principle of relationship or holism (everything is relational and connected) (Peng, Spencer-Rodgers, & Zhong, 2006). Consequently, it is not surprising to find that American and European understanding of the world and human life are Aristotelian in spirit, emphasizing coherence and constancy (identity), synthesis (non-contradiction), clear and unchanging entities or constructs (essence), and taking position (no middle ground), whereas, in contrast, Chinese thought emphasizes an approach that values holism, relationships, and is not averse to contradictions.

Western thought developed around the concept of *logos*, so that Galileo could observe that the world is like a book that just needs to be deciphered, which has led to embracing the discourse of science. Rather than the isolation of parts (concepts and ideas), and the definition of meaning, Chinese thought searched for the balance of opposites and has given more importance to the whole, to the context rather than to the parts:

> whereas the great minds in ancient China emphasized the role of relationships in discovering the truth the brilliant thinkers in ancient Greece believed that the truth can only be understood when the problem is analyzed step by step in isolation of its context.
>
> (Ji, Lee, & Guo, 2010, p. 165)

Subordinative and correlative thinking

The Chinese gave priority to correlative thought, which relates image or concept clusters in terms of their meaningful dispositions, whereas the West gave priority to causal thinking and logical analysis. Joseph Needham (1956) expresses succinctly the difference between the Western "subordinative" style of thinking and the "coordinative" or "associative" Chinese thinking: "in coordinative thinking, conceptions are not subsumed under one another, but placed side by side in a *pattern*, and things influence one another not by acts of mechanical causation, but by a kind of 'inductance'" (pp. 280–281).

Correlative thinking is not a-logical or proto-logical; we should resist this simplistic and ethnocentric temptation, although it is somehow opposite to Western *causal thinking*. Correlative thinking represents *another* logic and is best suited to "process" understandings of the world, whereas causal thinking better accommodates "substance" views (Randall Groves, 2010). Further, "coordinative" or "correlative" thinking is grounded in a binary system, and does not proceed toward integration, intended as *reconciliation* of different beliefs, or different theories. Chinese thought apparently does not consider integration as a sign of fine reasoning; it is not at the level of integration that it measures its effectiveness. This also means that contradictions have different implications in Western and Chinese dialectical thinking. For the former, the unity of opposites is temporary, transitory, and conditional; instead, for the latter the struggle of opposing tendencies is permanent (Peng & Nisbett, 1999). Contradictions exist in both systems, but in Chinese culture they are an opportunity for reaching balance and harmony.

Harmony and balance

Harmony and balance are two keywords in Chinese thought (Gao et al., 1996). Following Ji et al. (2010, p. 158): "the *zhong yong*, or the doctrine of the mean, advocates moderation and modesty in the interest of achieving and maintaining interpersonal harmony. Similar to holism, the *zhong yong* mode of thinking emphasizes looking at the whole picture." A balanced attitude will lead to interpersonal harmony, and possibly to harmony with the whole environment. One should then consider every position and not exclude or refuse any. As Chan (1999) states, "harmonization of the universe is achieved once a balance of the positive and negative side to things (black and white, good and evil, dark and light, female and male aspects) occurred." Following Ji et al. (2010, p. 164):

> Chinese are encouraged to argue for both sides in a debate (i.e. both arguments are correct), or to assign equal responsibilities in a dispute (i.e. no party is at complete fault). This presents an interesting contrast with the law of the excluded middle in Western philosophies, according

to which one ought to eliminate ambiguity or inconsistency by selecting one and only one of the conflicting ideas. Unlike the Chinese tradition, it assumes no merit in the middle ground.

Contrary to Aristotelian tradition, Chinese thought assumes that a median position will improve harmony and avoid conflict, and therefore the third is not excluded in Chinese thought. According to Wurmser (2011), harmony is a theme presented in both Confucianism and Daoism; understandably, harmony promotes balance rather than conflict, no matter whether it is a conflict between humans or an inner conflict. A median position may not be an option for overcoming conflicts in Western cultures; instead, it may create more conflicts, for example by increasing cognitive dissonance (Hoshino-Browne, Zanna, Spencer, & Zanna, 2004). Conflict is, however, intrinsic to the view of inner life in Western intellectual tradition, and is what stimulates critical thought and creativity. Conflicts exacerbate differences and lead to more distinctive positions. Instead, in Chinese cultures, conflicts are watered down by highlighting similarities and common ground, so as to achieve harmony between different individuals or different theoretical positions (Peng & Nisbett, 1999). According to Wurmser (2011), the Confucian man is not tragic because "he is not determined by the inner crisis of choice, decision, and guilt, but oriented toward action and toward the concentric circles of obligations surrounding him" (p. 118). To Wurmser, this deep and abiding antipathy to inner conflict may be one reason why the Chinese culture and tradition seems so peculiarly inimical to psychoanalysis.

Duality without dualism?

Both dualism and duality are grounded on the idea or belief that everything has two parts or principles. However, dualism is made of two parts that are clearly defined and mutually exclusive (*either* this *or* that), whereas duality is a conception of two things that cannot exist without each other (*both* this *and* that). There is symmetry at the base of dualism, where one part is versus the other; there is complementarity at the base of duality, where each part is necessary to the other. Duality is significantly different from dualism, yet it is irreducible to one, as in monism.

Confucianism is the philosophy par excellence of the two (Sun, 1991), where the two indicates a duality, but not a dualism. The two in Chinese thought never represents two elements that negate each other; thus we do not find a *thesis opposed to an antithesis*, which finally results in a *synthesis*. It is indeed different to say that something proceeds to make a whole or that it is an expression of *the one*, as opposed to it proceeding *two by two*:

> Western dialectical thought is fundamentally consistent with the laws of formal logic and aggressive in the sense that contradiction requires

synthesis rather than mere acceptance. The key difference is that the Chinese naïve dialecticism denies the reality of true contradiction, and never sees those contractions as logically opposite. Hence, it tends to [...] accept coexistence of opposites as permanent.

(Peng et al., 2006, p. 256)

Fang (2011) distinguishes between Chinese duality thinking (as expressed by the yin–yang) and Western dialectical thinking. Typical of the Western discourse is reasoning, proceeding per concept, isolating parts of the discourse and analyzing it by its *difference* from the rest. Instead, Chinese thinking proceeds by analogies, finding similarities among different elements, but it does not lead to any synthesis.

Yin and *yang* are together and interdependent. They are

an expression of a duality in time, an alternation of two opposite stages in time. [...] The day belongs to Yang, but after it reaches its peak at midday, the Yin within it gradually begins to unfold and manifest. Thus each phenomenon may belong to a Yang stage or a Yin stage, but always contains the seed of the opposite stage within itself.

(Maciocia, 1989, p. 16)

The principle of yin and yang reflects also a different notion of time; it has been said that European and American thinking is linear, whereas Chinese thinking is circular (Nisbett, 2003; Zuo, 2001).

In the so-called Order, or Pattern, or Organism (Needham, 1956) we can always distinguish the different elements composing it: there is never really a complete integration. In the yin–yang symbol the two dots in each of the two twirls mean that things exist only in *relation* to the opposite form. The relation is maintained, so that Chinese thought proceeds per *contrast* and *complementarity*, rather than per *integration*. In the Chinese language we have several examples of this paradoxical approach. For example, the word "thing(s)" is *dongxi* in Chinese; *dong* means east and *xi* means west. From a Chinese perspective, everything embraces opposite properties such as east and west. The yin–yang principle also explains many Chinese concepts and practices which look inconsistent and puzzling to Westerners but do not seem to disturb the Chinese mind as far as internal consistency and coherence are concerned, such as "one country; two systems" (*yi guo liang zhi*), "socialist market economy" (*shehuizhuyi shichang jingji*), and "stable development" (*wending fazhan*) (Faure & Fang, 2008). Here, opposite elements are not combined because they represent the two sides of the same coin; they are not simply expressions of the same principle (as it is in monism); instead, they are combined to produce another meaning. The two becomes three.

Chinese thought arose from duality, but apparently it does not turn into dualism, so that a contrast does not require a solution. Things are always connected and put in *relation*, mutually depending on each other. The two "ostensibly opposing but complementary forces are each in pursuit of the other's tail in a cyclical fashion, suggesting that a phenomenon will start regressing in the opposite direction once it reaches the extreme" (Ji et al., 2010, p. 165). The two is essential, but there is no symmetry between elements; the two is unsolvable, it never makes one. In Chapter 42 of the *Tao te Ching*, from the translation of James Legge, we find: "The Tao produced One; One produced Two; Two produced Three; Three produced All things" (Lao Tse, 2008, p. 42). This passage is well known; however, various translations are given: "The way produces one, one produces two; two produce three, three produce myriad beings" (Soho, 2010, p. 102). What is important is that the thousand things, or the myriad beings, are produced not by the two (two elements in opposition), but by the three, meaning when the dyad is broken. In Soho's commentary: "'One' is the absolute; 'two' is the sun and the moon; 'three' is sky, earth, and humankind. Sky, earth, and humankind produce myriad things. Look at this – originally they were all nonexistent" (Soho, 2010, p. 102).

Creating and transforming

We have mentioned before that (at least for the time being) the Chinese have not invented any remarkable counseling theory; at best, they have shown some concern about how to *adapt* the existing Western theories. Confucius (in Slingerland, 2003) defines himself a transmitter rather than an innovator:

【第一章】子曰、述而不作、信而好古、竊比於我老彭。

7.1 The Master said, "I transmit rather than innovate. I trust in and love the ancient ways. I might thus humbly compare myself to Old Peng."

However, this does not mean that Confucius did not promote creativity; quite on the contrary, he mentioned and encouraged it several times (Chan, 1963). Rather, he condemned inflexibility, rigidity, and taking arbitrary conclusions:

【第四章】子絕四、毋意、毋必、毋固、毋我

9.4 The Master was entirely free of four faults: arbitrariness, inflexibility, rigidity, and selfishness.

More likely, the difference between Western and Chinese traditions is the emphasis on the feature of *novelty* in creativity (Niu, 2012; Niu, & Sternberg, 2002). In Confucianism creativity does not indicate a process of *creatio ex nihilo* (creation out of nothing), but more likely a *creatio in situ* (Wen, 2009), meaning a constantly changing and continuous process. Ames (2005) defines the creation in situ as "the growth of the dynamic relationships that constitute things through the art of contextualization (*ars contextualis*), with the continuing emergence of something new and meaningful in those relations"

(p. 69). Novelty and creativity in Confucian tradition are obtained through a gradual but continuing change from the past more than a breakthrough, by receiving and transmitting knowledge, and implicitly transforming it and adapting it to the situation. Thus the word "appropriateness" (*yi*, 义), meaning doing what is fitting to the changing context or situation, may better express the Chinese concept of creativity (Niu, 2012).

In recent years, empirical research across mainland China, Taiwan, and Hong Kong has shown that characteristics relating to "humor" and "aesthetic appreciation" are normally missing in the Chinese perception of a creative person; and characteristics like "wisdom" and "self-confidence" are rated higher than "having original ideas." At the same time, Chinese culture promotes values like "obedience," "submission," "conformity," "following tradition," and "concerned with face" that are not indicative of a rupture with the past and the context, as novelty and creativity are normally understood in Western cultures (Rudowicz & Yue, 2000).

Bodde (1991) observed that Chinese thinkers have often adopted the method of "scissors-and-paste" or "composition by compilation," which means copying the works, without comment, of others into one's own new work; this was not seen as plagiarism but more likely as a reasonable process to build knowledge, and the application of this method can be seen in various fields of Chinese thought (this acritical "cut and paste" strategy is also very common among students). As Huff (1993) suggested, this phenomenon is likely due to the absence of dialectic tradition and faith in reason in Chinese intellectual thought. As a consequence, he concluded:

> the issue this technique raises is not that Chinese writers borrowed wholesale from the writing of their predecessors, but that this borrowing took place without the author's being aware that such a record is highly likely to contain contradictory assumptions and points of view, as well as contextually misplaced metaphors and allusions – of all which might confuse the reader.
> (Huff, 1993, p. 300)

A description that seems to fit well for the reception of counseling too.

The Chinese way: the combinatorial

Apparently, syncretic is not the term that best describes Chinese thinking, while the term eclectic may carry too much cultural connotation. It is suggested, then, that combinatorial may be more appropriate. According to the etymology of the word (that though is an English word), combining means "joining two by two." As we have mentioned before, the two in Chinese thought is original and irreducible to the one. There is no dualism, and thus no exclusion of one part, but duality and interdependency among elements. The combinatorial seems also to be at the base of the

Chinese language.² In particular, when comparing Western and Chinese thought, is easy to speculate that Chinese thinking radically differs from Greek-Christian thinking because of differences in the Chinese language and its writing system. A number of research studies have attempted to demonstrate how language* shapes the way we think. For example, Logan (2004) claims that the Chinese writing system may have hindered *abstract thinking* in China. Wenzel (2010) claims that a certain lack of morphology in the Chinese language invites the user to pay more attention to contexts. Bodde (1991) found a few weaknesses that made the Chinese language more ambiguous than Indo-European languages and far from ideal for scientific communication. Wright (1953) found that the Chinese language is relatively poor in resources for expressing abstractions and notions such as "truth" or "man" in a broader sense. My aim is not to evaluate whether every single hypothesis is grounded or not. However, some literature suggests that language has a fundamental role in shaping the way we think and how we understand the world (Boroditsky, 2001). Brown (2002, p. 15) suggests that the Chinese character and the Chinese language are the keys to understanding Chinese culture, and that

> the organization of the Chinese characters is what guides the organization of the other entities as well: cooking, medicine, history, and society. The manner in which the Chinese think about medicine, for example, is the same manner in which they think about history and cooking. Chinese culture is a cohesive unit, and each of these topics is intimately connected. [...] Western "science" is only one way of thinking and (that) it has its roots in Western languages.

The unique organization of the Chinese language may form the basis for thinking in Chinese. The Chinese language is said to be *morphosyllabic*, meaning that each character represents a single syllable and a single morpheme. The large majority of characters are composed of a radical (a morpheme that may suggest some possible meaning of the character) and a phonetic (that may suggest the pronunciation of the character) (DeFrancis, 1984). Further, in the Chinese language words are created by combining existing characters more than inventing or creating new characters. For example, different kinds of vehicles share one character (*che*); then, depending on the second character attached, this combination can refer to different vehicles such as adding the character *huo* (fire) to *che*, to make *huo-che*, train. Combinations are not only used to form single words, but can be used at different levels, to structure words into phrases which can be used to form sentences. Since Chinese is not an inflected language, combinations are the very system to form grammatical meaning, to pluralize, or to express verb tenses. There is one practical reason for this too: if every concept, every word, was just associated with one single character, the list of the total characters would be too long and too complex, even for those whose mother tongue is Chinese. Thus, combination is at the very heart of the Chinese language, whereas other languages may proceed differently. We can find similar examples in other languages too (e.g. in English "bumblebee", "honeybee", and "beehive" all contain the root word "bee"); however, these are infrequent relative to those in Chinese languages, so that this regularity of Chinese languages may focus Chinese children on patterns of association and category earlier and more systematically than does English (McBride-Chang et al., 2005). Similarly, another study on the development of morphological awareness in Chinese and English (Ku & Anderson, 2003) revealed that Chinese students' acquisition of derivational morphology lags behind that of compounding rules, likely reflecting the nature of Chinese word formation in that there are far fewer derivatives (a word formed from another word; words that are composed of a single lexical morpheme combined with one or more derivational/grammatical morphemes, e.g. self – noun, + ish – adjectivizer, + ly – adverbizer) than compounds (words that are composed of two free morphemes, i.e. "window-shopping", "blood-donors") in Chinese.

In Chinese, the juxtaposition of two or more elements is a common procedure. A distinction can be drawn between *hypotactic* and *paratactic* languages. According to the Oxford Dictionaries, hypotaxis is "the subordination of one clause to another." Parataxis, on the other hand is "the placing of clauses or phrases one after another, without words to indicate coordination or subordination, as in *Tell me, how are you.*" Linguists consider this as one of the most important typological distinctions between English or Italian and Chinese (Zhiping, 2003). English and Italian, for instance, tend to be more hypotactic (even though they can also be also paratactic, especially in the spoken language). Chinese, on the contrary, can be considered paratactic because in Chinese there are no connectors (and, also, in fact, even though, nonetheless, anyway, despite, etc.), so clauses can only be placed side by side, juxtaposed (another famous example, from Julius Caesar is: "I came; I saw; I conquered."). In English and Italian the speech should follow an order with a precise beginning and an end. Since the pre-Socratics, Western thought has developed rhetoric. Oration has some premises, which need to be exposed, argued, and demonstrated by some proofs before jumping to conclusions. The structure of discourse, the way elements are disposed, arranged (*taxis*), all reflect an attitude. Western thinking is normally said to be linear, causal, whereas the Chinese proceeding is more impressionistic, analogical: it is more paratactic. Much of Western philosophy, art, and even cuisine have normally reflected the *single thought*, the *perspective*, the *point of view*, the clearly defined and coherent theoretical approach (with a clear definition of what parts are subordinated). In Chinese cultures, instead, one does not go without the other, opposites go in association to gain balance. Thus, it may be that a similar logic influences the counselors' understanding of theories and their implementation in practice.

Notes

1 Terms that are defined in the Glossary are indicated by an asterisk.
2 The idea that language structures thought has a large number of opponents. Linguists like Chomsky are more concerned with what all languages have in common and they suggest that the diversity of linguistic phenomena is illusory. To them, language is governed by universal rules set in the human brain, so that speaking different languages actually makes little difference. Popper (Popper, 1970, in Chandler, 1994) also claimed that "even totally different languages are not untranslatable." This debate is intriguing, but it goes beyond the scope of this chapter. As a psychoanalyst who aims at listening to the unconscious (and as a person who has tried to learn a few languages), I find it hard to ignore the relations between language (intended both as a system including its rules for combining its components, then including all languages, and any specific spoken language), thought, and speech. Particularly, both my clinical and my personal experience lead me to think that as human beings we are *spoken by the language* (in a broad sense, again).

2 How to do research on psychoanalysis in Hong Kong

What constitutes psychoanalysis, and how does it work? It is rather difficult to say *what* psychoanalysis is. It is much easier to say what psychoanalysis is not. Indeed, psychoanalysis works quite well when applied to another discourse, but it itself is not a discourse. It is not a philosophical system and does not have its own set of values or beliefs, so it is also not a vision of the world (*Weltanschauung*). It is not just a supportive therapy, although it can also be. Finally, it cannot be reduced to a set of knowledge and therapeutic techniques (and evidently Freud dedicated only a minimal number of essays to it). Then, psychoanalysis has several features that distinguish it from other medical or philosophical practices.

Psychoanalysis and psychotherapy

The fact that only psychoanalysis is missing from Hong Kong may be an indirect confirmation that psychoanalysis is different from other forms of psychotherapy. Thus, we should start by examining this difference. Freud often attempted to distinguish psychoanalysis from other psychotherapies (he was mainly referring to hypnosis, psychology, and other treatments of his time). First, he described the greatest antithesis between suggestive and analytic technique with the formulas used by Leonardo da Vinci: *per via di porre* and *per via di levare*:

> Sculpture, however, proceeds per *via di levare*, since it takes away from the block of stone all that hides the surface of the statue contained in it. In a similar way, the technique of suggestion aims at proceeding *per via di porre;* it is not concerned with the origin, strength and meaning of the morbid symptoms, but instead, it superimposes something – a suggestion – in the expectation that it will be strong enough to restrain the pathogenic idea from coming to expression. Analytic therapy, on the other hand, does not seek to add or to introduce anything new, but to take away something, to bring out something.
>
> (Freud, 1905, pp. 260–261)

Psychoanalysis works by subtracting beliefs about the self and the world and by revealing the ambiguity of the words we use. Second, if healing is made possible by (suggestive) psychotherapy, Freud says that it is only with psychoanalysis that we can reach an understanding of the unconscious processes at work. Freud's interest was caught by the theorization, rather than just the treatment of patients: he generally considered the process of analysis as an opportunity for elaborating new theory rather than for curing patients. For him, each session was a chance to discover and not just apply a standardized method. Today, now that psychotherapies are operationalized and evaluated in terms of "effectiveness" it seems that the divide between psychoanalysis and psychotherapy is even greater. Third, the goal of psychotherapy is possible, whereas psychoanalysis is impossible. Freud (1925a) mentioned the joke of the three impossible professions in the preface to the book by August Aichhorn. These were: educating, curing, and governing. Later in "Analysis Terminable and Interminable" (Freud, 1937) he substituted curing with psychoanalyzing: "It almost looks as if analysis were the third of those 'impossible' professions in which one can be sure beforehand of achieving unsatisfying results. The other two, which have been known much longer, are education and government" (p. 248). The fact that Freud replaced the profession of curing in the original version of the joke with psychoanalysis seems to suggest that he might have considered curing possible and psychoanalysis impossible. This may seem paradoxical, considering that he is the father of psychoanalysis. However, such an ambiguous statement may allude to the ethics of the analyst, who is called to occupy a position that is not always gratifying (Freud assimilated the figure of the analyst to the surgeon whose only concern is for the operation s/he has to execute), and still is determined to hold that position and carry on the analysis. Psychoanalysis may be impossible because, although the cure may come to an end, the analysis is potentially interminable. As long as one speaks, thinks, and dreams, speech, and thus the unconscious are at work, so that the analysis is a never-ending process. Fourth, while psychotherapy aims to prevent "disorders" and treat "dysfunctions" by consolidation and defense, psychoanalysis considers symptoms as already one's attempt to heal ("compromise formations"), thus something meaningful for the person and a resource. Fifth, contrary to most psychotherapies, where the intervention is coded, psychoanalysis does not follow a standard procedure, except for only a few basic rules. (Freud gave the example of the game of chess, where only the openings and end-games moves can be standardized, whereas after the opening, the variety of possible moves is virtually infinite.) In psychoanalysis, the content and the style of intervention cannot be transferred from one analyst to another; there is not a psychoanalytical saying, or wisdom, nor is there a universal psychoanalytic knowledge that can be applied to every case. Regardless of its content, an interpretation, an act, a word can be "psychoanalytic" as long as it is able to produce an effect and be transformative. In psychoanalysis, an intervention will be effective *if it is* able to produce further associations; thus, it is measured by its effects (*après-coup*, or *nachträglichkeit**). Conversely, in psychotherapy, it is often thought that defining *in advance* the right words to say is possible; consequently, communication from the therapist to the client is only a matter of timing (as it was in hypnosis). More likely, in psychoanalysis the intervention of the psychoanalyst is effective when it is unexpected, surprising, and is able to break the representations that the analysand* holds. It does not come as a premeditated communication because it is dependent on what the analysand comes to say in that moment. Sixth, for all the reasons mentioned above, psychoanalysis cannot be a standard profession; its practice requires a sort of vocation. Either one is infected with the *plague*, or is not:

> Psycho-analytic activity is arduous and exacting; it cannot well be handled like a pair of glasses that one puts on for reading and takes off when one goes for a walk. As a rule psycho-analysis possesses a doctor either entirely or not at all. Those psychotherapists who make use of analysis among other methods, occasionally, do not to my knowledge stand on firm analytic ground; they have not accepted the whole of analysis but have watered it down – have drawn its fangs, perhaps; they cannot be counted as analysts.
> (Freud, 1933, pp. 152–153)

What psychoanalysis?

Today we speak of psychoanalysis as if it was one unitary discipline; however, it would be more correct to say that there are as many definitions of psychoanalysis as there are psychoanalysts. This is significant in the way psychoanalysis proceeds *by difference rather than by similarity*. This may also suggest that probably, everyone who wants to operate as a psychoanalyst will have to face intellectual solitude rather than large consensus; I am skeptical that psychoanalysis can proliferate in large groups or in institutions. The production of knowledge in psychoanalysis follows the singular logic of the unconscious; thus it is not something that can be transmitted or shared, as it is for other disciplines. We can also read in light of this the history of psychoanalysis, which is a history of (sometimes difficult and painful) separations (Bergmann, 2004). Psychoanalysis today is fragmented; however, here I will consider psychoanalysis as a whole.

Concepts like unconscious, transference*, and free floating attention* are cornerstones of Freudian psychoanalysis. Psychoanalytic theory is also known for its emphasis on sexuality, for its focus on dreams, and for terms like repression, superego, free associations, defense mechanisms, and drive, among others. However, psychoanalysis is a practice and not just a sum of concepts. Thus, research that aims to assess the reception of psychoanalysis in a foreign culture cannot simply measure the knowledge of a few concepts in a certain population. Simply asking local counselors if they know some psychoanalytic terms would not help us to understand the complex relations between psychoanalysis and Hong Kong Chinese culture. Furthermore, it may be that local counselors know some psychoanalytic concept without making use of it in their practice. Or, on the other hand, it may be possible that local counselors have an attitude similar to psychoanalysis in their practice, without being aware of it and without expressly referring to psychoanalysis. Therefore, it was not assumed in this research that psychoanalysis is simply missing from Hong Kong.

But then the problem was: how to do research on psychoanalysis where psychoanalytic theory is largely unknown? To begin with, it was argued that this study should not focus on some specific concepts. Instead, it was important to find an operational definition of psychoanalysis that: (1) allows us to conduct the research in such profoundly different contexts, for example not using any psychoanalytic jargon, (2) goes beyond the theoretical differences among various orientations and schools in psychoanalysis; and (3) could allow us to distinguish psychoanalysis from other counseling orientations. Thus, it was argued that a psychoanalytic attitude and a counseling/psychotherapy attitude should be described and then compared with the attitude shown by the local counselors.

It soon became essential to find an operational definition of psychoanalysis. Investigating the psychoanalytic attitude, rather than remaining at the level of the theory, allows us to investigate and compare different realities in which the psychoanalytic theory is not present, is not strong, or greatly differs. A psychoanalytic attitude seemed the most flexible and yet comprehensive concept, as it is not confined to one specific field.

Psychoanalytic attitude

Some scholars (Kernberg, 1993; White, 2001) have tried to describe the convergences and the divergences between schools inside the psychoanalytic movement. Wallerstein (1991) attempted to find "common ground" among different psychoanalytic orientations; however, as Green (2005) replied, this is likely to remain wishful thinking, impossible to realize.

Every psychoanalytic orientation and each school of psychoanalysis, analytic association, and analyst has his/her own theory and distinctions, and each of them tend to be dismissive of the others: this is what Freud named the *narcissism of minor differences**. Despite this, can we retrace something common among different psychoanalytic orientations? What do they share in the practice? What are the distinctive traits of psychoanalysis; and what are the basic assumptions that lead analysts to assume a particular attitude or disposition when listening to their clients? A hypothesis is that apart from the theoretical fragmentation or the imaginary divisions among schools, psychoanalysts share a common attitude toward the word and speech, which constitutes the core of their practice. *While concepts may be specific to one school, if a psychoanalytic attitude exists, it should be inclusive of different schools* *and orientations while distinguishing psychoanalysis from other disciplines at the same time.*

What are the characteristics of the analytic attitude?

Only a few authors (Schafer, 1983; Gorman, 2008; Hansell, 2008) have specifically addressed the question of what constitutes a "psychoanalytic attitude," while literature about theory and technique of psychoanalysis is copious.

For Schafer (1983), a psychoanalytic attitude implies that the psychoanalyst: (a) is non-judgmental and neutral; (b) avoids either–or thinking and simply analyzes; and (c) avoids the temptation to do more than that. First, it must be said that the term "neutral" raised numerous debates within psychoanalysis. It was proposed first by Freud for describing the position of the analyst toward the speech of the analysand. However, some argue that this was not the exact term chosen by Freud, and that a questionable translation is the cause of many misunderstandings and misinterpretations; for instance, Hoffer (1985) notes that the term "neutral" is an imprecise translation given by Strachey for Freud's less technical term *indifferenz*. It is likely Freud intended "indifference" to refer to the manifest meaning conveyed by the telling of the analysand and not to the person of the analysand. What was more likely an invitation to listen with hovering attention (not judging, not focusing on the explicit meaning or the fine reasoning, but listening to what is not being said) has instead been misinterpreted, and has led some to represent the analyst as a cold and distant person who refuses to manifest any emotion for others, and for the analysands in particular. Obviously the latter is just a parody of the analyst, an imaginary representation that results from a misinterpretation of the Freudian words. On the other hand, the image we have of Freud from his letters and the reports from his pupils and analysands is far from that of a cold and distant person (see, for example, Roazen, 1995). Second, saying that the psychoanalyst avoids *either–or thinking* is to simply consider the unconscious. The unconscious is the third non-excluded; then, psychoanalysts will listen to the contradiction and the paradoxes of the unconscious. The experience of psychoanalysis highlights precisely the fact that the truth can never really be said completely (as in the logic "either–or"). Speaking is revealing, so the psychoanalytic process is potentially unending. Indeed, the goal of the psychoanalytic process is not to uncover an original trauma, or realize a final truth. Third, the analyst should be concerned to analyze only, and avoid the temptation to do more than that, which would only interfere with the process of the analysis. As already mentioned, psychoanalysis is possible when a question is addressed by the analysand to someone in the position of the psychoanalyst. The analysis is possible because of a particular (analytical) disposition; but the operator, what makes the analysis possible, is the speech more than the person of the psychoanalyst. This implies that the analyst is not the expert, the master, or the guru; s/he is required instead to hold this position, without becoming too active, for example, imaging what s/he is supposed to do or say. Greenberg (1986) adds that the analyst: (a) does not try to make anything happen and does not try to bring about a certain kind of change because he/she believes in it in principle; and (b) totally repudiates any adversarial conception of the analytic relationship. Finally, Laurent (2006) remarks that: (a) there is no standard treatment, no general procedure by which psychoanalytic treatment is governed; (b) the transference bond presupposes the locus in which the unconscious is able to appear with the greatest degree of freedom; and (c) the analyst does not identify with any of the roles that his client wants to make him/her take on. Thus, a psychoanalytic attitude and approach to clinical work encompasses a number of distinct features about listening and how to conceptualize clinical process.

Some have tried to define a "psychoanalytic process," and various tools have been developed and used for evaluating it. However, Vaughan, Spitzer, Davies, and Roose (1997) stated that "there is no meaningful consensual definition of the term AP (analytic process)" (p. 964), and Schachter, Schachter, and Kächele (2012) concluded that "the concept of traditional psychoanalytic process may have provided in the past, it is no longer a viable or useful construct, and should be retired" (p. 19). Thus, a new perspective on defining the essence of psychoanalysis may be needed.

The analytic attitude: a different listening disposition

In this study it is claimed that *listening* is a key concept to describe and understand this psychoanalytic attitude, as listening is the axis where theory and practice merge. Psychoanalysis was first described as a talking cure, but listening (to the unconscious) is probably what best sums up and captures the essence of psychoanalysis, and the distinctive psychoanalytic listening is particularly clear when compared to any listening in counseling and psychotherapy.

At the same time, *listening* allows us: (1) to give an operational definition of psychoanalysis (with the advantage that it may overcome the conceptual differences among psychoanalytic schools); and (2) to distinguish psychoanalysis from other forms of psychotherapy and counseling. If it is impossible to describe a theoretical common ground, at least a psychoanalytic attitude or, better yet, a psychoanalytic listening, can be more pragmatic and can provide us with an easier operational definition. Furthermore, it is argued that by only assessing a "listening disposition" it is possible to understand not only what counselors think about their profession, their practice and eventually psychoanalysis, but also how they practice, and eventually how similar or different from psychoanalysis their practice really is. Finally, here, listening allows us to conduct cross-cultural research, and to assess the understanding and the use of psychoanalysis where psychoanalytic theory is marginal.

Listening as it emerged through Freud's recommendations

In 1912 Freud wrote the seminal text *Recommendations to Physicians Practicing Psychoanalysis*, in which he listed a number of technical rules for conducting psychoanalysis. Such guidelines implicitly describe psychoanalytic listening. First, "not directing one's notice to anything in particular and in maintaining the same 'evenly-suspended attention'" (Freud, 1912, p. 110) is the counterpart to the demand made to the patient to obey the fundamental rule of free association. Second, his advice is to avoid taking notes during analytical sessions. Third, he noted that the analyst should maintain emotional coldness "and concentrate his mental forces on the single aim of performing the operation as skillfully as possible" (p. 114). Fourth, the analyst should do everything not to become a censor of his own in selecting the patient's material (metaphor of the receiver). Fifth, educative ambition is of as little use as therapeutic ambition; every doctor should "take the patient's capacities rather than his own desires as guide" (p. 118). Finally, Freud advises against intellectualizing the psychoanalytic conversation as "mental activities such as thinking something over or concentrating the attention solve none of the riddles of a neurosis"; instead one should patiently obey "the psycho-analytic rule, which enjoins the exclusion of all criticism of the unconscious or of its derivatives" (p. 118).

In his recommendations, Freud advised against "various determined efforts to remember" (Jackson, 1992, p. 1626). He then specified that listening with free floating attention goes beyond the plan of explicit meaning, reasoning, and rational thinking. It is much more than just listening "without prejudices." The aim of psychoanalytic listening is not to come to a full comprehension or explanation; rather, it is an attitude of suspicion toward the apparent meaning. And, it is a listening that can be at best acquired through a personal analysis.

Psychoanalysis is often identified with the couch. But not everybody may know what led Freud to start using it. Indeed, the couch was part of a technical arrangement made to allow for better psychoanalytic listening. In his "On the Beginning of Treatment: Further Recommendations on the Technique of Psychoanalysis" Freud (1913, pp. 133–134) wrote:

> Since, while I am listening to the patient, I, too, give myself over to the current of my unconscious thoughts, I do not wish my expressions of face to give the patient material for interpretations or to influence him in what he tells me. The patient usually regards being made to adopt this position as a hardship and rebels against it, especially if the instinct for looking (scopophilia) plays an important part in his neurosis. I insist on this procedure, however, for its purpose and result are to prevent the transference from mingling with the patient's associations imperceptibly, to isolate the transference and to allow it to come forward in due course sharply defined as a resistance.

Listening to the unconscious through dreams, jokes, and negation

For Freud, most of the relevant material of analysis is unconscious; the main reason responsible for this is the mechanism of repression, which in fact is the "cornerstone of psychoanalysis." The process of analysis is to produce such knowledge, which is initially unknown to the speaker. However, there are several ways to elude the censorship of the unconscious, and they are those unintentional phenomena like dreams, jokes, lapsus, mot d'esprit, and slips of tongue that instead reveal a different truth than the speaker claims. Throughout his "Interpretation of Dreams" (1900) it is assumed that dreams are a way to overcome the internal resistance and the censorship of the consciousness, which indeed is lowered during sleep; dreams become in fact "the royal road to the unconscious."

The joke-work seems to be closely related to the dreams-work (that is to say: condensation, displacement, the representation of a thing by its opposite or by something very small, etc.), and in 1905 Freud writes "Jokes and Their Relation to the Unconscious," in which he analyzes the different ways humor operates in eluding the censorship and expressing unacceptable thoughts. Freud claimed that there are no innocuous jokes – jokes that have no relation to the people who share the joke, their stories, and of course their resistances and censorships. He reminds us in his later "An Autobiographical Study," that enjoyment derived from the joke is "due to the momentary suspension of the expenditure of energy upon maintaining repression" (Freud, 1925b, p. 63). This is probably the reason why Freud gave so much attention to jokes, and to popular stories, in making his theory. Indeed, he never overlooked them as non-scientific material; on the contrary, he considered them the best allies for psychoanalytic listening.

In a later essay that Freud wrote in 1925 on "Negation," he makes clear that the "content of a repressed image or idea can make its way into consciousness, on condition that it is *negated*. Negation is a way of taking cognizance of what is repressed" (Freud, 1925c, p. 236). The manifest meaning, what the patient "means" should not mislead the analyst. However, his truth lies in what the patient says, so it is precisely to the signifiers* that the analyst should give attention. Freud takes examples from his practice and how patients bring forward their associations during the work of analysis:

> "Now you'll think I mean to say something insulting, but really I've no such intention." We realize that this is a rejection, by projection, of an idea that has just come up. Or: "You ask who this person in the dream can be. It's *not* my mother." We emend this to: "So it *is* his mother." In our interpretation, we take the liberty of disregarding the negation and of picking out the subject-matter alone of the association.
>
> (1925c, p. 235)

This clearly represents a completely different attitude to listening than how it is generally intended in everyday life. Attention is given to what arises from the unconscious, not just to the conscious intention of the person speaking. For Freud, there are simply no "innocuous" communications that do not refer to another (unconscious) level. He even refutes the idea of an original distinction between subjective and objective. Indeed, there are no communications that can be objectified; all that comes from the analysand can be further analyzed and interpreted, everything that is said has value for consideration. The very function of the intellectual judgment, whose task is to affirm or negate the content of thoughts, would be an extension of the mechanism of repression:

> A negative judgment is the intellectual substitute for repression; its "no" is the hall-mark of repression, a certificate of origin [...] With the help of the symbol of negation, thinking frees itself from the restrictions of repression and enriches itself with material that is indispensable for its proper functioning.
>
> (Freud, 1925c, p. 237)

Listening in psychoanalysis after Freud

A number of analysts after Freud have expressly addressed the theme of psychoanalytic listening. Among them are some perspectives which are particularly relevant. Salman Akhtar (2007) defined psychoanalysis as the "listening cure" to match the celebrated label "talking cure" given to psychoanalysis by Sigmund Freud's early patient Anna O. (Breuer and Freud, 1893–1895). In a later work, Akhtar (2013) described four models of analytic listening: (1) *Objective listening*: great attention is given to how the patient is talking (pauses, hesitations, emphases, peculiarities of intonation, and slips of the tongue). The analyst relies less on his/her intuition and more on his/her intellectual capacity. (2) *Subjective listening*: the analyst's unconscious may pick up what the patient's unconscious is transmitting. The Kleinian concept of "projective identification" and its extended notion of "unthinkable thoughts" (beta elements) proposed by Bion fall here. (3) *Empathic listening*: the analyst actively seeks to resonate with the patient's experience, recognizing the inner state of the patient; and (4) *Intersubjective listening*: directed equally to the patient's subjectivity, the analyst's subjectivity, and the intersubjectivity they create together. Further, he suggests that "objective" and "intersubjective" models of listening lean toward the "skeptical listening" described by Killingmo (1989), which focuses on how the analysand is saying what s/he is saying, whereas "empathic" and "subjective" lean toward the "credulous listening," which focuses upon what the analysand is saying.

Arnold (2006) refers to the work of Reik and his often-forgotten "Listening with the Third Ear." Particularly interesting is the association between psychoanalytic listening and rhythmic sensitivity. Reik (1948) points out that the German word *Takt* (tact) refers to social feeling, but at the same time is synonymous with "musical beat, time, measure, bar." *Takt* is then a matter of timing: "to say the right thing is largely to say it at the right moment" (Arnold, 2006, p. 755). However, the advice given in Reik's text is predominantly negative:

> Reik more often tells clinicians what not to do than what to do. Clinicians should avoid interfering with the natural unfolding of the sequence of conjecture that flows from the detection of clues to their unconscious assimilation and the emergence of insight into consciousness. For the third ear to function smoothly, rational thought must be suspended until the right moment.
> (Arnold, 2006, p. 764)

Empathic and interpretive listening

A number of psychoanalysts have referred to the concept of empathy and empathic listening and suggested that it is an essential prerequisite for therapy (see Jackson, 1992 for a review). Deutsch referred to "intuitive empathy" with regard to the psychoanalytic process. Ferenczi introduced the notion of *tact* as one of the distinctive characteristics required of the analyst at work, particularly when interpreting. Greenson (1960) defined empathy as "emotional knowing, the experiencing of another's feelings" (p. 213).

Empathy sounds like a very intuitive and obvious concept, and it seems quite understandable that communication can improve within an atmosphere of trust and safety. But practically, empathy is difficult to operationalize and one may wonder whether being able to "put oneself in the place of the other" encourages speaking and listening or instead promotes the ideal of an imaginary and *immediate* (non-mediate by words) comprehension. One may even say that listening is possible precisely because of an *irreducible distance*, because we can never really know what the other feels or wants to say.

Stewart (1983) criticizes empathy as a way of listening, and instead he proposes what he calls an *interpretive listening*. To Stewart, listening is not only "listening to something" as part of a neutral act of perception; listening is productive, and listening to one's unconscious means that the speaker may be surprised at what was said: "In genuine conversation I actually do not know what I am going to say next, and interlocutors frequently surprise themselves with what 'comes out'" (p. 389). Furthermore, it is not clear what qualities would be required for empathic listening; instead, Stewart (1983) suggests that skills like paraphrasing, mirroring, asking clarifying questions, adding examples, and listening beyond, just to name a few, are easier to define and can help to maintain focus. Thus, listening is open, meaning that the object of listening is not known from the beginning (the so-called internal state, the self, the inner object, as if it was one and constant); so each conversation should be new, creative, unknown to both parties, and surprising.

For Schafer (2005), there is no distinction between listening and interpreting, as listening itself is an interpretive action. However, he suggests that the analyst is required to have some empathetic listening for ambivalence; psychoanalysts should be responsive to ambivalence and they should not take at face value what they hear from analysands, but listen critically to their speech, taking nothing for granted, so as to keep the door open for further meaning.

Further positions

Bohm (2002) suggests that the method of free association is no longer very popular among analysts, but Vehviläinen (2003, p. 574) gives a broader interpretation of it:

> the analyst treats a topic following another topic in the patient's talk as an *association* of that topic, that is, as essentially connected to the first topic by an unconscious link. If, for instance, the patient narrates a dream and then begins to talk about a recent incident at work, the analyst can treat the mentioning of the work incident as an association of that dream.

Working on the associative level of what is expressed by the analysand, rather than interpreting everything being said, might be what allows psychoanalysis to go beyond the imaginary level of the apparent meaning. Instead, following the flow of the speech may reveal the unconscious associations and throw light on the other story that is being repressed. As a consequence, the intervention of the analyst might be unexpected, because it is apparently unrelated to what is being verbalized. Analytic listening leads to listening to another story. This makes the psychoanalytic conversation difficult to explain out of the context in which it happens. Many times it is difficult to report what has been said in a session, because psychoanalytic listening aims at subverting the given meaning. As Freud has shown with dreams, jokes, and negation, psychoanalysis often plays with the apparent nonsense, more than sense. However, this attitude is often misunderstood, particularly by those who have not undergone this very peculiar experience: "One of the stereotypical assumptions about psychoanalytic interaction is that the patient talks in a monologue while the analyst mainly listens in total silence, or only occasionally informs the patient what her or his talk means psychoanalytically" (Vehviläinen, 2003, p. 579). In fact, it is a frequent oversimplification to think that the analysand speaks and the analyst listens and replies. Again, this simplification reflects the model of communication, where the message goes from one subject to another. In psychoanalysis there is not simply one person analyzing another; instead, attention is directed to the unconscious, so that both the analysand and the analyst must be listening. The very term "analysand" expresses the need for the client to become active in this process. The client too should enhance his/her listening and be able to analyze his/her speech. At the same time, the analyst does not simply reply to the analysand, and yet every word finds its answer. The psychoanalytic conversation is not just an exchange, a give and take. There may be much use of silence in a psychoanalytic session (Akhtar, 2013); however, a silence is not just that the analyst does not want to, or cannot, answer. A silence is not simply the moment before a psychoanalytic interpretation comes. Instead, silence may help to lead the analysand to listening and questioning his/her own words and, as such, a silence can already be a psychoanalytic interpretation.

Stensson (cited in Sjodin, 2006) distinguishes meditation from contemplation, and argues that the Freudian evenly hovering attention is similar to active contemplation. Indeed, meditation comes from the Latin *meditari*, and means to think reflectively. Instead, contemplation comes from *contemplari*, and means to look with attention. Furthermore, Stensson stresses that meditation has connotations of measurement, while contemplation is concerned with the immeasurable.

Bollas (2007, 2009) argues that for the most radical and effective theory of listening we should go back to Freud, who believed that if an analysand is allowed to speak long enough, the analyst can discover a line of thought in a chain of ideas, a logic sequence. However, he argues that classical psychoanalysts have abandoned this very core of Freud's practice, and have preferred to follow another approach:

> If we return to the history of psychoanalysis we can see that all theoretical schools adopted Freud's theory of repression and dropped his theory of reception. Instead of following the logic of sequence within the multiple lines of thought presented in a session, analysts opted to listen for derivatives of repressed material. They were, that is, engaged in a selective listening which unwittingly mirrored the selective activity of repression itself.
>
> (Bollas, 2009, p. 24)

Bollas suggests that the very revolution of Freud was to follow the patient's flow, rather than following some theoretical construct. Freud emphasized that it is the unconscious at work, more than the analyst. The analyst is required to literally learn to listen to the analysand's associations; constructing psychic models of the mind does not help listening. Bollas stresses that the analyst should not try to fix anything. Instead, s/he should catch the drift of the patient's unconscious with his/her own unconscious. More than relying on Freud's theory of repressed ideas, this is the way for accessing the unconscious. Another important issue related to this is that the analyst should maintain an attitude of openness and curiosity toward the analysand's flow of speech. S/he should be able to foster the analysand's curiosity toward what is being said in session. As a consequence, for Bollas (2009), stimulating further questioning is generally more beneficial to the analytical process than jumping to an interpretation. Or, at the very least, an interpretation should open up new scenarios, and not just answer a question, revealing a supposed truth.

Zeal (2008) criticizes the "here and now" total transference interpretation. Instead, he proposes a more discursive style of listening and interpreting, what he calls the oracular style of listening of Lacan. He contrasts "evocative listening," which he considers calling forth anything from within the domain of ego, to "oracular listening," meaning the listening for, and any speaking or dreaming from, the unconscious beyond ego. Indeed, he notices the paradox that our listening is receptive and evocative at the same time, but then: "even allowing for the fact that a greater part of the ego is unconscious of itself, is the ego an adequate word for the dreamer? Who is the dreamer who dreams?" (p. 97). In other words: who is the author of that speech, and where does that speech come from? Lacan emphasizes this question, as for him, the analysand should become responsible for his/her saying, by gradually developing a listening attitude themselves. As Widlöcher (2010) writes: "The analysand internalizes the mode of co-thinking, and, through a continuous process of elaboration, he or she little by little becomes his or her own psychoanalyst, at least in the best of cases" (p. 48). This means first of all that it is not only the analyst who should develop and maintain an analytic listening disposition; it is also the analysand who is called to do so. Indeed, psychoanalysis is a rather active process, in which the analysand is called to be protagonist (different from the medical relation, in which the patient lies down on a bed and is operated on passively). The role of the analyst is thus to preserve the setting of the analysis and let the analysand speak and enable his/her listening attitude:

> the analyst "must maintain a position of desire – desire for the patient to talk, dream, fantasize, associate and interpret" – regardless of any intensities of liking or disliking he may have. Therefore it can be said that, as the analyst is called upon to maintain this strictly analytically oriented desire in the work regardless of the personal, that all resistance to doing so is the analyst's resistance.
>
> (Zeal, 2008, pp. 97–98)

Widlöcher (2010, p. 47) distinguishes

> in any practice born from psychoanalysis a *psychoanalytic listening method per se* and a *psychotherapeutic listening method*. With J. Laplanche I consider that in the "cure-type"' of practice these two options are constantly "coasting" alongside each other. The psychoanalytic method is per se deconstructive, a pure discovery of the unconscious, its latent contents and process. It has no therapeutic value in itself, just knowledge of the psychic apparatus. But the major part of time during psychoanalysis is

devoted to reconstruct the personal history of the patient, his conflicts and traumatic memories. This second method underlies a process of "treating" the defenses that are intimately linked to unconscious fantasies, a process made possible through the psychoanalytical listening of free association and the analyst's interpretations.

According to Widlöcher, what distinguish psychoanalysis from psychotherapy are a "necessary associative listening" and an "unnecessary psychotherapeutic work":

> What characterizes the *psychanalytique* is the technique of listening, a pure associative and interpretative listening. The *psychotherapeutique* means how to use this technique to help the patient to extricate him or herself from his or her psychic suffering. From this perspective, I do not speak of the psychoanalytic and psychotherapeutic process, but of the psychoanalytic and psychotherapeutic technique of listening.
> (Widlöcher, 2010, p. 47)

All the conventions regarding the setting for psychoanalytic sessions (like the couch and the frequency of sessions) serve to preserve analytic listening, rather than being rules in and of themselves. Then "the analyst gives preference to a psychoanalytic, associative, listening, remaining as faithful as possible to the analysand's sequence of thoughts. The analyst will attempt to maintain this listening throughout the cure, through the variations of drive investments, present conflicts and interfering events" (Widlöcher, 2010, p. 53). This model may remain "utopian," whereas daily practice may be different and may turn into a psychoanalytic psychotherapy, different from the "cure-type": "there the therapeutic contract is formed to use the associative interpretative method to disengage the patient from the constraints issued from conflictual and defensive structures, which are the cause of its psychical suffering, and not to create discovery of its unconscious dynamic pressure" (Widlöcher, 2010, p. 48). This obviously has effects on the type of listening:

> In this way, our psychoanalytic listening is led astray by patients' successive, alternating, or indefinite requests. Instead of maintaining a way of listening strictly directed towards associative co-thinking between patient and analyst, we use our understanding of the dynamic play to clarify the nature of the conflicts, symptoms and defences, to help the patient disengage from his psychopathological structures.
> (Widlöcher, 2010, p. 48)

What transpires from this conception is a psychoanalytic listening that is radically different from a psychotherapeutic listening. The Freudian "evenly hovering attention" does not only indicate how to listen but precisely how "not to listen." Free floating attention suggests that listening arises from misunderstanding, because a signifier may open up to various and different meanings. It was not Freud, but those who came after him, who felt the need to specify what to listen for in the telling of the analysand. The fundamental rule of psychoanalysis, free association, simply invites one to speak and to follow the flow of thought; it does not suggest following a particular concept or construct.

Lacan criticized those analysts who, considering language and speech inadequate grounds for psychoanalysis, began to focus on illusory aspects situated beyond speech, which they claim they would know in an interpersonal and affective way. To Lacan, affects were effects of language and not something outside of the language. The speaker is not master of his/her speech. Thus, meanings are not created by the analysand or co-created by the analyst–analysand dyad. What emerges in psychoanalysis is not the meaning but the signifier without meaning; meanings are rather a consequence of how signifiers are disposed among each other. For Lacan (1977, p. 214), "we must listen to the speaker, when it is a question of a message that does not come from a subject beyond language, but from speech beyond the subject." As a consequence, one does not really know what one is saying. And thus, the goal of the analysis is to develop that listening disposition rather than reconstructing or giving meanings, as other postmodern narrative approaches would put it.

What the analysand is not aware of is the ambiguity of his or her words. In this sense, the meaning of his/her saying seems at first very clear, while indeed the signifier always opens up another meaning. The work of analysis is not to translate it so much as to rearticulate it. The intervention does not correct a false belief, or substitute an affect with another more adaptive, more functional belief. Instead, everything that comes within speech is structured and should be investigated and questioned.

Openness in psychoanalytic listening: listening to versus listening for

Central to psychoanalysis is the unconscious: "in contrast to other psychological theories or socially determinist ones, all psychoanalytic theories find common ground in the assumption that much of psychic life is unconscious" (Chodorow, 2003, p. 475). If both the individual and social levels converge into the unconscious, then every analysand shows something that the previous theory cannot fully predict or explain. The unconscious cannot be reified to a static entity that never changes. As such, listening should open to the new, it should allow a new saying; it cannot be reduced simply by retracing elements of a given theory. Bohm (2002) distinguishes between clinicians that are "*appliers* who apply a psychoanalytic school to their patients – and those who try to be psychoanalytic *explorers* using their school as the latest preliminary map" (p. 21). Chodorow (2003) suggests that analysts who are more driven by theory are likelier to listen for, while those driven more by individuality are likelier to listen to. "Ideally, in the clinical setting, listening *to* and listening *for* exist in a complex feedback loop" (p. 478).

What is probably needed, then, is to cultivate a disposition of openness: not just reading what is seen in light of what is known (the vision follows the speech; one sees what one thinks), but instead trying to find the nonsense and the paradoxes in what is heard; only this can open up new understanding. Personal analysis is the elective place for learning how to listen to one's own speech. A number of qualities are then required from both the analyst and the analysand. Instead of just knowledge, curiosity and uncertainty are necessary to a psychoanalytic process. "Curiosity and uncertainty enable or imply the recognition that things are not necessarily as they seem, that the analysand's current self-understanding or current ways of feeling may not be inevitable" (Chodorow, 2003, p. 479). An attitude of openness means that what is said should not simply be explained or reduced to an existing theoretical framework. It is not just a matter of translating a foreign language into a more comprehensible one.

Then, ideally, we should be listening *to* the speech, *to* the telling, *to* the associative chains, and we should be listening *for* lapses, *for* forgetfulness, *for* contradictions, and *for* any other formations of the unconscious.

In conclusion

After extensive literature review about psychoanalytic listening, it can be summarily deemed that: (a) while *hearing* is directed toward what is being said, *listening* is directed toward what is *not* being said; (b) there is speech beyond the speaker and his/her intended meaning, and this "beyond area" should be the focus of the analyst; (c) the analyst listens to what remains implicit and what is not being verbalized, including his/her feelings and reactions toward the analysand; (d) psychoanalytic listening is not intentional; the analysand is required to free associate and say whatever comes to mind, while the analyst is required not to focus on anything in particular; (e) listening and questioning are intertwined, and together they may lead to a different disposition that allows unconscious material to emerge; (g) there is no dialogue in analysis, but instead, an asymmetrical conversation; (h) the aim of the psychoanalytic conversation is to reflect to the analysand his/her speech; (i) the content of communication should be read in the light of the transference between analyst and analysand; (j) generally, the analyst sits behind the analysand, so as to avoid eye contact and interfere as little as possible with the flow of the analysand, who instead lies on a couch; (k) psychoanalysis is more effective when it sustains the formulation and the articulation of questions rather than the production of answers; and (l) the analyst's engagement in the treatment is more important than the mastery of any techniques.

It should be noted that psychoanalytic listening is not a unified construct. Psychoanalysis has gone through its own developmental process, and the recommendations made by Freud in his early technical papers have been challenged over the past century. In particular, current developments in relational psychoanalysis represent a major rethinking of psychoanalytic technique toward a more dialogic attitude. Then, the above-mentioned criteria should not be considered as conclusive and representative of all psychoanalytic orientations. The conceptualization of psychoanalytic listening presented here is influenced by the European tradition of Freud and Lacan more than other approaches.

What is counseling?

As emerged from the literature review, psychoanalysis and counseling reflect two very different attitudes to listening and how to conceptualize the clinical process. Psychoanalysis and counseling are influenced by different theories of language. In short, they answer differently the question: *who is speaking?* For the psychoanalyst, it is the unconscious who is speaking; the person is not fully aware of what is s/he saying (as Freud said, the ego is not master in his own home). The reference is always Other: the speech comes first, the speaker can only follow. This is also the very etymology of *subject*: one who is under control or domination of another. As a consequence, in psychoanalysis, a lapsus, a thought, or a fantasy is not simply right or wrong; a fantasy is like a dream, which is meaningful for the analysand, and then it should be investigated to see where it originates and how it is relevant within the psychic organization. In contrast, in counseling, the client is normally considered the author of his/her speech and talk; then, it may be that what the client says or does is maladaptive, dysfunctional, or irrational, and must be corrected, or substituted, through an appropriate technique. However, beside theoretical differences, psychoanalysis and counseling/psychotherapy are informed by different conceptions of language and speech, which is what orientates the listening disposition of clinicians.

Under the label "counseling" fall a multitude of practices very diverse in terms of ontology, epidemiology, and methodology. For example, one may argue that behavioral modification is on the opposite spectrum to narrative therapy. To some extent, this is likely true. However, listening in counseling and in psychotherapy generally arise from the traditional theory of communication (Berlo, 1971; Shannon, 1948), which is the matrix common to all counseling and psychotherapeutic practices. Different attitudes toward language between different counseling orientations do exist (Elliott, 2008; Neimeyer, 2009); however, they are understood as minor differences within the same main paradigm, so that finally they appear all to be on a continuum. Only psychoanalysis is radically different (Clemens, 2013; Mounin, 2013). A different conception of the language is what distinguishes psychoanalysis from any other kind of psychotherapy or counseling practice. In psychoanalysis, speech is not just a tool for communicating. The subject is inhabited by the language, and is thus divided, or "spoken." As a consequence, the analysand is not only supposed to talk but, most important, s/he is supposed to listen to his/her words. A popular saying goes "think before you speak"; however, the experience of psychoanalysis shows that this is not possible, and that instead what matters most is that one can listen to what one is saying and start from there. This means that there is not simply a dyad in psychoanalysis, for example between analyst and analysand. This peculiar conception of the language has fundamental implications for the theory and for each aspect of the practice; for example, it is at the basis of the theorizations of transference, free association, interpretation of dreams, and psychoanalytic conversation, as well as the understanding of the psychoanalyst and the analysand.

In this study, the definition of "counseling listening" has been preferred to "psychotherapeutic listening." Indeed, it is claimed that counseling listening may be more comprehensive of a wide spectrum of psychotherapeutic, supportive, and helping practices, led by different professionals from various fields. Counseling listening is a more general and more inclusive definition, which is also more suitable for the sample of this study. In fact, psychotherapy is not regulated in Hong Kong as it is in Western countries. Likewise, there are no officially recognized psychotherapists in Hong Kong, but several professionals, with different education, who deliver counseling. Thus, for both theoretical and practical reasons, the definition of "psychotherapeutic listening" has been discarded.

Purdy and Borisoff (1997, p. 1) describe seven qualities that characterize an effective listener:

> (a) will to listen; (b) focus of attention: if our minds are wandering [...] we are apt to miss important information; (c) awareness of all elements of message, speaker and context; (d) listening involves interpreting, which includes understanding. In interpreting a message we naturally make sense of that message in terms of our own experience; (e) remembering: we need to consciously and actively include listening skills that help us retain what we have heard; (f) response: after understanding a complete thought it is important that we give feedback to the speaker, or respond in such a way that the speaker has an idea of how we have understood and interpreted what he or she has said; and (g) care about the relationship: while we listen for information, we must also keep in mind that information is colored and given meaning by a person's needs and concern.

The listening as it emerges from the analytic experience has nothing to do with the *will*, with focusing the attention or with an active process where a subject would put effort in to interpret or listen to something in particular, trying to bear in mind everything the speaker says. As the psychoanalytic experience shows, listening to another meaning is not simply a matter of will; another meaning is the meaning that emerges from the ambiguity of the signifier. It is not necessarily a *deep* meaning.

Reading these seven principles one can easily notice that they go in the opposite direction to the few pieces of advice that Freud gave. For example, in introducing free floating attention he answered to the issue of how to retain all the information that an analyst hears. His answer was quite the opposite, as in his conception this was already a false problem. Freud's advice was to let the speech operate, to place faith in (or entrust) the unconscious, rather than try to impose a direction on the process.

Wolvin and Coakley (1982) identified five categories of listening: discriminative, comprehensive, critical, appreciative, and therapeutic. In particular, they suggest that five skills are essential to therapeutic listening: focusing attention, demonstrating attending behaviors, developing a supportive communication climate, listening with empathy, and responding appropriately. Similarly, Purdy (in Purdy and Borisoff, 1997) describes the kind of listening in which we all engage during our everyday life: discriminative, critical, evaluative, therapeutic, and appreciative listening. According to Purdy, two types of listening from the humanistic field are useful for describing therapeutic listening: "reflective listening," described by Rogers (1951); and "active listening," defined in the same tradition by Gordon (1977), a follower of Rogers. The term reflective listening is a cornerstone of Rogerian client-centered therapy, or non-directive counseling, and it emphasizes that the content of another person's story should not be altered. Similarly, the rationale for active listening is to prevent or minimize misunderstandings in person-to-person communication by the use of specific techniques and strategies (e.g. eye contact, body posture, vocal qualities, and verbal tracking) (Gordon, 1977). Active listening is intended to enhance empathy and acceptance; however, ideally, its main goal is to reduce as much as possible distortions in interpersonal communications. The structure of active listening is explained by Gordon with terms that clearly recall the basic theory of communication: "Active listening is certainly not complex. Listeners need only restate, in their own language, their impression of the expression of the sender. It's a check: is my impression acceptable to the sender?" (p. 62). With active listening, Gordon defined the kind of listening that arose in counseling, brought to different settings, mainly in work environments. His techniques became particularly known among managers and those who train managers to become leaders.

The main discrepancy between psychoanalytic and counseling listening concerns the position of the analyst with regard to the discourse of the analysand. Active listening is intended as an effort toward comprehending the (conscious) logic, the reasoning, and the discourse of the speaker. As a consequence, it may then be easier to either agree or change one's perspective or attitude. In psychoanalysis, however, the aim is to go beyond the intended meaning, which is what the other believes and (unconsciously) wants us to also believe. From this, the psychoanalyst does not focus on the meaning, or the sense, of words. On the contrary, the analyst will try to remain "distracted" by the manifest meaning, trying to grasp that signifier that opens to another, different story. In psychoanalysis, there are many schools, and many orientations. Some analysts may try to play with words, whereas others may try to answer with a silence. However, it is argued that a common attitude among psychoanalysts of different schools is that they generally try not to be overwhelmed by the discourse of the analysand. Probably, a psychoanalyst would not follow the intended meaning in the analysand's speech, regardless of the meaning; instead, s/he would be more interested in *how* the analysand expresses his/her story and what else emerges from the various associative chains formed by speaking in session. The disposition of psychoanalytic listening is rather cautious, suspicious, and opposite to putting oneself "momentarily into the other person's shoes," as described by Gordon. One could say that if the goal of counseling is to comprehend the other's perspective, conversely, listening in psychoanalysis attempts to create an openness in the analysand's speech, pointing out the inconsistencies, the gaps, and omissions of the discourse presented. The miscomprehensions are highlighted, because from them a different understanding may be possible (Leclaire, 1998).

Is listening tiring?

In an attempt to defend the role of listening in the counseling profession from over-medicalization and standardization of treatments, Graybar and Leonard (2005, p. 4) give some illuminating perspectives on how listening in counseling and psychotherapy is normally intended:

> Listening is not quick or easy. It can be a complex task that is incredibly draining. Deep, active listening is time consuming. It takes time to allow clients to gather their thoughts and express their feelings. It takes additional time to convey that we care, that we have listened to what has been said and have understood what has been meant. Devouring even more time and demanding even more skill (and therapeutic metal) is listening for and decoding client hopes for, fears about, and disappointments with, therapy or the therapist. Given that listening can be time-consuming, difficult, and stressful it is not surprising that listening finds itself in the cross-hairs of managed care, de-emphasized in many brief, manualized treatments, and nearly eliminated by the 15-minute-medication check.

One may ask why listening should be incredibly draining. It is not specified, but one has the impression that listening in counseling is intended to mean listening "more": to retain *more* information and have *more* elements to elaborate on. This is also what clients normally think, particularly during the initial sessions; some persons can talk non-stop for the whole session, trying to give every detail (at least, those details that they consider essential) of the reason that brought them to our consultation room, imagining that if they are able to provide every single detail their therapist would find it easier (and quicker) to provide them with the answer and solution. This is not necessarily wrong; however, "all" cannot be said and what is being presented is only what one tells oneself. It is important to start from here; however, by paying attention to the exact words that are being used one can listen to a different story. And by continuing questioning and speaking, one might only realize that there is more to say beyond what was initially imagined.

The model of listening that orientates counseling reflects the conception of a speaker who is actively discerning what to say and what to omit, and a receiver who is there to receive, decode, store, and elaborate all the information conveyed, so as to finally provide the answer. We can see here the metaphor of man as information processor; thus, given these premises, listening can indeed be extremely demanding. However, this is quite different from listening in psychoanalysis. Freud had already addressed this question more than hundred years ago when he was asked how he could keep in mind all the names, dates, detailed memories, and fantasies communicated by each client in the course of months and years of treatment. What makes it possible to master such an abundance of material? Precisely, it is the evenly suspended attention. Instead, for Freud,

> as soon as anyone deliberately concentrates his attention to a certain degree, he begins to select from the material before him; one point will be fixed in his mind with particular clearness and some other will be correspondingly disregarded, and in making this selection he will be following his expectations or inclinations. This, however, is precisely what must not be done. In making the selection, if he follows his expectations he is in danger of never finding anything but what he already knows; and if he follows his inclinations he will certainly falsify what he may perceive. It must not be forgotten that the things one hears are for the most part things whose meaning is only recognized later on.
> (Freud, 1912, p. 112)

Freud seems to say that *listening happens whether the analyst wants it to or not*. Indeed, whether material said is relevant or not may be understood only when associated with other material. It may be unclear at the beginning, and for this reason it is important not to discard anything that seems irrelevant at first. Instead, the conception of listening as it arises from counseling always refers to the qualities of the counselor, such as his or her will or intention to listen, or skills:

> We believe at its most basic level listening is a function of time and intention. Having the time to listen, but not the intention is one problem. Having the intention, but not the time is yet another. We suspect, in fact it is our thesis, that both time and intention to listen are frequently lacking in brief, manualized, and/or biological treatments. A clinician may have the intent to listen, but without time intention is of little worth.
> (Graybar & Leonard, 2005, p. 5)

Thus, listening in counseling is considered as complex and tiring because it requires lots of cognitive resources and personal effort to process all the information coming from the other; instead, listening in psychoanalysis might be complex because the psychoanalyst first has to overcome his/her own resistances and temptation for quick comprehension. The former is a listening that happens between "you" and "me" (between two conscious parts) and aims for full comprehension; the latter is a listening to the unconscious, which necessarily cannot lead to a full and conclusive explanation.

Finally, I suggest that a difficulty of listening in psychoanalysis is that the psychoanalyst needs to always keep distance from the meaning that the analysand is consciously trying to convey; it is not always easy not to be overwhelmed by the countless (misleading) details that are mentioned, or by the meaning the client is trying to impose on his/her speech, sometime with the unconscious goal of reducing the psychoanalyst to a mute listener.

Counseling listening includes the following elements: (a) speaking and listening are both intentional processes; (b) it focuses on the content of the message, and particularly on the speaker's intended meaning; (c) when listening to clients, the counselor tries to show the other party that what they are saying is being heard (by gestures of the body, or restatements, etc.); (d) communication is most effective in a vis-à-vis encounter; (e) it aims at clear communication. The counselor reflects or paraphrases the meaning ascribed to what s/he has heard, so as to give clients a chance to correct any misunderstanding; (f) it provides advice and information to help clients to acquire skills and coping strategies; (g) it helps clients to recognize and address problems involving their emotions, attitudes, motivation, or personalities; (h) the alliance between the counselor and the client is a collaborative partnership to which each brings important expertise; (i) an empathic, supportive, yet directive counseling style provides conditions under which change can occur; (j) it develops strategies to reduce symptoms; (k) it maintains positive behavior/attitude/mood; (l) it explores and resolves grief and loss issues, conflicts, and stress; (m) it focuses on specific problems. In individual or group sessions, problem behaviors and problem thinking are identified, prioritized, and specifically addressed; (n) it encourages people to rely on their own strength sets to minimize the problems that exist in their everyday lives; (o) the therapist actively directs clients to the discovery of central thinking problems; and, (p) it focuses on the resolution of current, specific problems, providing a clear structure and focus to treatment.

What are the major criticalities against psychoanalysis?

Since its inception, psychoanalysis has occupied a prominent position in the helping professions and had a profound impact on intellectual lives in most of Western societies. As its popularity grew well beyond the patient consultation room, no other therapeutic method has been so divisive, or has provoked so many contrasting reactions among academics, intellectuals, clinicians, and laymen. Even today, psychoanalysis has a great number of both supporters and detractors.

Over the years, psychoanalysis has been criticized: (1) as a method; (2) as a set of theories; and (3) as a therapeutic process. As a method, its theoretical basis and approach have been criticized by philosophers of science and linguists among others, for lacking adequate scientific credibility (Chomsky, 1978; Grünbaum, 1985); for not being falsifiable (Popper, 1988); and for behaving unscientifically in demonstrating and testing what it holds as its core truths (Schlesinger, 2013). Theoretically, psychoanalysis (particularly in its earlier Freudian version) has been criticized by anthropologists, historians, psychologists, and feminists for: (a) being conservative, reductionist, and positivistic (Chandran, 2011); (b) being too biologically deterministic, too sexist, too pessimistic, and too focused on sex and aggression as intrinsic motives (Sandy, Boardman, & Deutsch, 2000); (c) its emphasis on women's "innate" passivity and dependency and its belief that motherhood is "the only goal" (Marecek, 1974); and (d) being slow to change and adapt to the realities of postmodern life (Maroda, 2009). As a therapeutic process, psychoanalysis has also been criticized for being too expensive because of its labor intensity (Swartz, Gibson, Richter, & Gelman, 2002); for being slow to compete actively with other forms of treatment (Maroda, 2009); and for its overt emphasis on separation and individuation (Roland, 1989).

Psychoanalysis: social work, psychology, and counseling

Historically, psychoanalysis has often been intertwined with counseling/psychotherapy, social work, and psychology, showing substantial overlap and occasional divergence with these fields. In both Europe and America, the psychoanalytic perspective, although it has a long tradition in counseling psychology, has never held a central position (Robbins, 1989). Starting with Freud's work (1919), which distinguished "the pure gold of analysis" from the "copper of direct suggestion," psychoanalysts have often tried to describe what differentiates psychoanalysis from other psychotherapeutic/counseling approaches. Conversely, counselors tend to consider psychoanalysis as one of the many healing tools available for their use (Hansen, 2002). Psychoanalysts often see some incompatibilities between psychoanalytic theory and different counseling approaches, and they tend to rationalize that psychoanalysis is structurally different from counseling/psychotherapy because the two orientations pursue goals that are somehow antithetical (for a review see Alperin & Hollman, 1992). However, counselors are also generally more eclectic and receptive to various techniques, and might be more interested in the similarities between such practices.

In regard to social work, the profession was more enamored with psychoanalysis in the 1960s; however, it still holds potential for social workers' client-centered work. For instance, Edward (2009) suggested that the profession's values, ethics, and focus on its person-centered work might positively influence its approach to the practice of psychoanalysis. He further contended that a psychoanalytic framework, which puts transference at the center of clinical practice, offers an important model for many mental health professionals, including social workers. Federn (1992) noted that social workers who receive analytic training may improve the overall quality of their interventions. Similarly, Nathan (1993) suggested that a psychoanalytic perspective can advance social work thinking, especially at a time when undue emphasis is being given to a more managerialist approach.

Although psychoanalysis was once central to mainstream psychology, by the early 1960s, it had become increasingly marginalized within both clinical and academic communities, which were dominated instead by more positivist approaches (Bornstein, 1999). From a theoretical point of view, a significant divide still exists between psychoanalysis and psychology, as the former goes from the individual to the universal (as such, a case study serves to gain an understanding of one's psychic life), whereas the latter evolves from the universal to the individual (the norm/standard serves as a term of reference for the individual). However, the heuristic value of psychoanalysis is robust, thus psychoanalytic ideas are often co-opted by theoreticians and researchers in other areas of psychology (Bornstein, 2005).

Over time, psychoanalysis gradually became more popular among artists, literates, and intellectuals, rather than social scientists. Consequently, in many universities it has been better received in departments of humanities (e.g. literature and modern languages, history, philosophy), rather than in more traditional departments of psychology and social sciences, implying it has more appeal for its heuristic value than for its clinical application.

However, these claims do not completely explain why only psychoanalysis as a "helping intervention" generally finds such overt resistance among clinicians and counseling professionals. Literature on this indicates that this can be attributed to a number of other concerns, namely those which are specifically theoretical issues about psychoanalysis, its practical applicability, and its transmission. Additional explicit concerns include: its ineffectiveness, complexity, eclecticism, and training. These will be briefly elaborated here.

Its ineffectiveness

There is a belief, particularly in some academic circles, that psychoanalysis lacks empirical support, or that scientific evidence shows other theories and approaches are more effective. In addition, psychoanalysis is sometimes described as being rather obsolete, not as well developed as other counseling techniques, and in some instances not suitable for many clients. This may be partially due to the historic attitudes of psychoanalysts being against empirical research; however, this belief does not resonate with the scientific evidence available today (Shedler, 2010; Leichsenring, 2005). In Hong Kong, a few factors may influence whether local clinicians consider psychoanalysis effective or not. The first of these is *causality*, a milestone of Western philosophy, though it seems to be less relevant in Chinese thought. Several studies (e.g. Choi, Nisbett, & Norenzayan, 1999; Morris & Peng, 1994) show that Westerners interpret behaviors by looking at the inner qualities of the person, whereas the Chinese give more emphasis to circumstances and tend to explain behaviors based on situations. Hong Kong people generally hold a much lower sense of mastery over their lives than North Americans (Stewart et al., 2002). The sense of community in Hong Kong may be very supportive, but also very normative and overwhelming to the individual, to the point that people might perceive they have little room for individual change. Thus, it might be that psychoanalysis, which stresses the importance of everyone finding their own responsibility in what happens in their life, is perceived as of little help, and that other approaches that emphasize adaptation are better received.

The second factor is *technique*: following Chong and Liu (2002), Chinese people value "knowing how to" more than "knowing why," and emphasize practice rather than conceptual thinking. Similarly, this seems to be the tendency in Hong Kong, as there is a strong focus on how to "make use" of Western theories, meaning how to apply them. This attitude obviously reduces a theory to a technique, and the counseling process to the application of one or more techniques. This disposition toward the theory influences the reception of psychoanalysis, which in contrast is an impressive theory with a relatively limited number of standardized and defined techniques. Given such emphasis on technique only, it might be that psychoanalysis is perceived as obsolete, or not as developed as other approaches, or even not as scientific.

A third factor is *concrete thinking vs abstraction*: Chinese thinking has been described as practical and concrete (Hall & Ames, 1998; Jullien, 2004; Randall Groves, 2010; Liang, Cherian, & Liu, 2010). Nakarama (as cited in Redding, 1990, p. 76) summarizes five characteristics of Chinese thinking: (1) emphasis on perception of the concrete; (2) non-development of abstract thought; (3) emphasis on particulars, not universality; (4) practicality as central focus; and (5) concern for harmony and balance. Interestingly, the word concrete literally means "to grow together" (from *com-* "together" + *crescere* "to grow"), thus referring again to the idea of a group, which is so central to Chinese culture. Hong Kong Chinese culture emphasizes concreteness and a straightforward attitude. Psychoanalysis instead proceeds most likely by abstraction, which means being "withdrawn or separated from material objects or practical matters" (nevertheless, psychoanalysis aims at being *pragmatic*). The literature seems to suggest that today Chinese people might strongly prefer visualization rather than abstract thinking, and answers rather than questions.

Finally, a fourth factor is *introspection*: introspection has no tradition in Chinese culture and some Chinese psychiatrists suggest that insight-oriented psychoanalysis is not suitable for the Chinese (Haag, 2014). Furthermore, Haag (2014) observed that Chinese psychoanalyst candidates frequently work in a supportive way rather than maintaining a more psychoanalytic position. She suggested that Chinese therapists might find it difficult to refuse to fulfill clients' wishes and encourage them to develop their resources because of their Confucian backgrounds (where the counselor is expected to be closer to a teacher or master rather than a psychoanalyst). Particularly in this context, the neutral position of the analyst and his/her attitude of not interfering with the associative work of the analysand may be misunderstood and be perceived by the latter as lack of interest in his/her story; thus, such a position might be considered as less effective than that of a more traditional counselor. However, previous experiences in teaching psychoanalysis in China have demonstrated that it can at least partially be received and practiced in this context. For example, Zhiyan and Zachrisson (2014) reflected on transference and countertransference in a Chinese setting and suggested that the psychoanalytic conception of this is largely valid in China as well. In their opinion, in a Chinese context and with Chinese clients, there are variations in the way transference is expressed, but normally this should not call for significant modifications of the psychoanalytic technique.

Its perceived complexity

Psychoanalysis is indeed much more complex than other counseling approaches. A major obstacle here is that psychoanalytic language may appear unclear and almost "esoteric"; in fact, psychoanalysis tends to give different meanings to terms taken from other fields, or it simply coins its own words. In addition, psychoanalysis spreads differently in different cultural contexts, and the original Freudian theory has been reinterpreted in very different ways. Some terms that Freud expressed in his German language were already misinterpreted and distorted when translated into English, Italian, French, and Spanish. The difficulty of psychoanalysis in a Chinese context, where even terms like *unconscious* do not find correspondence, is therefore quite understandable (Plänkers, 2013; Busiol, 2012b, 2015). As noted by Brandell (2013), discomfort with the complexities of psychoanalytic theory on the part of both students and non-analytic colleagues may lead to confusion and intellectual resistance. In mainland China, psychoanalytic candidates reported that the main factors negatively influencing their practice and motivation are the difficulties that they encounter working with patients. Specifically, their feeling incompetent with therapeutic work, being unclear how to deal with a client, or being unsure that their intervention can be beneficial (Li, 2014). Furthermore, psychoanalysis is often considered as lasting too long (particularly from a Hong Kong perspective), both for counselors and for clients. For clients, it generally requires an undefined number of sessions and offers no quick answers. For counselors, it requires a long (and virtually unending) training protocol before one can actually practice. Psychoanalytic training requires several years and great personal involvement. Instead, training in Hong Kong mainly consists of academic training, which is brief and limited to didactic courses, and in some cases even limited to a three- or four-year bachelor's degree. More important, psychoanalytic training cannot proceed without personal analysis, which should be continuous and may take several years; however, the great majority of counselors in Hong Kong have never been in therapy before, and probably can see no reason for it. Finally, here, Chinese therapists receiving psychoanalytic training have been described as posing concrete questions to clients, and wishing to receive practical answers, similar to how Chinese clients wish to obtain quick fixes from their therapists (Xu et al., 2014; Schlösser, 2009). According to Fishkin and Fishkin (2014), even CAPA supervisees (thus, Chinese professionals) found it difficult to deal with their patients' "characterological or cultural lack of understanding of the reflective nature of psychodynamic psychotherapy; instead, these patients manifest an 'action-orientation'" (p. 213), meaning that they want advice and directive therapy rather than an experience of discovery.

Eclecticism

Eclecticism is the technical, relatively atheoretical combination of clinical methods about "what works," regardless of its theoretical grounds (Norcross, 1990). Chan and Lee (1995) found that the majority of psychologists in Hong Kong endorsed more than one orientation, meaning that "much of the therapeutic practice in psychology in Hong Kong is best characterized as eclectic in nature" (p. 62). Tsoi and Lam (1991) also found that what is practiced in Hong Kong is a form of technical eclecticism. Eclecticism aims at addressing formative questions such as "*what* treatment, by *whom*, is most effective for *this* individual with *that* specific problem, and under *which* set of circumstances" (Paul, 1967, p. 11). Essentially, eclecticism emphasizes technique over theory, and as such, this could be limiting the understanding of psychoanalysis. An eclectic approach may thus fail to readily apply to psychoanalysis, so that it might be summarily rejected.

Psychoanalytic training

According to research conducted by Li (2014), psychotherapists from mainland China reported that the three top factors for learning psychoanalysis were: receiving supervision, theoretical seminars, and undergoing personal therapy. The lack of psychoanalytic training in Hong Kong is confirmed by reading the programs for the current or the coming academic year of the various Bachelor's and Master's degrees in Psychology, Counseling, or Social Sciences of the University of Hong Kong, the Chinese University of Hong Kong, Hong Kong University of Science and Technology, The Hong Kong Polytechnic University, Baptist University, the City University of Hong Kong, Lingnan University, and Shue Yan University. Apparently, today, only the last of these offers some introductory courses dedicated specifically to psychoanalysis. Outside academic circles, training opportunities are in general scarce and limited to sporadic events. This could be a serious limit to the understanding and development of psychoanalysis in Hong Kong. Psychoanalysis is clearly a "learning by doing" process. Besides attending theoretical seminars (common to every counseling training), psychoanalysts to be are normally required to have had their own ongoing personal (training or didactic) analysis. A conversation from the couch may be impossible to report outside, because the analytic conversation (which is not just a dialogue) happens in a peculiar setting, is influenced by transference, and follows the so-called free association. Thus, psychoanalysis cannot be taught simply through academic seminars; it must be experienced with a personal analysis. However, the lack of opportunities to receive a personal analysis in Hong Kong may seriously limit its understanding and development.

Other implicit factors

In addition to these, other implicit factors may influence how counseling/psychotherapy and psychoanalysis are understood and received, both consciously and unconsciously. For example, Scragg, Bor, and Watts (1999) examined how personality influences the choice of one's theoretical models, among a sample of prospective candidates for a program in counseling psychology, and found that candidates who expressed interest in the more directive models of counseling such as cognitive behavioral therapy, scored higher on scales assessing interpersonal boldness, systematizing, and conforming in comparison to those who expressed an interest in non-directive therapies such as psychoanalysis, who scored greater on intuitiveness. Other studies revealed similar findings, as Barrio Minton and Myers (2008) showed the association between intervention styles, cognitive styles, and theoretical orientation, and Murdock and colleagues (1998) built a model to predict the counselor theoretical orientation on the basis of philosophical assumptions, interpersonal control, and theoretical match with supervisor.

Culture is another factor that affects how psychoanalysis is understood and practiced. We can find many examples of this in the history of psychoanalysis. Psychoanalysis was hatched in the unique intellectual milieu of *fin-de-siècle* Vienna, and Bettelheim (1990) suggested that it could not have been invented anywhere else, as the understanding of ambivalence, hysteria, and neurosis was a natural consequence of the Viennese culture of the time, which was a rare paradoxical combination of provincialism and cosmopolitanism, tradition and modernism. Later, psychoanalysis was spread differently in Anglo-Saxon countries than in Latin and South American ones, while in others it remains almost unknown, after more than a hundred years since its inception.

The concept of culture seems to be clear, concrete, and almost measurable, but the fact that it has so many different definitions may be indicative of its complexity and abstraction. Etymologically, the term culture derives from a Latin verb *colere* meaning cultivation and, figuratively, to take care/guard, and is related to the root *cultus*, which refers not only to cultivation in the agricultural sense, but also to training, style, refinement, sophistication, and civilization (Toadvine, 2007). Thus, on the one hand, culture might be understood as "shared meanings," and could be measured by what is transmitted, perpetuated, and achieved. Bates and Flog (1990) defined culture as "a system of shared beliefs, values, customs, behaviors, and artifacts that members of a society use to cope with one another and with their world, and that are transmitted from generation to generation" (p. 466). Conversely, culture may be understood as how one "makes sense" of things, meaning the "process" of how knowledge is produced. Language is central to culture because meanings can only be constructed and transmitted through our common access to language. Thus, culture is not just a *set of beliefs*, or a collection of particular values and behaviors, but a *set of signifying practices*, which are reflected in how various members of a group see and interpret the world. In this regard, "culture depends on its participants interpreting meaningfully what is happening around them, and 'making sense' of the world, in broadly similar ways" (Hall, 1997, p. 2). The first, narrower, definition of culture was adopted in this study for identifying a set of values and beliefs to form the Conflicts with Hong Kong Chinese Culture scale (CHKCC). The second, broader, definition was instead adopted for exploring (and possibly explaining) associations between the CHKCC scale and the variables from the Psychoanalysis Use/Non-Use scale (PUNU).

In Hong Kong, it seems that identification with mainland China and what it represents is no longer possible. Precisely the "border closure in the early 1960s and British assimilation of extant refugee populations created the Hong Kong identity on a foundation of Mainlander 'otherness'" (Price & Ho, 2012). Today, Hongkongers hardly recognize themselves as being part of mainland China; nevertheless, the feeling of being members of the Chinese race remains strong (Public Opinion Program, the University of Hong Kong, 2014). For this reason, here traditional Chinese culture and Hong Kong culture have been described separately.

Conflicts with Chinese culture

Xu et al. (2014) suggest that some, but not necessarily all, Chinese psychiatrists and psychotherapists see psychoanalysis as incompatible with the Chinese ingrained ways. Generally, in the Chinese context, there is a remarkable individual disposition for controlling one's emotions. This is particularly true when referring to anger/conflict or aggressive feelings, as well as sexuality-related issues. Faure and Fang (2008, p. 198) observed that in China:

> social harmony is achieved through controlling feelings, appearing humble, avoiding conflict and even hiding competition. The expression of emotion is carefully controlled because of the risk of disrupting group harmony and hierarchies. Those who do not follow this code of behaviour would be considered as face losing and shameless. Thus, in relationships

things are suggested, not told in a straightforward manner. [...] Chinese medicine radically bans excessive expressions of emotions. Saying "no," being negative would be perceived as a clear lack of good manners. Not showing ignorance seems more important than telling the truth.

Normally, any expression of such emotions in public is frowned upon and repressed. Similarly, public expressions of intimacy and desires are still quite inhibited, when compared to European or North American contexts. For instance, according to Okazazi (2002), "sex is a taboo subject in contemporary Chinese culture, where sex education in schools is minimal and parents as well as health professionals are reluctant to discuss sexuality and sexual information" (p. 35).

However, in recent years, some changes have been observed. For example, an emerging expectation of love and intimacy among both men and women, together with the rise of a consumer individualism supporting the legitimacy of sexual desire, has been described, subsequently, more Chinese men are now apparently able to report their sexual problems in therapy and seek treatment for them, while women are increasingly able to see and express their right to sexual enjoyment (Scharff, 2014).

Not all Chinese values are necessarily antithetical to psychoanalysis, but some more than others seem to encourage the repression of feelings and desires, such as: keeping oneself disinterested and pure; having few desires; being a "gentleman" or "lady" at all times; the sense of righteousness and integrity; having a sense of shame; conformity and group orientation; loyalty to superiors; hierarchical relationships by status and observing this order; harmony between man and nature; and fatalism (Fan, 2000). Zhong (2011) suggested that *oneness* is the most important idea in Chinese culture for understanding the relationships between humans and nature, and that concepts like freedom, autonomy, separation, and individuality are somehow antithetical. For these reasons, several authors claim that contemporary cognitive and behavioral therapies are less in conflict with traditional Chinese values than more in-depth approaches, suggesting that they might be more effective for Chinese populations (Hodges & Tian, 2007).

Conflicts with Hong Kong Chinese culture

Although many describe Hong Kong as a place where East and West meet, Staples (2002) observed that "Hong Kong culture is dominated by Chinese cultures rather than Western culture and as such may not be regarded as a 'hybrid' culture, but as a conglomerate of independently used cultures" (p. i). Using the five Hofstede cultural dimensions, Li (2013) found that Hong Kong's culture is remarkably similar to China's. Further, Hong Kong culture includes features like: subordination of the individual, education for action, social cohesion, bureaucratic tradition, self-confidence and moralizing certitude (Au, Tsai, & Leong, 2009).

The Chinese socialization process emphasizes structure, hierarchy, and defined roles and responsibility, which suggests that Chinese people might prefer a directive and structural counseling approach to a non-directive one (Qian et al., 2002), at least initially. Hong Kong Chinese clients are described as expecting directive, goal-oriented, time-limited, and pragmatic counseling (Chong & Liu, 2002). Furthermore, Chinese clients may perceive therapists as being effective only when they take partial responsibility for the process as well as the result of the counseling and play an active role in providing clear and concrete suggestions, advice, and solution-giving methods which facilitate clients' actions (Lin, 2001). According to Lo (2005), "Hong Kong is a fast-moving society and its people prefer time-limited and 'fast-food' type services" (p. 464). Particularly today, in the fast-paced Hong Kong, the time given to reflection and thinking is very limited, and immediate comprehension seems to be the priority: everything must be quick. This immediacy can be better guaranteed by images rather than by words. Instead, too many spoken words can produce what is perceived as confusion. Evidently, this is a big limitation for psychoanalysis, which typically starts with the analyst's statement: "What's the first thing that comes to your mind?" so that direction is not given by the analyst (who is generally not directive), but is given by the client's speech.

Westerners are traditionally more concerned with analyzing problems, comprehending the causes, and searching for the *truth* than the Chinese are (Hall & Ames, 1998); *why* did something happen? *what* to do? As a core of a reflective and analytical dimension, the Western discourse relies much on logic and argumentation. In contrast, the Hong Kong Chinese attitude leaves little room for complex speculations, and the literature shows that they tend to be more practical than analytical, meaning that they focus more on *solving problems* rather than analyzing, understanding, or discussing them extensively (Cheung, 2001; Chong & Liu, 2002). The Western discourse emphasizes reasoning and theorization, although simply "understanding the problem" does not necessarily lead to change and it can even lead to an excessive *psychologization*. In Chinese thinking, there is not the "systematic doubt characteristic of European philosophies" (Plänkers, 2013, p. 94). Instead, the Hong Kong Chinese attitude seems to be generally very *practical*, meaning, for example, a focus on the action, which is in the present, rather than on thoughts, which belong to the past or the future. If being practical is defined by a criterion of "usefulness," "understanding the past" is no longer a priority.

3 The research study

Introduction

One of the objectives of my research journey was to explore what hinders the understanding and practice of psychoanalysis in Hong Kong. As I could not study Hong Kong society as a whole, I specifically focused on local counselors and how they listen to their clients. This chapter will introduce the main tools that were developed and used for this research. Because both the target population and I are not native English speakers language barriers represented a concrete obstacle for conducting quality in-depth interviews, so a quantitative approach was preferred. Furthermore, quantitative research was deemed to be appropriate for testing a number of hypotheses that emerged from the literature presented in the previous chapter.

The main research tool for this study is a questionnaire, developed and validated by me and completed by Hong Kong counseling professionals (social workers, psychologists, and counselors). The questionnaire was divided into three parts. The first part was to collect demographics about the respondents, their academic and professional training, work setting, client population, preferred counseling approaches and reasons for them. Using some of the items from this section, a scale named Combining Approaches was developed so as to gain further understanding about how various approaches are combined together by local counseling professionals, as this attitude appeared very common among the majority of participants in this study. Respondents were also asked if they had received any training in psychoanalysis, and if they made use of it in their practice. However, whether counselors simply refer to psychoanalysis, or make use of it, is not sufficient for the purpose of this study. Therefore, the second part of the questionnaire presented a list of items that aimed to differentiate the psychoanalytic listening from the counseling attitude; this item list was largely based on the literature presented in the first part of the second chapter of this book. Answers from the participants were analyzed using the statistical program SPSS, and two scales were developed, namely the Psychoanalytic Attitude towards Clinical Work Scale (PACWS), and the Counseling Attitude towards Clinical Work Scale (CACWS). The listening profile of the participants was then compared with these two scales. Finally, the third part of the questionnaire investigated the reasons why use of psychoanalysis is limited in Hong Kong. The items presented in this part were based on the literature review presented in the second part of the second chapter of this book. Two scales were here developed, namely the Psychoanalysis Use/Non-Use (PUNU) and the Conflicts with Hong Kong Chinese Culture (CHKCC) scale. Finally, a multiple regression analysis was run in order to understand what variables affect psychoanalytic listening, counseling attitude and the use of psychoanalysis, particularly in this context. Details about the participants, the process of scale development, and the findings are presented below.

The study

Participants

Although there exist some local regulatory registration requirements for counselors, psychiatrists, social workers, and psychologists in Hong Kong, registration is not mandatory, and is not always required in local employment settings. As a consequence, it is practically impossible to determine the precise number of professionals delivering "counseling services" among Hong Kong's 7.2 million citizens. Further, selecting a representative sample of this population was difficult, so a purposive sample was used. Because only a few individuals practice as psychoanalysts in Hong Kong, participants were selected from among the population of counseling professionals. Potential participants were invited from the Social Welfare Department and some of the main local non-governmental organizations (NGOs). A number of counselors in private practice recruited by direct contact or snowball techniques became study participants. Targeted participants had to meet the following requirements: (a) hold a university degree in psychology, social work, or counseling; (b) deliver counseling as part of their routine practice; and (c) have at least two years of work experience in counseling.

It was assumed that all three of these disciplines (social work, psychology, and counseling) would have differences in their education and their use and/or non-use of psychoanalysis. As a consequence, a clustered sample representing these three cohorts was selected. A total of 550 questionnaires were distributed by hand and administered anonymously. This study was presented in general terms, as a study on how local professionals conduct counseling; psychoanalysis was never mentioned as the focus of the study. An information cover page assured respondents that this was not a test with right or wrong answers, and that their personal opinion and experience was the only concern.

Eventually, a total of 223 questionnaires were returned (representing a favorable response rate of 40 percent) and 217 were considered usable. Participants received no monetary rewards and their participation was voluntary. The majority of respondents were women (72 percent), between 31 and 40 years of age (43 percent), with a university degree primarily in social work (70 percent), and were Christians (53 percent). Almost all participants received their educational training in Hong Kong (98 percent). Less than one third of respondents (29 percent) had personally received counseling before (23 percent among social workers, and 41 percent among those with a degree in psychology or counseling), or were personally receiving counseling themselves at the time of the study. Of those, the majority (64 percent) had undergone counseling for less than a year. The majority had less than eight years of working experience (63 percent). The number of clients counseled varied: 22 percent reported having counseled fewer than 30 clients, and 42 percent more than 100 clients. Only 15 percent of respondents reported working in more than one type of treatment setting; the most common settings were NGOs (76 percent) and schools (18 percent), whereas only 10 percent were in independent practice and 7 percent worked in hospitals. The great majority (94 percent) practiced individual therapy, whereas 56 percent engaged in family counseling, 44 percent in couple counseling, and only 26 percent in group counseling. The professional groups reporting the greatest incidence of independent private practice were psychologists and counselors (19 percent), compared to 6 percent of social workers. In most cases, respondents provided counseling to adults (62 percent), followed by youth (53 percent), children (42 percent), and elderly (27 percent).

Almost all of the sample (93 percent) reported using two or more counseling approaches. The most commonly endorsed counseling approaches reported by participants were: cognitive behavioral therapy (CBT) and/or cognitive therapy and/or behavioral therapy (72 percent of respondents reported at least one of these approaches, with 56 percent reporting CBT, 28 percent cognitive therapy and 27 percent behavioral therapy), person-centered therapy* (44 percent), narrative therapy* (29 percent), positive psychology* (27 percent), play therapy* (27 percent), group therapy (24 percent), systemic therapy (23 percent), brief therapy* (21 percent), art therapy (16 percent), task-centered therapy* (15 percent), psychoanalysis (11 percent, but more specifically, only 8 percent among social workers, and 17 percent among those with a degree in psychology or counseling), and gestalt therapy (10 percent). No counselor in the sample reported psychoanalysis as their only therapeutic approach. Furthermore, this survey does not reveal the level of training any of these counselors have had. Among those who reported using psychoanalysis, more than two thirds (71 percent) reported using it together with CBT, cognitive therapy and/or behavioral therapy, followed by positive psychology (48 percent), person-centered (48 percent), or art therapy (38 percent).

Scale development

Following standard criteria for the development of valid and reliable questionnaires (Gillham, 2000; MacKenzie, Podsakoff, & Podsakoff,

2011; Worthington & Whittaker, 2006), five scales were constructed and validated. The Combining Approaches scale is a uni-dimensional scale (three items, α = 0.77) that determines to what degree participants use different theoretical approaches in combination. The PACWS assesses the degree to which counseling professionals may operate psychoanalytically, without being aware of it and without expressly referring to psychoanalysis. It includes three subscales, namely: Transference (five items, α = 0.70), Unconscious (six items, α = 0.80), and Free Floating Attention (seven items, α = 0.72). The CACWS assesses the degree to which counseling professionals adhere to three counseling/psychotherapeutic dimensions: Directivity of the Cure (five items, α = 0.79), Restoration (six items, α = 0.76), and Focused Attention (four items, α = 0.71). The PUNU measures specific factors that might hinder the understanding and development of psychoanalysis. It comprises seventeen items in four domains: Perceived Ineffectiveness of Psychoanalysis (five items, α = 0.86), Perceived Complexity of Psychoanalysis (five items, α = 0.76), Eclecticism (four items, α = 0.70), and Psychoanalytic Training (four items, α = 0.74). Finally, here, the CHKCC is a uni-dimensional scale (nine items, α = 0.87) to determine whether respondents think that psychoanalysis is in conflict or not with Chinese culture and values and Hong Kong clients' expectations for counseling.

All items were assessed on 6-point Likert scales, ranging from 1 = strongly disagree to 6 = strongly agree, thus having a theoretical mid-point at 3.50. The 6-point scale was preferred to a 5-point one, so that respondents could select a position rather than being "neutral," and a 6-point scale tends to have better discrimination and reliability values than a 5-point one (Chomeya, 2010). Scores from 1 to 3 were considered to be in the Disagree range, scores from 4 to 6 were considered to be in the Agree range, and scores that ranged around 3.50, the mid-point, were considered to be uncertain.

Scale construction and validation

These self-report questionnaires were designed specifically for this study. Content validity, construct validity, and external validity were established in the following manner. Initially, for each scale a list of items based on the literature review was compiled by me. These initial lists were then subjected to expert judgment for redundancy, content validity, and clarity. The experts, both Western and Chinese psychoanalysts and counseling professionals, were informed about the purpose of the list and asked to give their opinions regarding the validity of the items, and to indicate those items that had little relevance with regard to the local context, and/or were confusing, and those that were deemed grounded and worthwhile items. At the end of this process, some items were deleted and others reworded. The reduced lists of items were then presented to participants in the study (all items were translated from English into Chinese and were presented in both languages).

When the questionnaires were returned, the items were analyzed again and some were removed. To test the factor structure and determine the construct validity of each scale, Bartlett's test of sphericity and the size of the Kaiser–Meyer–Olkin measure of sampling adequacy were first calculated, so as to ensure that the items of the scales had adequate common variance for factor analysis. Second, Parallel Analysis (with 5,000 random permutations), Minimum Average Partials (MAP) tests and scree plots were used to determine the number of factors to extract for each scale. Third, Exploratory Factor Analysis* (EFA) (Principal Axis Factoring and/or Maximum Likelihood) with Promax rotation were performed. EFA revealed the distribution of items across factors and the magnitude of item loadings, indicating what items were to be included in what subscales. An oblique (i.e. Promax) rotation was applied because it was not assumed the factors would be independent. When a clear factor structure emerged, factorial validity was interpreted as evidence of the usefulness and validity of the proposed scale. Finally, the external validity for each scale was assessed by performing independent sample *t*-tests among different subgroups. This procedure determines whether a scale can discriminate among groups based on variables such as academic major, age, gender, history of therapy, work experience, and number of clients. Statistical details of the scale construction and validation process are available in specific publications elsewhere (e.g. Busiol, 2015, 2016).

Combining Approaches scale

A few items were used to gain further understanding about how various approaches are thought to coexist (Table 3.1). In particular, the development of this scale was deemed to be necessary so as to operationalize the variable "combinatorial" (introduced in the last part of Chapter 1) and assess its relation with other variables, meaning how this cultural feature affects psychoanalytic listening and the understanding and use of psychoanalysis in Hong Kong. Factor analysis showed that three items heavily loaded on the same factor, and Cronbach's alpha showed that they formed a statistically reliable scale. Cronbach's alpha*, means (M), standard deviation (SD)*, skewness*, kurtosis* and confidence interval* are reported in Table 3.1.

Subgroup analysis did not show any significant differences when the group was split by gender, years of working experience, number of clients, history of therapy, university major, or age, suggesting that the attitude of combining various approaches rather than adopting only one might be culturally embedded.

Results suggest that participants considered different approaches as not necessarily contradicting each other but rather complementing each other, and that a multimodal approach potentially offers more opportunities for

Table 3.1 Descriptive statistical properties of the Combining Approaches scale (N=217)

Scale items	Cronbach's alpha (α)	M	SD	Skewness	Kurtosis	95% confidence interval of the mean	
						Lower	Higher
Overall scale statistics	0.77	4.88	0.72	−0.24	−0.23	4.78	4.98
1. Different approaches can balance each other		4.86	0.89	−1.04	2.79		
2. Different approaches compensate each other's blind spots		5.04	0.80	−0.82	1.49		
3. Different approaches can coexist remaining distinct		4.74	0.93	−0.58	0.80		

Scores: Based on a 6-point Likert scale with anchors 1 = strongly disagree and 6 = strongly agree.

understanding their clients than a single theoretical approach. This also suggests that participants tend to *combine* various approaches together, and this is a feature of their style.

Psychoanalysis (PACWS) and counseling (CACWS) scales

For the PACWS, a list of items was determined by reviewing: (a) the existing literature describing psychoanalytic attitude, psychoanalytic listening, and common grounds of psychoanalytic practice; and (b) the existing literature describing the common grounds of the psychotherapeutic/counseling approaches. Items were generated based on their satisfaction of both the following two principles: (1) they should be applicable to psychoanalysis in a broad sense, meaning that they should encompass best the similarities and commonalities among different orientations (ideally they describe a practice rather than a theoretical perspective), and (2) they should be able to distinguish between psychoanalysis and other psychotherapeutic or counseling approaches. Particularly, concepts that belong only to some psychoanalytic schools but not others were rejected; likewise, items that are controversial within the psychoanalytic field, like the notions of countertransference or empathy, were not considered. Likewise, items that may be common to psychoanalysis, psychotherapy, and counseling were discarded.

Specifically, the development and validation of the PACWS was intended to assess the degree to which individuals with a university degree in psychology, social work, or counseling who delivered counseling as part of their practice in Hong Kong share a psychoanalytic attitude in their clinical work, without being aware of it and without expressly referring to psychoanalytic theory. However, the PACWS did not aim to be pan-theoretical and relevant to psychoanalysis regardless of school of thought or grouping.

The CACWS was constructed adopting a similar rationale, but with the aim of making a comprehensive list for counseling which at the same time did not include psychoanalytic features.

Cronbach's alphas, means, standard deviation, skewness, kurtosis and confidence interval of all subscales of PACWS and CACWS are reported in Table 3.2 and Table 3.3, respectively. For all subscales, the distribution of the scores did not deviate substantially from normality.

PACWS

There are probably numerous ways of defining psychoanalytic attitude. However, in this research, an exploratory factor analysis supported a three-factor solution (Table 3.2); this is the simplest yet the most meaningful solution that has emerged. The three components identified are: Unconscious, Free Floating Attention, and Transference. Such factors are intended to be descriptive of psychoanalysis more than other psychotherapy/counseling approaches.

CACWS

Exploratory factor analysis has suggested that a three-factor solution is what best serves for describing the attitude toward clinical work in counseling (as opposed to psychoanalysis). The three factors are as follows.

Focused Attention

These items concern the counselor's effort or will to listen to what the client verbalizes, and the gestures that accompany his/her speaking; his/her ability to remain focused, aware, and perceptive; his/her ability to understand the (intended) message; and his/her ability to give feedback.

Restoration

These items sum up some goals of the counseling process. A common factor may be that they aim at "restoring" the individual's ability to cope with his/her environment by "restructuring" so-called patterns of thought, maladaptive cognitive structures, and cognitive distortions. Clients are shown these negative beliefs, are led to re-examine them, and helped to replace them with more functional, more adaptive ways of viewing life. This way is intended to produce rapid symptom shifts, and to solve main problems.

Table 3.2 Descriptive statistical properties of the PACWS (N=217)

Scale items	Cronbach's alpha (α)	M	SD	Skewness	Kurtosis	95% confidence interval of the mean Lower	95% confidence interval of the mean Higher
Transference	0.70					4.63	4.79
1. The words of the client carry much more meaning than it seems		4.71	0.59	−0.09	0.06		
		4.91	0.86	−0.59	0.27		
2. The client may re-experience feelings, directed at the therapist, which he/she has had for important people in the past		4.78	0.81	−0.70	1.80		
3. I think that both the therapist and the client have internal resistances that might affect the therapeutic process		4.75	0.87	−0.31	−0.15		
4. Clients sometimes show some unconscious resistance to change		4.72	0.85	−0.23	−0.33		
5. It is normal that the client experiences ambivalent feelings toward the therapist, and this is part of the process		4.39	0.97	−0.28	0.19		
Free Floating Attention	0.72					4.21	4.37
1. I let clients start talking from where they prefer		4.29	0.58	0.12	−0.05		
		4.64	1.04	−0.69	0.21		
2. I encourage clients to reflect and question their own words		4.48	0.74	−0.20	0.44		
3. My feelings and reactions to clients are meaningful to understanding the client and the treatment		4.46	0.83	−0.43	0.37		
4. Therapy proceeds depending whether I am really engaged, more than for the other techniques that I master		4.18	1.05	−0.14	−0.59		
5. I help clients formulate new questions rather than giving them answers		4.14	0.99	−0.55	0.47		
6. I follow the client's associations rather than trying to impose a direction to the helping process		4.12	1.04	−0.48	0.22		
7. I encourage clients to keep their questions open-ended		4.00	0.94	−0.21	−0.36		

Table 3.2 (cont.)

Scale items	Cronbach's alpha (α)	M	SD	Skewness	Kurtosis	95% confidence interval of the mean	
						Lower	Higher
Unconscious	0.80					3.29	3.49
1. In the unconscious we can find the logical and rhetorical foundations of our discourse		3.39	0.79	−0.01	−0.07		
		4.07	0.93	−0.14	0.21		
2. Most of the client's material is unconscious		3.36	1.06	0.12	−0.28		
3. Unconscious is central to my practice		3.35	1.10	−0.16	−0.34		
4. I use the technique of the free association		3.28	1.20	−0.14	−0.63		
5. Investigating the client's unconscious fantasies and beliefs is the core of my approach		3.16	1.23	0.15	−0.68		
6. Dreams have a particular relevance in my practice		3.11	1.17	−0.01	−0.49		

Scores: Based on a 6-point Likert scale with anchors 1 = strongly disagree and 6 = strongly agree.

Table 3.3 Descriptive statistical properties of the CACWS (N=217)

Scale items	Cronbach's alpha (α)	M	SD	Skewness	Kurtosis	95% confidence interval of the mean Lower	95% confidence interval of the mean Higher
Focused Attention	0.71					4.71	4.87
1. I maintain eye contact with the client		4.78	0.62	−0.41	0.86		
2. I show my clients that I am listening by my body language (e.g. head nods)		5.13	0.79	−0.64	0.26		
		5.05	0.77	−0.53	0.27		
3. I focus harder on the client's speech when I have trouble understanding		4.65	0.89	−0.73	1.33		
4. When my mind wanders, I recover my concentration right away		4.32	0.92	−0.20	−0.10		
Restoration	0.76					3.86	4.06
1. Counseling should help the client to adapt to his/her environment		3.96	0.72	0.14	0.42		
		4.73	0.84	−0.38	−0.13		
2. It is important to help clients to build good reality-testing skills		4.70	0.78	−0.11	−0.39		
3. After counseling, clients have more answers		4.13	1.07	−0.27	−0.40		
4. Counseling serves for feeling good		3.55	1.22	−0.28	−0.32		
5. Aim of counseling is to teach clients to control their emotions		3.45	1.19	−0.04	−0.37		
6. Formation of counselors should focus primarily on intervention techniques and strategies		3.17	1.26	0.19	−0.42		

Table 3.3 (cont.)

Scale items	Cronbach's alpha (α)	M	SD	Skewness	Kurtosis	95% confidence interval of the mean	
						Lower	Higher
Directivity of the Cure	0.79					3.76	3.96
1. I teach clients techniques to address problem areas		3.86	0.73	−0.24	1.04		
		4.36	1.00	−0.71	0.83		
2. I give explanations to clients		4.09	0.95	−0.65	1.14		
3. I actively give direction to the client		3.76	0.95	−0.15	0.54		
4. I focus my intervention on solving the symptom		3.55	1.04	−0.26	0.01		
5. After listening to the problem, I usually tell the client what he should do next, how to cope with it		3.51	1.04	−0.13	0.04		

Scores based on a 6-point Likert scale with anchors 1 = strongly disagree and 6 = strongly agree.

Directivity of the Cure

These items refer to how the counselor sees his/her role in the counseling relation, with particular attention as to whether s/he thinks that therapeutic work can advance by actively giving explanations, advice, or direction.

Correlations among variables

All correlations among subscales are reported in Table 3.5.

Intra-correlations

All three subscales of the PACWS were positively correlated with each other (albeit at a low level, with r ≤ 0.30), suggesting that the items generated might assess different portions of the same dimension. Concerning the CACWS, only Directivity of the Cure and Restoration were correlated ($r = -0.38$, $p < 0.001$), whereas Focused Attention did not show statistically significant correlation with the other two dimensions. Results were in line with expectations.

Correlations between psychoanalytic (PACWS) and counseling dimensions (CACWS)

Focused attention is negatively correlated to Unconscious ($r = -0.18$, $p = 0.011$); this is in line with expectations, and supports the Freudian hypothesis that when focusing the attention on the manifest meaning, understanding of the unconscious may be limited. Focused Attention also positively correlates with Transference ($r = 0.27$, $p < 0.001$), as much attention is given to the behavior and the reaction of the clients for understanding advancements of the therapy. Focused Attention and Free Floating Attention are positively correlated ($r = 0.29$, $p < 0.001$), suggesting that both subscales assess the same dimension. However, this result suggests a particular listening attitude emerging from this sample, which will be discussed later.

The variable Directivity of the Cure has no statistically significant correlations with any of the psychoanalytic scale; this is in line with the theoretical premises, as a psychoanalytic approach is not supposed to be directive.

The variable Restoration has correlations with all psychoanalytic variables: higher with Unconscious ($r = 0.35$, $p < 0.001$), and lower with Transference ($r = 0.19$, $p = 0.007$) and Free Floating Attention ($r = 0.22$, $p = 0.002$). These associations of psychoanalytic dimensions and Restoration may indicate that psychoanalysis is normally understood as a counseling/psychotherapeutic technique among others.

Subgroup analysis

In order to further assess the discriminative validity of the two scales, independent t-tests (with a Bonferroni adjustment for multiple statistical tests) were performed to compare different groups. If psychoanalytic and counseling/psychotherapeutic attitudes were structurally different dispositions toward clinical work, subgroup differences should be found only when assessing variables such as professional training, and the history of therapy, and not demographic characteristics of the therapist, such as gender, years of working experience, and/or number of clients.

The main group of respondents was split by: (a) gender, (b) university major, (c) years of practice experience, (d) number of clients, (e) history of therapy, (f) age, and (g) use of psychoanalytic theory. For statistical purposes, the following continuous variables were dichotomized according to predefined cut-off points, so as to have subgroups with similar numbers of respondents: (a) years of practice experience (≤ 8 vs > 8 years); (b) number of clients (≤ 100 vs >100); (c) age (≤ 30 vs ≥ 31). Finally, the variable of university major was dichotomized as social work vs non-social work.

As expected, for both scales, significant findings were related to history of therapy and university major, but not years of practice, number of clients, or age.

PACWS

Social workers ($M=3.51$, $SD=0.76$) reported significantly higher Unconscious than psychologists and counselors ($M = 3.12$, $SD = 0.81$, $t = 3.29$, $p = 0.005$). In addition, social workers scored around the theoretical mid-point of 3.50 (from a low of 3.38 to a high of 3.62), whereas psychologists and counselors scored below (between 2.92 and 3.33).

Respondents who had been in therapy before ($M = 4.91$, $SD = 0.60$) gave significantly more attention to Transference than respondents who had not been in therapy ($M = 4.62$, $SD = 0.55$, $t = -3.39$, $p = 0.001$).

Respondents who had been in therapy before ($M = 4.48$, $SD = 0.57$) reported significantly higher Free Floating Attention than respondents who had not been in therapy ($M = 4.21$, $SD = 0.58$, $t = 3.03$, $p = 0.003$).

CACWS

Social workers ($M=4.06$, $SD=0.71$) reported significantly higher Restoration than psychologists and counselors ($M = 3.74$, $SD = 0.69$, $t = 3.06$, $p = 0.003$).

Respondents who had been in therapy before ($M = 3.56$, $SD = 0.66$) reported significantly lower Directivity of the Cure than respondents who had not been in therapy ($M = 3.98$, $SD = 0.81$, $t = 3.94$, $p < 0.001$).

Respondents who had been in therapy before ($M = 3.77$, $SD = 0.70$) reported significantly lower Restoration than respondents who had not been in therapy ($M = 4.03$, $SD = 0.70$, $t = 2.45$, $p = 0.015$) (ns after correction).

Participants who used psychoanalytic theory ($M = 3.50$, $SD = 0.77$) reported significantly lower Directivity of the Cure than participants who did not refer to it ($M = 3.89$, $SD = 0.73$, $t = 2.29$, $p = 0.022$) (ns after correction).

Psychoanalysis Use/Non-Use scale (PUNU) and Conflicts with Hong Kong Chinese Culture scale (CHKCC)

These scales aimed at assessing factors that might hinder the understanding and development of psychoanalysis, considering separately explicit factors (concerning psychoanalysis), and implicit ones (concerning the background of the counseling professionals). Secondly, this study aimed to assess the association between culture and the other variables (from PUNU, PACWS, and CACWS), meaning how culture may be related to the professionals' attitude toward psychoanalysis and counseling. Descriptive statistics of the two scales were then determined. Their respective Cronbach's alphas, means, standard deviation, skewness, kurtosis and confidence intervals are reported in Table 3.4.

Intra-correlations: PUNU

Of the four subscale variables of the PUNU, three (namely, Perceived Complexity of Psychoanalysis, Perceived Ineffectiveness of Psychoanalysis, and Eclecticism) were moderately to strongly correlated with each other (Table 3.5). These are variables that assess possible criticalities and limitations to the reception of psychoanalysis in Hong Kong; in contrast, the variable Psychoanalytic Training aims at assessing the potential counselors' interest in pursuing further training in psychoanalysis. Not surprisingly, this last variable measures an attitude rather opposite to the other three. Indeed, the variable Psychoanalytic Training was significantly (and negatively) correlated only with the subscale Perceived Ineffectiveness of Psychoanalysis ($r = -0.25$, $p < 0.001$), implying that the more psychoanalytic training a counselor has received, the more likely s/he will perceive psychoanalysis as effective.

Correlations between PUNU and CHKCC

When analyzing the relationship between the CHKCC scale and the PUNU subscales (Table 3.5), what emerged is that the former correlated with Perceived Ineffectiveness of Psychoanalysis ($r = 0.57$, $p < 0.001$), Perceived Complexity of Psychoanalysis ($r = 0.34$, $p < 0.001$), and Eclecticism ($r = 0.36$, $p < 0.001$), but not with Psychoanalytic Training. Although it is not possible to determine the causality in a correlation (the independent and dependent variables), results showed that culture, understanding of psychoanalysis, and theoretical assumptions about counseling had some empirical associations in this sample. Interestingly, the CHKCC scales had no association with the interest in receiving psychoanalytic training.

What has emerged from the correlations between the scales is that a counseling approach is probably perceived as ineffective when the theoretical grounds are perceived as too complex and potentially in conflict with Chinese values. Ineffectiveness of psychoanalysis is also correlated with eclecticism;

Table 3.4 Descriptive statistical properties of the PUNU and CHKCC (N=217)

Scale items	Cronbach's alpha (α)	M	SD	Skewness	Kurtosis	95% confidence interval of the mean Lower	Higher
Psychoanalytic Use/Non–Use scale (PUNU)							
Perceived Complexity of Psychoanalysis	0.76	4.09	0.71	−0.21	0.77	3.99	4.19
1. It takes too long time to become a psychoanalyst		4.47	0.97	−0.27	0.10		
2. Psychoanalysis takes too long		4.12	0.99	−0.70	1.34		
3. Psychoanalysis requires too much effort and involvement		3.89	0.92	−0.40	1.26		
4. Psychoanalysis is too complex and complicated		3.88	0.94	−0.21	0.62		
5. Psychoanalytic language is not clear		3.62	0.92	−0.09	0.37		
Psychoanalytic Training	0.74	4.03	0.83	−0.81	2.40	3.91	4.14
1. I would undergo a personal analysis, if this was possible		4.15	1.20	−0.63	0.26		
2. I might be interested in learning and practicing dream analysis		4.14	1.07	−0.85	1.44		
3. If I could get more training in psychoanalysis, I might be interested in joining		3.97	1.02	−0.68	1.00		
4. I would not pursue psychoanalysis training, even if this was available ** R)		3.88	1.33	−0.34	−0.40		
Eclecticism	0.70	4.00	0.70	0.28	0.70	3.91	4.09
1. I feel more convenient combining different theories together, instead of specializing in one only		4.45	0.91	−0.36	0.49		
2. An eclectic approach can offer more solutions		3.95	1.03	−0.42	0.45		
3. An eclectic approach can be more effective than one theory only		3.83	1.03	−0.10	−0.02		
4. A single theory cannot be as effective as a combination of techniques		3.76	1.05	−0.13	−0.16		

Perceived Ineffectiveness of Psychoanalysis	0.86	30.20	0.79	−0.17	0.63		3.31
1. Psychoanalysis is not very scientific		3.44	0.98	0.07	0.27	3.09	
2. Psychoanalysis is not very helpful for my clients' problems		3.32	1.03	0.09	−0.09		
3. Psychoanalysis is not very practical		3.30	0.93	0.07	0.77		
4. Psychoanalytic technique is not as developed as other forms of psychotherapy		3.07	1.02	−0.05	0.06		
5. Psychoanalysis is obsolete		2.93	1.07	0.14	0.11		
Conflicts with Hong Kong Chinese Culture (CHKCC)							
Overall scale statistics	0.87	3.49	0.76	−0.15	0.42	3.38	3.59
1. Chinese culture does not welcome recognizing aggressive feelings		3.96	1.09	−0.33	−0.10		
2. Chinese culture does not welcome recognizing inner desires and sexuality		3.86	1.15	−0.05	−0.46		
3. Chinese culture does not welcome talking about emotions		3.45	1.19	0.03	−0.58		
4. My clients may not be interested in speculative argumentations		3.42	0.90	0.05	0.68		
5. My clients do not want to investigate their inner desires		3.41	1.03	0.10	−0.18		
6. Hong Kong people don't want to engage in in-depth counseling		3.37	1.22	0.13	−0.37		
7. Psychoanalysis is too individualistic to work in Chinese society		3.36	1.01	0.14	0.08		
8. Psychoanalysis conflicts with Chinese values		3.28	1.08	0.21	−0.01		
9. Hong Kong people are little interested in pursuing a knowledge about themselves		3.18	1.08	0.18	−0.37		

Scores: Based on a 6-point Likert scale with anchors 1 = strongly disagree and 6 = strongly agree.
**(R) item negatively worded; in the table are the reported scores after recalculation.

this probably reflects the need for a simpler and clearly defined approach. If the effort and involvement required by psychoanalysis may lead to conflicts with Hong Kong Chinese values, and if the (perceived) complexity of psychoanalysis may have an effect on ineffective practice (theory difficult to handle, which causes poor therapeutic results), then the counselors may be more inclined toward an eclectic approach, which they perceived as more effective.

Correlations between the PACWS, the PUNU, and the CHKCC

As expected, the variables from the psychoanalytic listening scale and the variables from the criticalities against psychoanalysis scale are generally poorly correlated (Table 3.5). Psychoanalytic Training is correlated with Unconscious ($r = 0.26$, $p < 0.001$) and Transference ($r = 0.16$, $p = 0.025$), suggesting that specific training can refine the reception and use of such concepts. Unconscious is also correlated to possible conflicts with Hong Kong Chinese culture ($r = 0.31$, $p < 0.001$); because respondents scored low on these variables (interpretation of the unconscious, and CHKCC), this suggests that local counselors see little reason for investigating the unconscious fantasies of their clients.

Correlations between the CACWS, the PUNU, and the CHKCC

As noted before, Focused Attention did not correlate with other counseling dimensions, but correlated with three psychoanalytic listening subscales (Table 3.5); thus, it may not be surprising that it does not correlate with Perceived Complexity of Psychoanalysis and Perceived Ineffectiveness of Psychoanalysis. At the same time, Focused Attention does not correlate with Psychoanalytic Training; this is important because it confirms that focused attention is not a mode of psychoanalytic listening. Instead, it shows a little correlation with Eclecticism ($r = 0.14$, $p = 0.043$), meaning that focused attention is indeed selective. Finally, here, Focused Attention reported a moderate negative correlation with conflicts with Hong Kong Chinese culture ($r = -0.14$, $p = 0.047$); although here it is not possible to identify the independent variable, this may suggest that high engagement in the counseling process by the clinician may overcome cultural norms and values that normally would limit the participation of the client.

Unsurprisingly, the variable Restoration correlates with all the other subscales. Similarly, the variable Directivity of the Cure correlates with all variables except for Psychoanalytic Training; this is also understandable, as psychoanalysis is not a prescriptive or directive practice.

Subgroup differences

This sample was further analyzed in order to gain more understanding of the possible relations between professional formation, psychoanalytic training, and use of psychoanalysis. Independent *t*-tests (with Bonferroni correction) were performed, computing the independent variables: (a) university major; (b) history of therapy; (c) age; and (d) use of psychoanalysis (Tables 3.6 and 3.7).

(a) When social workers (N = 152) were compared to psychologists and counselors (N = 65) on the PUNU and the CHKCC, both groups showed the same order among subscales; however, social workers (M = 3.64, SD = 0.70) scored significantly higher on the CHKCC than psychologists and counselors (M = 3.16, SD = 0.79, *t* = 4.3, $p < 0.001$). Furthermore, for the CHKCC, while for social workers, the confidence interval lies completely above the theoretical mid-point (from a low of 3.52 to a high of 3.74), meaning that the great majority of them think that psychoanalysis is in conflict with Hong Kong Chinese values and clients' expectations, for psychologists and counselors, it lies below (from a low of 2.96 to a high of 3.36), showing that they have the opposite opinion.
(b) Respondents who had been in therapy before (N = 63; M = 2.87, SD = 0.74) reported statistically significant lower perceived ineffectiveness of psychoanalysis than respondents who had not been in therapy (N = 154; M = 3.32, SD = 0.76, *t* = 3.9, $p < 0.001$).
(c) Respondents of 30 years old or younger (N = 65; M = 4.25, SD = 0.62) reported statistically significant higher psychoanalytic training than respondents of 31 years or more (N = 152; M = 3.93, SD = 0.89, *t* = 3.0, $p = 0.009$).
(d) Finally, respondents who adopted psychoanalysis (N = 21) reported:

    statistically significant lower perceived ineffectiveness of psychoanalysis (M = 2.56, SD = 0.74), than respondents who do not adopt psychoanalysis (N = 196; M = 3.27, SD = 0.76, *t* = 4.0, $p < 0.001$);
    statistically significant higher psychoanalytic training (M = 4.54, SD = 0.64) than respondents who do not adopt psychoanalysis (N = 196; M = 3.97, SD = 0.83, *t* = -2.9, $p = 0.004$).

Predictors: multiple regression analysis

The primary scope of the regression analysis is to see if there is a statistically significant relationship between two or more variables and to investigate the possible causal relationships. The amount of variation explained (R square) is relatively less important here.

Running a multiple regression analysis first requires to test for residuals, outliers, and influential cases, as well as checking for the assumptions of non-multicollinearity, independence, normality, homoscedasticity, linearity; no particular problems among these variables were found.

Table 3.5 Correlations among variables (N=217)

Scales	M	SD	1	2	3	4	5
Psychoanalytic dimensions (PACWS)							
1. Unconscious	3.39	0.79					
2. Free Floating Attention	4.29	0.58	0.30***				
3. Transference	4.71	0.58	0.28***	0.28***			
Counseling dimensions (CACWS)							
4. Focused Attention	4.79	0.62	−0.18*	0.29***	0.27***		
5. Directivity of the Cure	3.86	0.73	0.08	0.07	0.06	0.10	
6. Restoration	3.96	0.72	0.35***	0.22**	0.19**	0.01	0.38***
Psychoanalysis Use/Non–Use scale (PUNU)							
7. Perceived Ineffectiveness of Psychoanalysis	3.20	0.78	0.12	−0.08	−0.01	−0.12	0.33***
8. Perceived Complexity of Psychoanalysis	4.09	0.71	−0.01	0.04	0.10	−0.03	0.34***
9. Eclecticism	4.00	0.69	0.04	0.05	0.22**	0.14*	0.34***
10. Psychoanalytic Training	4.03	0.83	0.26***	0.07	0.16*	0.03	0.03
Conflicts with Culture scale (CHKCC)							
11. Conflicts with Hong Kong Chinese Culture	3.49	0.76	0.31**	0.07	0.12	−0.14**	0.24**
Major							
12. Social work	0.70	0.46	0.22**	0.04	−0.03	−0.04	0.11
13. Psychology/Counseling	0.28	0.45	−0.18*	−0.02	0.05	0.03	−0.13
Theoretical orientation							
14. Use of Psychoanalytic Theory	0.10	0.29	0.05	0.08	0.07	0.04	−0.16*
History of therapy							
15. In therapy	0.29	0.45	−0.01	0.21**	0.23***	0.08	−0.27***
Multimodal logic							
16. Combining Approaches	4.88	0.72	0.20**	0.20**	0.13	0.04	0.10

Scores based on a 6-point Likert scale with anchors 1 = strongly disagree and 6 = strongly agree.
*** Correlation is significant at the 0.001 level (2-tailed); ** Correlation is significant at the 0.01 level (2-tailed); * Correlation is significant at the 0.05 level (2-tailed).

6	7	8	9	10	11	12	13	14	15

0.30***

0.14*   0.34***

0.22**   0.38***   0.35***
0.12   −0.25*** −0.10   −0.05

0.38***   0.57***   0.34***   0.37***   0.10

0.20**   0.06   −0.13   0.02   0.04   0.29***
−0.20** −0.07   0.14*   −0.01   −0.05   −0.26*** −0.96***

−0.09   −0.27*** −0.10   −0.05   0.20** −0.15*   0.18**   −0.16*

−0.17*   −0.26*** −0.10   −0.03   0.08   −0.13   −0.19**   0.18**   0.27***

0.29***   0.14*   0.05   0.25***   0.06   0.12   0.08   −0.07   −0.12   −0.01

Table 3.6 Correlations among variables (N=155) – social workers

Scales	M	SD	1	2	3
Psychoanalytic scale (PACWS)					
1. Unconscious	3.50	0.75			
2. Free Floating Attention	4.30	0.55	0.29**		
3. Transference	4.70	0.57	0.25**	0.35***	
Counseling scale (CACWS)					
4. Focused Attention	4.77	0.64	−0.09	0.37***	0.28**
5. Directivity of the Cure	3.91	0.72	0.25**	0.12	0.11
6. Restoration	4.06	0.71	0.42***	0.21*	0.27**
Psychoanalysis Use/Non–Use (PUNU)					
7. Perceived Ineffectiveness of Psychoanalysis	3.23	0.77	0.25**	0.02	−0.04
8. Perceived Complexity of Psychoanalysis	4.03	0.66	0.02	0.06	−0.02
9. Eclecticism	4.01	0.66	0.12	0.17	0.19*
10. Psychoanalytic Training	4.05	0.70	0.22**	0.02	0.17*
Conflicts with Chinese Culture (CHKCC)					
11. Conflicts with Hong Kong Chinese Culture	3.63	0.70	0.26**	0.13	0.08
Theoretical orientation					
12. Use of Psychoanalytic Theory	0.06	0.25	−0.03	−0.03	−0.05

Scores based on a 6-point Likert scale with anchors 1 = strongly disagree and 6 = strongly agree.
*** Correlation is significant at the 0.001 level (2-tailed); ** Correlation is significant at the 0.01 level (2-tailed); * Correlation is significant at the 0.05 level (2-tailed).

The subscales of PACWS (Unconscious, Transference, and Free Floating Attention) and CACWS (Restoration, Directivity of the Cure, and Focused Attention), as well as the variable Use of Psychoanalytic Theory, were considered as the dependent variables. The independent variables were the four subscales from the PUNU (Perceived Ineffectiveness of Psychoanalysis, Perceived Complexity of Psychoanalysis, Psychoanalytic Training, and Eclecticism), the CHKCC, the variables Major and History of Therapy, and the scale Combining Approaches. As a consequence, the dependent variables were seven (PACWS + CACWS + Use/Non-Use of Psychoanalytic Theory), and the independent variables were eight (PUNU + CHKCC + Major + History of Therapy + Combining Approaches). Because for regression analysis only one of the (seven) dependent variables can be assessed at a time (whereas the independent variables are entered simultaneously), this operation has been computed seven times. Table 3.8 summarizes the analysis results.

Use of Psychoanalytic Theory: the multiple regression model with five predictors produced $R^2 = 0.142$, $F(5, 188) = 6.12$, $p < 0.001$. As can be seen in

4	5	6	7	8	9	10	11
0.06							
−0.01	0.38***						
−0.13	0.23**	0.32***					
0.09	0.37***	0.17*	0.26**				
0.13	0.32***	0.24**	0.36**	0.26**			
0.13	0.20*	0.21*	−0.25**	0.12	0.05		
−0.08	0.26**	0.34**	0.60***	0.47***	0.45***	0.01	
−0.01	−0.09	−0.12	−0.25**	−0.03	−0.04	0.16	−0.09

Table 3.8, Major in social work had a (small but) significant negative regression weight (implying that a major either in psychology or counseling is a contributor); further, History of Therapy was a contributor to Use of Psychoanalytic Theory. Perceived Ineffectiveness of Psychoanalysis, Psychoanalytic Training, and CHKCC did not contribute to the multiple regression model.

Unconscious: three out of four correlating variables resulted as predictors in this model; all predictors had significant positive regression weights, producing $R^2 = 0.188$, $F(4, 179) = 10.39$, $p < 0.001$.

Free Floating Attention: both History of Therapy and Combining Approaches resulted as contributors, producing $R^2 = 0.081$, $F(2, 188) = 8.30$, $p < 0.01$.

Transference: Psychoanalytic Training, Eclecticism and History of Therapy produced $R^2 = 0.134$, $F(3, 200) = 10.35$, $p < 0.001$.

Restoration: the multiple regression model with seven variables produced $R^2 = 0.223$, $F(7, 163) = 6.70$, $p < 0.001$. As can be seen in Table 8, only CHKCC and Combining Approaches had significant positive regression weights.

Table 3.7 Correlations among variables (N=62) – psychologists/counselors

Scales	M	SD	1	2	3
Psychoanalytic scale (PACWS)					
1. Unconscious	3.17	0.81			
2. Free floating Attention	4.27	0.64	0.28*		
3. Transference	4.76	0.62	0.32**	0.12	
Counseling scale (CACWS)					
4. Focused Attention	4.81	0.57	–0.34*	0.14	0.32*
5. Directivity of the Cure	3.71	0.71	–0.25	–0.16	0.04
6. Restoration	3.74	0.71	0.12	0.26*	0.04
Psychoanalysis Use/Non–Use (PUNU)					
7. Perceived Ineffectiveness of Psychoanalysis	3.12	0.81	–0.14	–0.24	0.02
8. Perceived Complexity of Psychoanalysis	4.25	0.78	0.01	0.08	0.26
9. Eclecticism	3.99	0.72	–0.08	–0.09	0.32*
10. Psychoanalytic Training	3.96	1.09	0.35**	0.13	0.15
Conflicts with culture (CHKCC)					
11. Conflicts with Hong Kong Chinese Culture	3.19	0.80	0.23	–0.04	0.16
Theoretical orientation					
12. Use Of Psychoanalytic Theory	.18	0.39	0.24	0.21	0.22

Scores based on a 6-point Likert scale with anchors 1 = strongly disagree and 6 = strongly agree.
*** Correlation is significant at the 0.001 level (2-tailed); ** Correlation is significant at the 0.01 level (2-tailed); * Correlation is significant at the 0.05 level (2-tailed).

Focused Attention: two predictors in the model produced $R^2 = 0.072$, $F(2, 196) = 7.56$, $p < 0.001$. Specifically, Eclecticism had significant positive regression weights, whereas CHKCC had significant negative regression weights.

Directivity of the Cure: the multiple regression model with five predictors produced $R^2 = 0.250$, $F(5, 183) = 12.19$, $p < 0.001$. Perceived Complexity of Psychoanalysis and Eclecticism had significant positive regression weights, whereas Perceived Ineffectiveness of Psychoanalysis and CHKCC did not contribute to the model.

The three components of psychoanalytic listening

Although listening is the core of psychoanalysis, this is probably the first time that a definition and operationalization of *psychoanalytic listening* has been attempted. The PACWS represents a simple yet meaningful solution; however, other ways of defining psychoanalytic listening might be possible.

4	5	6	7	8	9	10	11
0.17							
0.11	0.34**						
−0.12	0.49***	0.21					
−0.13	0.32*	0.16	0.47***				
0.27*	0.33**	0.16	0.35**	0.44**			
−0.11	−0.21	0.08	−0.26	−0.37**	−0.17		
−0.20	0.18	0.39**	0.54***	0.23	0.19	0.24	
0.12	−0.22	0.04	−0.30*	−0.29*	−0.07	0.27*	−0.14

What makes psychoanalytic listening?

The psychoanalytic attitude to clinical work that emerged from this study was constituted of three components: unconscious, transference and free floating attention. Because these three components are positively (albeit slightly) correlated with each other, we may argue that together they describe a common dimension: psychoanalytic listening. The fact that the correlations are relatively small (from 0.28 to 0.30) should not be overlooked; in fact, when too high correlations occur it may be due to multiple loadings of items and unclear factor structure (which is not the case for these scales). Thus following the findings from this study, we may say that psychoanalytic listening is grounded on a tripartite system (unconscious, transference and free floating attention), and that *listening can be said to be psychoanalytic only when the three components are present simultaneously.*

For example, scores from this study suggest that participants are receptive toward what the client expresses and are sensitive about the relationship with

Table 3.8 Predictors for PACSW, CHKCC and use of psychoanalytic theory

	Use of Psychoanalytic Theory	PACWS ||||	CACWS			
	β	Unconscious β	Free Floating Attention β	Transference β	Restoration β	Focused Attention β	Directivity of the Cure β
Perceived Ineffectiveness of Psychoanalysis	ns	–	–	–	ns	–	ns
Perceived Complexity of Psychoanalysis	–	–	–	–	ns	–	0.23**
Eclecticism	–	–	–	0.24**	ns	0.24**	0.24**
Psychoanalytic Training	ns	0.19**	–	0.18**	–	–	–
CHKCC	ns	0.24**	–	–	0.23**	-0.23**	ns
Major: social work	-0.14*	0.17*	–	–	ns	–	–
History of Therapy	0.20**	–	0.21**	0.21**	ns	–	-0.23**
Combining Approaches	–	ns	20**	–	0.27**	–	–

*p < 0.05; **p < 0.01; ns = non-significant.

their clients (scores from Transference and Free Floating Attention subscales fall in the Agree range). Nevertheless, they cannot be said to be doing psychoanalytic listening because they lack one fundamental concept of it: the unconscious (scores from the Unconscious subscale fall in the Disagree range). An obvious consequence of not having a theory of the (Freudian) unconscious in mind when listening to clients is that a great many unconscious motives and fantasies, repressed thoughts, defense mechanisms, lapses, and various unconscious formations may be misinterpreted or missed completely. A less obvious consequence is that lacking a theory of the unconscious will also reflect on the understanding and conceptualization of the other two components. For example, being sensitive toward the relationship with the other is surely a quality that any good listener should have; however, it is only an understanding of the unconscious that can open up an understanding of psychoanalytic transference, which is something that goes far beyond what is enacted in the present relationship. Similarly, it is only a theory of the unconscious that can help with listening to and understanding the (unconscious) associations among various chains of thoughts; thus, attention toward what the other person says should be described as "free floating" in a psychoanalytic sense only when it is oriented to grasp the unconscious motives and associations beyond the intended meanings.

Psychoanalytic listening is therefore not simply "listening between the lines" as listening in counseling can be. Psychoanalytic listening requires more than a set of skills; it requires a theory of the unconscious. This implies that psychoanalytic listening is not just constituted by a few components separately but more so by the interactions of each component with the others. It is both *listening to* and *listening for*. Thus, *we may say that each of these three components is like a ring that ties the other two together; losing one ring would break the whole chain.*

In contrast, the three CACWS dimensions are not correlated among each other, suggesting that they do not assess a common dimension such as a hypothetical *counseling listening*; instead, they describe a set of skills or dimensions that can exist quite independently alongside each other (their intensity depends mainly on the choice of the clinician) and they do not necessarily refer to a specific theory.

Psychoanalytic listening vs counseling attitude

The psychoanalytic and counseling dimensions that emerged from these scales are not necessarily *in opposition* to each other, which suggests that psychoanalysis and counseling are really distinct and to some extent incomparable practices. For example, the three CACWS subscales describe the goals of counseling and the direction imposed by the therapist; in contrast, the three PACWS dimensions describe the various components that form psychoanalytic listening but do not describe the intervention of the psychoanalyst. Interestingly enough, at the initial stage of scale construction, a few items concerning a psychoanalytic intervention were included; however, these items did not produce any valid and reliable subscales. The fact that the subscale intervention was not supported by factor analysis is likely a further confirmation that a psychoanalytic "intervention" cannot be standardized or defined in advance, but it can only occur as a result of listening. This suggests that psychoanalysis and counseling really operate along different directions.

Insights from the subgroup analyses

In addition, as shown by the subgroup analyses, significant differences were found among the PACWS dimensions when the group was divided by history of therapy and university major, but not when the variables examined were years of practice, number of clients, gender, or age. This should be interpreted as a confirmation that psychoanalytic listening is structurally different from listening as practiced in other counseling orientations, and as such, it cannot simply change as a consequence of time (as measured by age or years of practice or number of clients) or by demographics; instead, a substantial change in listening requires specific training and a personal therapy experience.

Similarly, whether respondents reported making use of psychoanalytic theory or not, this has not influenced any psychoanalytic dimensions (the 21 counseling professionals who reported to use psychoanalytic theory did not score significantly differently in any PACWS subscale than other participants). This is actually in line with what was expected. In fact, an academic knowledge of some psychoanalytic concepts does not necessarily enhance understanding of the unconscious, transference, or free floating attention, which instead can be better experienced in a clinical setting. On the other hand, not adopting or not knowing psychoanalytic theory does not necessarily (always) hinder psychoanalytic listening or understanding. *These findings simply indicate that knowledge of psychoanalytic theory is not what guarantees that a psychoanalytic listening occurs.* Thus we can argue that one does not always listen or operate "psychoanalytically" simply because one has a title or an academic qualification as a psychoanalyst. And, at least theoretically one can listen psychoanalytically even if one has not mastered psychoanalytic theory. Finally, adopting a specific theoretical orientation or the analyst's experience or knowledge does not guarantee the results of a practice, which instead is dependent on other factors like transference.

Further understanding of the three psychoanalytic variables emerging from this study

Unconscious

First, this is predicted by psychoanalytic training, meaning that the level of psychoanalytic training one receives will reflect on understanding of the unconscious. This is a significant finding, because, although unconscious does not belong to the local culture, it can nevertheless be received. Second, conflicts with local culture (as represented by the CHKCC) can open up the understanding of the unconscious. However, there is substantial difference between social workers and psychologists/counselors. In fact, correlation analyses revealed an association between perception of the clients' resistance to talk and open up (i.e. CHKCC) and the interpretation of the unconscious among social workers (Table 3.6), but not among psychologists/counselors (Table 3.7). This suggests that the former but not the latter may interpret resistance to psychoanalysis as due to some unconscious motives. Indeed, among this sample, a degree in social work shows a positive correlation with the variable unconscious, whereas a degree in psychology/counseling shows an opposite attitude (see Table 3.5). This is reflected in multiple regression analysis too; in fact, a major in social work resulted as a contributor to the understanding of the unconscious, whereas a degree in psychology and counseling resulted as a suppressor. *This may suggest that social workers and psychologists/counselors develop different understandings of the unconscious.* Thus, both academic and professional training play a role in understanding the unconscious. Further, history of therapy is not a predictor for the variable Unconscious, among this sample; this might seem odd at first, but we should consider that none of these counseling professionals had undergone psychoanalysis. It is argued instead that receiving psychoanalysis might be an important factor for having an understanding of the unconscious (this could be tested in further research). Finally, here, the variable Combining Approaches is non-significant as a predictor in this model; however, its p value was just above the threshold value used for testing a statistical hypothesis, meaning that it may be not totally unrelated. It is suggested that a combinatorial attitude is closely related to the functioning of the unconscious, even though in this model this did not clearly emerge; by refining the assessment and measurement tool it is possible that future studies will provide more evidence to support this link.

Free floating attention

Two variables resulted as significant predictors, namely History of Therapy and Combining Approaches. This is a meaningful finding. On the one hand, it means that free floating attention cannot be directly taught by academic training, but it needs to be experienced through personal psychotherapy or psychoanalysis (findings from this study lead us to consider that even non-psychoanalytically oriented psychotherapy may enhance free floating attention, meaning that psychoanalytic effects may occur in various contexts). On the other hand, it means that free floating attention does not respond to the linear Aristotelian logic of the excluded third; instead, combining approaches might reflect that "combinatorial logic" is what gets closer to the functioning of free floating attention. Proceeding per combination, or even per contradiction, is what potentially opens up psychoanalytic listening (combination and not "eclecticism," which did not result as a predictor).

Transference

Eclecticism, psychoanalytic training and history of therapy are the three significant predictors. Personal psychotherapy or psychoanalysis is an optimal condition for transference to emerge; further, specific training might enhance understanding. Most important, although a relational inclination might be embedded within the local culture, these two variables resulted as significant predictors even among this sample, suggesting that undergoing personal analysis and receiving specific psychoanalytic training might be essential components for an understanding of transference as it originated in psychoanalysis. Finally, it is not completely clear how eclecticism can contribute to transference; however, previous studies (Berger, Zane, & Hwang, 2014) showed that among community mental health clinicians, therapists with an eclectic orientation reported greater multicultural awareness and better multicultural counseling relationships with their clients than therapists with a humanistic or psychoanalytic orientation. Thus, it might be that eclecticism serves as a sort of adaptation for interpreting the various expressions of transference in different cultural contexts, as is the case of this sample.

Attention

It is particularly interesting that Free Floating Attention (PACWS) and Focused Attention (CACWS) are positively correlated (Table 3.5). This may seem counterintuitive at first, as one may hardly imagine focused attention to be an elective practice of psychoanalysts; at least, the way the psychoanalytic settings is organized (with the couch, for example) seems to suggest the opposite. However, the fact that the two scales are not negatively associated might simply mean that they assess the same dimension, namely "attention". In the first case (focused attention), it is the attention of a subject toward another subject, whereas in the latter case (free floating attention) it is attention to the unconscious. Not surprisingly, then, the two predictors of Focused Attention (Eclecticism, as a contributor, and CHKCC as a suppressor; see Table 3.8), are not significant predictors for Free Floating Attention, which instead is partially explained by History of Therapy and the Combining Approaches scale, in this model. Free floating attention is openness toward the unconscious, meaning what goes beyond the representation of the Other*: the very function of the couch was indeed that of isolating the function of listening in psychoanalysis, separating it from the gaze/look. As such, the psychoanalytical "free floating attention" is not at all a "lack" of attention; instead, we can say that *it is genuine and absolute attention*, which is oriented toward the signifiers and what emerges beyond the manifest meaning. Conversely, in the face-to-face dialogue is easy for this manifest or intended meaning to remain in the foreground, for example because we might tend to find in the expressions of the other a confirmation or disapproval of our fantasies, thoughts, fears. Thus, the gaze/look may produce a fixation on the imaginary meaning or sense, which also works as a resistance against listening to the words we are saying and the Other meaning they reveal.

Focused attention is oriented to the other person in front of us; thus, his/her participation or withdrawal from the conversation can influence the effort spent on actively listening (and vice versa). This might explain why, for example, clients' expectations (CHKCC) might be a suppressor of active listening: the resistance of the client may limit and reduce the active participation of the therapist. On the other hand, it might also be that the participation of the therapist can help overcome the resistance of the client. In contrast, psychoanalytic listening should not be affected by the client's resistance (Table 3.8); Freud suggested something similar when he urged the psychoanalyst to just concern him/herself with conducting his/her operation as well as possible.

4 Is there psychoanalysis in Hong Kong?

Absence of psychoanalytic theory from Hong Kong

When asking local counselors whether they refer to psychoanalysis or not in their practice, 21 respondents out of 223 were positive. This suggests that psychoanalytic theory is not completely unknown in Hong Kong, but it remains marginal. In fact, none of the respondents from this sample reported adopting psychoanalysis alone, but always in combination with several other techniques, such as cognitive behavior therapy (CBT), person-centered therapy, cognitive therapy, narrative therapy, positive psychology, play therapy, behavioral therapy, group therapy, systemic therapy, brief therapy, art therapy, or task-centered approaches.

Psychoanalytic theory ranked low in popularity among counseling professionals, in contrast to Europe and North America, where it is considered an important orientation in counseling, after behaviorism/cognitivism and humanism (Hansen, 2000, 2002); not to mention that psychoanalysis in Europe and America is normally practiced by psychoanalysts, and only secondarily by counselors.

Further, there are some serious issues concerning the effective training that one can receive, and about how psychoanalysis is actually practiced: (1) at present, teaching about psychoanalysis is limited to some introductory courses in some universities; and (2) the lack of psychoanalysts means that professionals are normally not able to undergo a personal analysis or receive psychoanalytic supervision.

Why are behaviorism/cognitivism and humanism more popular in Hong Kong?

As mentioned before, the very notion of counseling matches the Hong Kong Chinese culture better than psychotherapy or psychoanalysis; at the same time, the counselor more than the psychoanalyst is more readily accepted by the Chinese. What historical, cultural, and social grounds have determined the prevalence of counseling over other approaches?

Psychoanalysis is a complex theory that requires lengthy training and offers only a few guided techniques; it requires a peculiar curiosity and desire for investigating the unconscious; it can be very effective from the beginning, but potentially remains a never-ending process. A distinction may be made between the Chinese cultural bias against psychoanalysis in general and the Cantonese cultural bias against psychoanalysis specifically. The former is characterized by a Confucian bias against the Freudian concepts of libido and sexuality (Hong, Yamamoto, Chang, & Lee, 1993); the latter is characterized by a Cantonese emphasis on efficiency, technique, and practicality by Hong Kong people. This partially explains why CBT is more popular in Hong Kong. Behaviorism emphasizes finding solutions to problems over short periods of time. Behaviorism and humanism put very little emphasis on understanding and analyzing the underlying structure and unconscious mechanisms. Humanism emphasizes empathy with the client, a sense of sharing feeling and experience. Behaviorism and humanism have very different theoretical backgrounds; however, some professionals may find that such approaches are complementary and may combine them in their practice. In contrast, psychoanalysis is probably too distant, both in theory and in practice, from any counseling orientation, and it cannot be mixed so easily.

Pragmatism and humanism in Western and Chinese cultural traditions

It is striking to see how popular some counseling orientations are in Hong Kong. For example, humanism in counseling finds its roots in a cultural context and time that is very distant from Hong Kong. Hansen (2000) observed that humanism has combined much of the existential and phenomenological philosophy originating in Europe with the optimistic American mind-set. Sass (1989) described the four essential elements of humanism as: freedom, uniqueness, privacy, and self-transparency. However, nothing seems more distant from Chinese culture, and from Chinese values, than these elements. Freedom, uniqueness, privacy, and self-transparency are at opposite poles to the Chinese and Hong Kong way of living. However, Wu (1998, p. 314) maintained that "the pragmatic thinking in both America and China is humanistic" (meaning that the vision of life may be different, but both cultures emphasize the value of human beings), but while for Americans, "thinking is an activity of solving problems; ideas must make a difference to human life; the earth can be civilized through scientific technology" (pp. 316–317), in China, "to think is to meditate, to live and to act" (p. 319). Thus, despite profound differences, both US and Chinese cultures might reflect two forms of humanism (Halliwell & Mousley (2003) name at least eight different types of humanism). For instance, Chan (cited in Wu, 1998) described "the pragmatic spirit of the Chinese humanism as 'not the humanism that denies or slights a Supreme Power, but one that professes the unity of man and Heaven'" (p. 317). Normally, client-centered therapists attempt to "empathize" with their clients and adopt what they call an attitude of unconditional positive regard toward them (Hansen, 2000). Empathic feeling and unconditional positive regard might be precious in a context like Hong Kong, where pressure from society, and thus criticism, can be very high; thus, such values, even though they may originally arise from different grounds, are particularly appreciated. In contrast, the neutrality of the analyst and his/her attitude of not interfering with the associative work of the analysand may easily be misunderstood and be perceived as lack of interest in the client and his/her story (particularly in a Chinese cultural context, see for example Haag, 2014).

Integration or eclecticism?

In this study, a total of 221 counselors reported their theoretical orientation. Of them, 206 (93.2 percent) have reported making use of more than one counseling technique. Of the remaining thirteen professionals: two reported to refer only to CBT, three reported to use only play therapy and to treat only children, two reported to adopt only client-centered therapy, four reported some other orientations not included in the list, two did not complete this section.

What are the criteria for combining different theories?

Four questions aimed at better understanding what criteria drove the adoption of more than one approach are shown in Table 4.9.

Among the 206 participants who currently adopt more than one counseling orientation, a consistent part reported having adopted more than one approach from the beginning (89.8 percent), while the remaining part (10.2 percent) initially referred to a single theory and then shifted to a multimodal approach later. The majority of counselors adopt different approaches in different clinical situations (93.6 percent), combine those approaches that are distant and complementary (62 percent), and do have a preferred theoretical approach (68.3 percent). Two thirds of the respondents (68.3 percent) reported not having any preferred approach but that they considered various approaches as equally important; only less than one third (31.7 percent) reported having a main theoretical orientation and incorporating techniques from other approaches.

These results may be in line with an eclectic model, where techniques are chosen regardless of their theoretical distance; indeed, in most cases an eclectic approach tends to merge together techniques that are distant and complementary, and where no specific orientation emerges over the others.

Brook (1993) noted that in the Chinese context, Buddhism, Daoism, and Confucianism live together with a considerable degree of harmony; they are

Table 4.9 What are the criteria for combining different theories? (N=206)

	Percent
Question 1: Have you previously adhered to a specific theoretical orientation (only one)?	
a) No, I have never adopted one approach only	89.8
b) Yes	10.2
Question 2: If you normally adopt two or more approaches, please indicate the criterion that drives your selection (choose one)	
a) It depends on the case treated (kind of client, objectives, etc.). I can adopt different approaches in different clinical situations	93.6
b) Structured approach, and normally I tend to use the same techniques	6.4
Question 3: How do you choose to combine different approaches (please choose one)?	
a) I combine those approaches that are distant and complementary	62.0
b) I combine those approaches that share some theoretical background	34.5
c) Other	3.5
Question 4: How would you describe your theoretical orientation?	
a) I have no adherence to any preferred approach; I adopt different approaches and they are equally important	68.3
b) I have a main theoretical orientation, but with experience I like to incorporate techniques from other orientations	31.7

equal in principle, equally available, and free to associate and interact in a multitude of ways. He described this relation with the term "condominium." Apparently, the same can be said about counseling. For instance, the majority of counselors adopt CBT and a person-centered approach, but they do not seem to consider such orientation more important than another. Each counselor apparently has his/her own set of tools and techniques where s/he can pick from each time, depending on the case; however, different techniques are free to be combined differently each time, and it is hard to describe a stable profile, or one approach that clearly prevails over others. In conclusion, when considering eclecticism and integration, we can say that Hong Kong counselors are more likely to be eclectic. This result is in line with previous findings in the literature.

Effects of covariance

Interrelationships among factors (effect of co-variances) have been examined, so as to verify if, for example, years of work experience affected counselors' choices to adhere to a specific theoretical orientation or not. The four questions have been computed, considering the variables: age, gender, experience, major, history of therapy, religion, and number of clients. For questions 1 and 3 (Table 4.9), no statistically significant associations were found. Concerning question number 2, only the two variables "history of therapy" and "age" were shown to be significant. The majority of respondents (93.6 percent) reported making use of different approaches in different clinical situations, depending on the case treated; however, this is particularly true for the group of respondents who have not been in therapy before. Further, respondents older than 41 are relatively less likely than their younger colleagues to adopt different approaches depending on the case treated. In respect of question 4, the variables gender, major, history of therapy, and age were shown to be statistically correlated. Precisely, female professionals showed less adherence to a specific theoretical approach; likewise, social workers are more inclined to consider all orientations equally important and not have a preferred theoretical orientation; respondents who have not been in therapy before do not have particular preference for a specific theoretical orientation; finally, younger professionals are more likely to consider different techniques in their practice. Conversely, men, non-social workers, and professionals who are older than 40 and have been in therapy before appear relatively more inclined toward having a preferred theoretical orientation.

Finally, among this sample of Hong Kong counseling professionals there emerged a strong inclination toward technical eclecticism rather than theoretical integration; this is somehow opposite from what emerges among counseling professionals from Europe and North America,[1] where eclecticism is most likely to be perceived as a lack of professionalism, and a single orientation or theoretical integration are preferred. Furthermore, in Hong Kong eclecticism seems to be embedded within the local culture and is primarily due to dissatisfaction with any specific counseling orientation; in fact, the large majority of participants reported that they adopted a multimodal approach from the beginning. This is also in contrast with findings from Western countries, where instead eclecticism appears in most cases to be caused by dissatisfaction with a single orientation and is not culture specific. Eclecticism seems to be descriptive of the approach of all counseling professionals in this sample. A tendency toward eclecticism was shown to be partly influenced by history of therapy and other variables like major, age, experience; however, at present, it is difficult to say that a higher level of professionalism among Hong Kong counseling professionals will greatly change this eclectic approach.

Overview of the listening orientation

Given that psychoanalysis is not so popular in Hong Kong, local counselors were expected to be very distant from any psychoanalytic attitude. Furthermore, the fast-paced life in Hong Kong, and the pragmatic nature of Chinese thought, all lead to the belief that counselors were oriented toward a quick, directive, and solution-focused counseling, to the detriment of psychoanalytic listening. It was therefore expected that respondents would score higher on the three counseling dimensions (CACWS) and lower on the psychoanalytic dimensions (PACWS). Results are shown in Table 4.10.

Table 4.10 Listening profile of the respondents (N=217)

Subscale	Rank	Scale	Mean	SD	95% confidence interval of the difference	
					Lower	Upper
Focused Attention	1	Counseling	4.79	0.62	4.71	4.87
Transference	2	Psychoanalysis	4.71	0.59	4.63	4.79
Free Floating Attention	3	Psychoanalysis	4.29	0.58	4.21	4.37
Restoration	4	Counseling	3.96	0.72	3.86	4.06
Directivity of the Cure	5	Counseling	3.86	0.73	3.76	3.96
Unconscious	6	Psychoanalysis	3.39	0.79	3.29	3.49

Scores based on a 6-point Likert scale with anchors 1 = strongly disagree and 6 = strongly agree.

The scales are listed together and classified in descending order. Scales at the top are those that best describe the Hong Kong counselors' attitude toward clinical work.

Quite surprisingly, Hong Kong counselors do not simply belong on one dimension or another. Grouping the six subscales together and listing them in descending order, shows that local counselors reported a peculiar profile that combines characteristics of both counseling attitude and psychoanalytic listening. In particular, two psychoanalytic scales (Transference, and Free Floating Attention) scored unexpectedly high, ranking second and third.

Beside the subscales order, another important parameter to consider is the theoretical mid-point. The theoretical mid-point sets a term of reference for interpreting the scores and the respondents' attitude toward a dimension. For instance, in this case, the theoretical mid-point is at 3.5. This means that values above 3.5 describe general agreement on a variable, while values below 3.5 indicate general disagreement. However, it is not possible to take into account only the mean score, rather, the whole confidence interval has to be considered. The confidence interval for each variable is calculated and shown in Table 4.10.

Concerning the CACWS, Focused Attention, Directivity of the Cure, and Restoration had confidence intervals above the theoretical mid-point of 3.5 (with both means being positioned between "slightly" and "moderately" agree on the 6-point Likert scale). Concerning the PACWS, Free Floating Attention and Transference had confidence intervals above the theoretical mid-point, whereas Unconscious benchmarked below the theoretical mid-point (from a low of 3.29, to a high of 3.49), which leads us to conclude that the unconscious is not a relevant concept for our sample. *Because one essential component of psychoanalytic listening is missing, we should doubt that their listening is psychoanalytic at all.*

Altogether, the fact that Focused Attention, Free Floating Attention, and Transference scored higher than other subscales suggests that local counselors are particularly receptive, attentive toward clients, their needs, their feelings, what they verbalize, and what they don't. On the other hand, a low score on Unconscious and a relatively higher score on Directivity of the Cure and Restoration lead to the suggestion that the respondents may be more inclined to find solutions to problems rather than critically analyzing questions. However, this aspect deserves further investigation. In particular, one should be cautious when interpreting these results because, in the absence of any kind of baseline statistics, it is not possible to know how therapists in general respond and make meaningful comparison.

Finally, here, psychoanalysis as a theory is little known among Hong Kong counselors; only a very few respondents referred explicitly to psychoanalysis, and even more fundamental psychoanalytic concepts find little resonance here. Although from a theoretical point of view, the participants apparently share the basic assumptions of a brief, focused and goal-oriented counseling, their practice reveals some inclination toward Free Floating Attention and a marked sensitivity toward Transference. Nevertheless, they cannot be said to have a psychoanalytic listening profile because they lack of one fundamental component of it: the unconscious.

Influence of Hong Kong culture over the PACWS subscales

Because psychoanalytic theory and techniques were not much used by this sample, low scores on the Unconscious dimension were not surprising; the concept of unconscious does not belong to Chinese culture (Zhang, 1992) and could only be provided by specific training.

However, scores largely above the theoretical mid-point of Free Floating Attention and Transference were more surprising. In general, participants scored higher on those dimensions that assess being receptive of others. On the one hand, this tendency possibly derives from clinical and social work education, as the free-value, non-judgment, and client-centered principles have been emphasized throughout training in general. On the other hand, this may also reflect an attitude embedded in Hong Kong Chinese culture. For example, some aspects of the Chinese listening disposition may overlap with some dimensions of what we have identified as psychoanalytic listening.

Free floating and focused attention

Participants scored relatively high on Free Floating Attention (Table 10). Not much in Chinese culture is expressed through spoken words. According to Gao et al. (1996), Chinese communication is governed by five distinctly alternative rules: (1) *hanxu* (implicit communication) 含蓄; (2) *tinghua* (listen-centeredness) 听话; (3) *keqi* (politeness) 客气; (4) *zijiren* (a focus on insiders) 自己人; and (5) *mianzi* (face-directed communication strategies)

面子. The first two rules, *hanxu* and *tinghua*, seem particularly relevant to explain why Focused Attention and Free Floating Attention scored higher than other subscales. In Chinese, *han* means "to contain," "to embody" or "to reserve"; *xu* means "to store," or "to save." Thus, *hanxu* suggests an implicit and indirect Chinese approach to communication:

> *hanxu* refers to a mode of communication (both verbal and nonverbal) which is contained, reserved, implicit, and indirect. To be *hanxu*, one does not spell out everything but leaves the "unspoken" to the listeners [...] The value of *hanxu* also explains the importance of nonverbal communication in Chinese culture. Meanings often reside in unspoken messages. A hand movement, a smile, and a shrug, for example, convey embedded meanings. Chinese may smile to express embarrassment, frustration, or nervousness. In addition, nonverbal communication often provides important cues for interpretation of verbal messages.
> (Gao and Ting-Toomey, 1998, p. 37)

Tinghua, instead, translates literally as "listen talks." Chinese culture encourages listening, not speaking. "To Chinese, there are conditions associated with speaking, and not everyone is entitled to speak. Thus, a spoken 'voice' is equated with seniority, authority, age, experience, knowledge, and expertise. As a result, listening becomes a predominant mode of communication" (Gao & Ting-Toomey, 1998, p. 42).

PASSIVE IN SPEAKING, BUT ACTIVE IN LISTENING

Attention is then necessarily oriented to silence, and to what is not being said. This is to say that in Chinese culture, attention is normally directed to the meaning behind words. Traditionally, in knowledge creation and transfer processes in Asian cultures, "the invisible, the tacit, the spoken, and the implied are inevitably privileged over the visible, the explicit, the written, and the articulate" (Chia, 2003, p. 957). In Chinese culture, understanding greatly relies on the receiver, and this applies to different fields. The way in which Chinese philosophers and artists expressed themselves is also inarticulate:

> Suggestiveness, not articulateness, is the ideal of all Chinese art, whether it is poetry, painting, or anything else. According to Chinese literary tradition, in good poetry "the number of words is limited, but the ideas it suggests are limitless." An intelligent reader of poetry reads what is outside the poem; and a good reader of books reads "what is between the lines".
> (Fung, 1966, p. 12)

The emphasis on listening rather than speaking may be due to the societal structure of Chinese societies. In most cultures, the status one has within a relationship influences how much one speaks, if any, and how one speaks, and this is particularly true in the hierarchical structure of Chinese society. In fact,

> Chinese speaking practices in the context of status and role relationships are portrayed as listening-centered, asymmetrical, and deferential. Given that the ability to listen is stressed, promoted, and rewarded in the context of hierarchy and role relationships, Chinese constantly seek to cultivate and refine their listening skills. As a result, they are more likely to detect any nuance and subtlety embedded in verbal messages.
> (Gao and Ting-Toomey, 1998, p. 42)

Being receptive and good at listening becomes even more important as communication is implicit and indirect in Chinese culture: "communication in Asian cultures is receiver-centered. [...] It can be argued, however, that Chinese communication appears to be 'passive' in speaking, but it emphasizes 'activeness' in listening" (Gao, 1998, p. 174).

In Chinese culture not everyone is allowed to express everything, because harmony in relationships is more important than the truth. As a consequence, something always remains unsaid, and the attention (of the receiver) should always be floating, so as to also capture what the speaker cannot express. Gestures and body communication therefore also acquire more importance (what has been grouped in the variable Focused Attention); every minimal gesture becomes relevant to communication.

ALLUSIVE SPEAKING

Chinese culture emphasizes listening, but at the same time it lacks a conception of the unconscious. Thus, listening is normally intended as listening to the relevant other, and to his/her needs. Speaking in Chinese culture is already "speaking of something" (Jullien, 2001, 2004), and listening is "listening to someone." A message could then be easily interpreted on a personal level, for example as a request or a suggestion (because if there is no such thing as the unconscious, then there is no Other reference; a talk is already a dia-logue). However, since communication has to undergo some politeness rules, the speaking is usually allusive:

> In conversation, Chinese tend to use small "modifiers" to condition their meanings the way Westerners often find strange and disconcerting. The ubiquitous Chinese use of "perhaps" and "maybe" is one example. If the Chinese say "Maybe I will come with you," "Perhaps it is too far for you to walk," and "inconvenient," they actually mean "I'm coming," "There's no way I'll let you walk," and "impossible" respectively. Here, the words "maybe" and "perhaps" are used to help create a harmonious atmosphere and prevent the parties involved from losing face. For a

professor, an indirect way to suggest something to his student could be for instance to ask him if he is not too hot. Any Chinese student would immediately understand that he has to open the window.

(Fang & Faure, 2010, p. 328)

LISTENING AND SPEAKING IN CHINESE COMMUNICATION

Chinese schools emphasize listening skills, writing skills, and reading skills, but rarely give importance to speaking skills (Lu, 2001). Chen and Chen (1988) found that nonverbal reasoning skills were rated equally by two groups of Chinese and English students; however, the Chinese group tended to rate verbal reasoning skills as less relevant to measuring intelligence than did the English group. Traditionally, verbal abilities are not very much considered as indicating intelligence in Chinese culture, and verbalization is not encouraged. Indeed, the Chinese often have a feeling of distrust that the spoken word can lead to a satisfactory communication. Numerous expressions in the Chinese language reflect this inclination:

yan bu jin yi (言不尽意), "not saying all that is felt"; *yan wai zhi yi* (言外之意), "more is meant than meets the ear"; and *zhi ke yi hui, bu ke yan chuan* (只可意会不可言传), "can be felt, but not be expressed in words" all emphasize the inadequacy of spoken words in constructing meanings. Hence, the ability to surmise and decipher hidden meanings is highly desirable in Chinese culture.

(Gao, 1998, p. 169)

Other expressions include:

yi zai yan wai (意在言外), "meaning lies beyond words"; and *yi zai bu yan zhong* (意在不言中), "meaning lies in the unspoken." In Chinese culture, children are taught and encouraged to apply *cha yan guan se* (察言观色), "examining a person's words and observing his [her] countenance" in their communication with others.

(Gao, 1998, p. 170)

This has some important implications; it means that the responsibility for effective communication largely lies upon the receiver rather than the speaker (as it does instead in Western cultures), and thus one should become as attentive and receptive as possible:

In conversational exchanges, one thus is required to make inferences, read between the lines, and draw connections through *ti hui* (体会), "to apprehend or to experience," and *zhuo mo* (琢磨), "to contemplate or to ponder." The ability to *ti hui* and *zhuo mo* is highly emphasized and essential to accurate interpretations of messages in Chinese culture. As a result, direct expressions in Chinese culture tend not to carry the same weight or be as meaningful as those that are indirect.

(Gao, 1998, pp. 170–171)

SILENCE

In most Western countries, speech needs to be loaded with information. Silence is perceived as an empty awkward and embarrassing pause. People even find it as expressing a lack of interest and unwillingness to communicate, a sign of hostility, rejection, or interpersonal incompatibility; anxiety or shyness; or a lack of verbal skills. On the other hand, when not used to refute the other's point, silence might imply consent. In China, however, "silence holds a strong contextual meaning, such as showing obedience to senior people, or being a sign of respect for the wisdom and expertise of others, or disagreement while avoiding direct confrontation, or a time interval for sorting out ideas, depending on the context of the time" (Gu, 2003, p. 58).

Silence in Chinese culture is not just a lack of saying; conversely, it is full of information which remains unsaid because of community rules. In a society where group harmony is valued over individual expression of inner thoughts and feelings, contradicting someone else may be perceived as taking one side of an argument and becoming an opponent. Silence becomes then a form of respect for the other who shows a different idea, since taking distance from such ideas could also mean taking distance from the person. On the contrary, in the West, discussion serves to clarify opposite points of view, as well as leading to mutual understanding.

Transference

Transference is not a phenomenon that can be observed only in psychoanalysis; transference is a psychoanalytic term that refers to a supposed universal phenomenon (thought it might have different expressions in different cultures). However, only in psychoanalysis has it acquired that centrality and received that much attention. In Western contexts, among various psychoanalytic schools the concept of transference has gained quite different interpretations, concerning both the very nature of the transference and how it should be handled. However, transference is normally considered the motor of the cure; a therapy advances because of transference.

The variable Transference scored unexpectedly highly among this sample, ranking second out of the six subscales (see Table 10). This was unexpected in a context where psychoanalysis is very marginally applied. Given that the literature normally describes counseling in Hong Kong as time limited and solution oriented (Lo, 2005), transference was expected to receive less attention. One hypothesis to interpret this result is that attention to relational aspects is embedded in Chinese culture. As already mentioned, this is probably rooted in the different philosophical grounds of Western and Chinese cultures. Daoism and Confucianism shape Hong Kong Chinese thought and society. The social structure of Chinese societies has perhaps favored interdependency among people rather than developing individual critical thinking. Relationships are central, rather than abstraction and philosophical speculations. As a consequence, speech serves very different goals, and "in contrast to Western cultures, where communication is often seen as an expression of 'self,' Chinese cultures treat 'communication' as a means of reaffirming the communicator as a member of society and of maintaining existing relationships, social harmony and status differentials" (Chang, 2001, p. 158).

Literature suggests that the counseling relation is perceived very differently by Westerners and Chinese. On one hand, clients can have very high expectations and be rather passive in counseling:

> Asian clients may develop a positive idealized feeling very readily, construing the therapist as an authority figure, much like a teacher, with warmth, benevolence, and an expectation that the therapist's wisdom and knowledge can help them. The client also readily assumes the role of a patient or a student. In doing so he or she may not say much, expecting instead that the guidance and structure come from the therapist.
>
> (Yi, 1995, p. 311)

Asian American clients have also been described as greatly influenced by a highly hierarchical culture which prescribes rules of conduct with authority figures, as therapists are. For this reason, the concept of transference "is quite unfamiliar to Asian American clients. The importance of examining the clients' relationship to the therapist may not be immediately apparent to the client. Its value to the therapeutic process may need to be explained and elaborated over time" (Chin, Liem, Domokos-Cheng Ham, & Hong, 1993, p. 128).

On the other hand, Chinese therapists might tend to respond to their clients and somehow collude with their idealization:

> The dyad is structured like this: The idealization and trust on the part of the junior person are responded to with fulfillment of their needs by the authority figure whose self-esteem, in turn, is heightened by the junior person's idealizing attitude. However, when either or both in the dyad cannot fulfill the expected role or responsibility, the mutual idealizing cannot be maintained, resulting in loss of face, shame, disappointment, and resentment.
>
> (Yi, 1995, p. 311)

This cultural feature might be a limit to the understanding of transference as conceptualized in psychoanalysis, because transference is not simply the relation between the two. For instance, visiting China in 1987, Joseph noted that "the formal terminology of transference was alien to the Chinese and unacceptable. However, if this term was not used in discussion periods but rather one spoke of relationships between the patient and the therapist, the Chinese hosts could then present their own examples and experiences" (in Fine, 1987, p. 97). This suggests that Chinese counseling professionals are attentive to the relational dimension of the counseling process; however, sensitivity toward the relational dimension does not necessarily imply that transference is analyzed or interpreted for the advancement of the therapy; more likely, it is used for imposing direction on the client. In fact, Joseph's description of the therapist–client relation in China is more reminiscent of the classic medical doctor–patient dyad than psychoanalyst–analysand. Chinese clinicians were presented more as

> authoritarian, paternal figure, with the patient as passive, obedient, dependent, and accepting member of the pair. They were aware that the patient is not always as obedient as he seemed, but felt that whatever treatment was offered [...] it was most successful if the patient accepted it without question. If the patient behaved otherwise, efforts were made to overcome his reluctance (which analysts would call resistance) by reinforcing the authority rather than by attempting to understand the reason for such resistance.
>
> (Fine, 1987, p. 97)

However, it has to be noted that among this sample, the variable Transference is correlated with the other two psychoanalytic variables, Unconscious and Free Floating Attention, with Restoration, but not with Directivity of the Cure (Table 3.5), which makes the interpretation inconclusive.

In Hong Kong Chinese culture, much attention is given to the other (not any other, but only the relevant others; there is a fundamental difference between insiders and outsiders), and thus to the relation; however, one might wonder if *an understanding of psychoanalytic transference can really be possible when a theory of the unconscious is lacking*. Being more sensitive or more caring to the relationship with the other does not necessarily illuminate one's relation with the Other and thus transference.

It may be the case that Freud came to a theorization of transference because, in a Western context, transference expressions were perceived as more outstanding and striking than in a Chinese context (where instead deference toward authority is stronger, roles in relationships are clearly defined and thus transference expressions might be weaken or interpreted in a different framework). Freud needed some time before theorizing transference; only by occupying the position of the psychoanalyst was he able to experience what the analysand was projecting onto him, or expecting from him, or accusing him of. Only by occupying the place of the Other, could Freud experience that his clients were not simply speaking to his person. Recognizing transference means recognizing that one is being addressed a demand, a request, or even an accusation because one is currently occupying the place of the Other; this implies that there is a difference between the person of the psychoanalyst and his/her position in a discourse. Transference is obviously a normal condition, but in some circumstances (for example, when one is addressed as a psychoanalyst), this phenomenon massively emerges.

Interestingly, Haag (2014) also found that Chinese candidates often work in a supportive way rather than maintaining a more psychoanalytic position. This seems to confirm that they might focus on the actual relation more than on transference. Haag suggests that Chinese therapists might find it difficult to refuse to fulfill clients' wishes and encourage them to develop their resources because of the Confucian background (where the counselor is expected to be more like a teacher or master than a psychoanalyst). Further, Haag suggests that Chinese candidates find it difficult to understand transference because in the Chinese context there are rather fluid boundaries (less separation) between self and object; in her opinion, this makes it more difficult to perform the therapeutic "splitting" that would allow the therapist to understand the inner life of the client without becoming too involved in it, as well as to distinguish the transference and countertransference aspects from the relationship with the so-called "real" person of the analyst.

Finally, here, Zhiyan and Zachrisson (2014) reflected specifically on transference and countertransference in a Chinese setting and found that the psychoanalytic conception of it is largely valid in China as well. In their opinion, in a Chinese context and with Chinese clients we might see variations in the way transference is expressed, but normally this should not call for significant modifications of the psychoanalytic technique. Teaching psychoanalysis in China, Gullestad (2014) found that psychoanalytic transference can be received, and that verbatim accounts of therapy sessions was the best way to help Chinese candidates to understand latent transference patterns.

UNCONSCIOUS

The Unconscious subscale scored as one of the lowest among all subscales, below the theoretical mid-point (see Table 4.10). This confirms that the concept of the unconscious is largely unknown in Hong Kong, and that even among counselors, it does not represent a reference concept. More likely, local counselors do not refer to the unconscious when they listen to clients; and they do not interpret in terms of the unconscious what they hear from them. Thus, their "listening" means listening to the other person rather than to the unconscious; this is very different from psychoanalytic listening. However, this study has shown that introduction of this concept in the local context may follow some specific psychoanalytic training.

The unconscious is a difficult concept to render in Chinese culture, and in the Chinese language. This problem is not new and has been debated for more than 80 years, but there are still no satisfactory translations into the Chinese language. Importantly, such difficulties in translating (or reinventing) the unconscious in Chinese may indicate that the unconscious is still perceived as something abstract.

As said, not only is the term "unconscious" not significant to many, but in Chinese a specific word for unconscious does not even exist. Zhang (1992, p. 43) notes that this is an issue that has been debated for a very long time, from the arrival of psychoanalysis in China:

> The Japanese way of translating the term was "muishiki" [無意識], which means, in Chinese, "without consciousness or non-conscious," an erroneous way of understanding the Freudian concept of the unconscious. Chinese translators debated about whether to use the Japanese coined-word "muishiki" or to create a new term. There were several Chinese translations for the Freudian term "the unconscious": (1) "qian shi" 潛識, "yin shi" 隱識, "yin ji" 隱機, "qian yishi" 潛意識, (2) "xia yishi" 下意識, (3) "wu yishi" 無意識, "bu qi yi shi de" 不起意識的. The three groups refer to the unconscious, the subconscious, and nonconsciousness, respectively. Some writers pointed out that "wu yishi" (nonconsciousness) originated from Buddhism and has a special connotation of "Manovijnana," the level at which the awareness of self originates and creates evil karma. The word "qian" in "qian yishi" is metaphorical and has a double meaning of "hidden, latent" and "submerged".

The term "wu yishi" 無意識, which corresponds to the Japanese term "muishiki," is clearly inappropriate for describing the psychoanalytic unconscious, as it refers to a state of non-consciousness. Unfortunately, today this version is still quite commonly adopted. Another version ("qian yishi" 潛意識) is normally used, but this is also questionable as this translation recalls more of the "subconscious" than the "unconscious":

> Zhu Guangqian initiated discussion specifically about the unconscious in 1921. [...] He thinks that "yin ji" is an ambiguous term for the unconscious, which cannot reflect Freud's intention because instinct and impulse also belong to "yin ji." [...] He suggests that it is better to use "qian" (submerged) or "yin-" (hidden) "yishi" than to use the ready-made Japanese term "muishiki." [...] Although "qian yishi" may seem to be the best term in Chinese for the Freudian concept of the unconscious, the debate for the proper translation of the Freudian term "the unconscious" continues well into the 1980s, and people tend to repeat the same questions asked and explored over fifty years ago.
> (Zhang, 1992, pp. 43–44)

Probably, a brand new combination of characters for unconscious should be invented. I find it relevant and interesting that Chinese thought has never encountered or theorized the unconscious.

Interestingly, according to historian of psychoanalysis Hannah Decker (1977), even in Western contexts, the issue of the unconscious was a greater barrier to the acceptance of psychoanalysis than was the issue of sexuality. This might indicate that a psychoanalytic training cannot be simply limited to academic teachings, as general knowledge *about* the unconscious is not enough to have an understanding of psychoanalysis or to produce psychoanalysts. Thus, it may be that the key for introducing psychoanalysis among counselors in Hong Kong is to have them experience the unconscious in a personal analysis.

Even in Western cultures and among Western professionals the unconscious is not clearly defined, as sometimes it is considered as a noun, sometimes as an adjective, and sometimes it is confused with a state of non-consciousness. A lack of conceptualizing the unconscious in Chinese culture and language is probably the biggest limitation for the reception of psychoanalysis in Hong Kong. On the one hand, a theory of the unconscious would allow a better understanding of transference and free floating attention and their place in therapy. On the other hand, an understanding of the unconscious would orient the listening and promote intellectual curiosity and articulation of theoretical questions, thus potentially opening the way to the practice of psychoanalysis.

Listening across cultures

Contemporary Western philosophy perceives the signifier as introducing a multiplicity of meaning, *difference* in Derridean terms. While traditional Chinese thought tends to emphasize similarities, Westerners value difference more, along with independent thinking and speaking as a way for developing one's own perspective. Westerners are much concerned with the truth, and with the idea that the truth should be put in words and communicated. Moreover, the subject is a subject of free will, in Western philosophy, and together with the free will goes the idea of freedom of speech. But Chinese culture has developed a different attitude, not based on the idea of free will or on the freedom of speech. Generally, European and North American societies have been defined as independent cultures, whereas Chinese societies have been described as interdependent (Liu and Rau, 2012; Yang et al., 2011). Becoming an individual (thus someone different from others) is generally a positive value in European and American societies, whereas interdependent societies emphasize being part of the group. Interestingly, *the former have also emphasized speaking, while the latter have emphasized listening*. There thus appears to be a relation between societal structure and the disposition toward speech: "results show cultural influences on listening styles such that individualist cultures stimulate a greater degree of action-oriented listening while collectivist cultures stimulate more people-oriented listening styles" (Dragan & Sherblom, 2008, p. 174).

Listening is obviously much more complex than just hearing; what generally is not sufficiently taken into account is that there are more listening styles. For example, Watson, Barker, and Weaver (1995) developed the Listening

Styles Profile (LSP) to analyze individual differences in listening-style preferences. The LSP defines four types of listening: people oriented (concern for others' feelings and emotions), action oriented (receiving concise, error-free presentations), content oriented (receiving complex and challenging information), and time oriented (brief or hurried interactions with others). The authors found that

> people-oriented listeners tried to find areas of common interest with others and respond emphatically to them. [...] Action-oriented listeners appeared to be particularly impatient and easily frustrated when listening to a disorganized presentation. [...] Content-oriented listeners tended to evaluate facts and details carefully before forming judgments and opinions. [...] Time oriented listeners tended to let others know how much time they had to listen or tell others how much time they had to meet.
>
> (Watson et al., 1995, p. 3)

Further cross-cultural research has supported and expanded the hypothesis of listening differences across cultures; for example, using the LSP in their investigation Kiewitz, Weaver, Brosius, and Weimann (1997) found US participants to be time- and action-oriented listeners, whereas German participants preferred a more content-oriented listening style. Imhof's (2003) study, which used the instrument to compare German and US participants, suggests that Germans place more emphasis on behavior orientation than Americans do. Imhof and Janusik (2006) used the scale to show that German and US participants view listening differently. Their US participants conceptualized listening as a sustaining activity which affects the listener's knowledge structure and set of attitudes. Their German participants conceptualized listening as interactive and focused on the person and activities that support monitoring the conversation. These results demonstrated US participants to be more action oriented and German participants more people oriented. In another study (Lewis, 1999), it was found that US listeners expected to be entertained and persuaded, while the Germans more valued receiving detailed information and learning about the context. Veenstra (2004) found that the more collectivist Arabic societies emphasize the feelings of the people involved in the interaction during the process of listening; in contrast, people from the United States generally have a preference for cause–effect arguments and a linear form of communication. Dragan and Sherblom (2008) found the US listeners significantly more action oriented and the post-Soviet group significantly more people oriented.

Although no specific data refers to the Chinese context, a first conclusion one can draw is that societal structure is an important variable that greatly influences the listening attitude of a population. Specifically, in high-context cultures, such as the Chinese, Japanese, and Vietnamese cultures, personal relationships are highly valued and people in this type of high-context culture prefer a more people oriented listening style. In low-context cultures, such as the German, Swiss, Scandinavian, and US cultures, people focus on completing tasks and there is [...] a greater preference in this type of low-context culture for an action oriented style.

(Dragan & Sherblom, 2008, p. 177)

Chinese culture obviously lies among the high-context cultures, together with other Asian cultures. It is then reasonable to expect the Hong Kong Chinese people to be normally more people oriented in their listening. A people-oriented listening style is what may explain the high scores in the three subscales Focused Attention, Transference, and, partially, Free Floating Attention. The peculiar listening profile of the Hong Kong counselors should be understood in light of the cultural variable, specifically because the particular societal structure leads people to focus less on the content of communication and more on the relational aspects.

It was difficult to assess the weight of culture in details at the beginning of this research. Literature about counseling and psychoanalysis across cultures usually refers to culture in general terms. But in this case, the cultural factor has been expressed and analyzed in terms of listening differences, and studies about listening across cultures come from fields marginally related to counseling or psychoanalysis. These results also show that listening is probably influenced more by the culture than by the adoption of a specific counseling theory. Indeed, different counseling theories can sometimes explain differences in subscales. In this study, the order of the subscales is very similar among subgroups (age, gender, major, experience, etc.), which may be understood as the influence of the culture over academic and professional training.

Interpretive and empathic listening

In Western philosophical tradition, listening has been mainly identified as a function of the conscious mind, and it has been normally considered a cognitive process; normally, listening has been equated with interpreting the meaning, within a framework informed by Aristotelian logic based on the excluded third. As mentioned above, the majority of counseling approaches based on the classical theory of communication tend to consider listening simply as a consequence of a person's effort, thus suggesting that the more one applies, the more one can listen.

In recent years, probably in contrast to this mind/body division that reduced listening to a cognitive process, another kind of listening has become popular in counseling (and partially in some post-Freudian psychoanalytic schools): empathic listening. This kind of listening seems to counterbalance the active/cognitive listening to what is verbalized with a more bodily or affective understanding of what remains unspoken; to some extent, it is more of a listening with the body.

However, such a distinction between interpretive and empathic listening may be misleading. On the one hand, it is not surprising that listening in Hong Kong is not interpretive, given that traditionally Chinese cultures have been little interested in logic, rhetoric, or philosophy. On the other hand, empathy is a Western concept, and it may be inappropriate for describing a listening that arose in a non-Western culture:

> it is important to emphasize that empathy is a Western concept. Chinese and Japanese dictionaries describe empathy as a newly coined word that has been borrowed from Western languages. […] In Asian cultures, references to empathy actually more closely approximate the Western concept of sympathy, to be concerned about another.
>
> (Chin et al., 1993, pp. 36–37)

As mentioned before, empathy in counseling is generally intended as "the patient's actively putting something into the analyst's mind" (Akthar, 2013, p. 9). It is a term that mainly refers to one's ability to project one's personality into the object. In contrast, sympathy is more related to affinity with things, conformity of feelings:

> Sympathy, a concept related to empathy but more closely associated with condolence, pity, and agreement, emphasizes heightened attention to one's own feelings and assumes a kind of internal reverberation. In sympathy, we assume a similarity between the feelings of both the person who is sympathetic and the person who stimulates the feelings. Both projections (an unconscious attribution of one's desires or wishes) and identification (an unconscious modeling of oneself in thought, feeling, or action after another person) are examples of sympathy where a person is preoccupied with his or her own feelings in response to another person.
>
> (Chin et al., 1993, pp. 42–43)

Sympathy is thus much related to the ability to reverberate to the "resonance" described by Needham (1956). Resonance is indeed a keyword when speaking of Chinese thought (Nisbett, 2003); it is the idea that every event is related to all other events, and that everything one does has an effect on other events, a principle in line with a holistic conception of life.

> Empathy focuses attention of the feelings and context of the other person, rather than only on our own internal state. When we are sympathetic we understand the other person because of an awareness of our internal state; when we are empathic we go beyond our own emotional awareness and use information we have acquired in our conversation with them. If we only intuit what the other person feels without inquiring from the other person whether our intention is accurate, then we have sympathized with the other person. If we notice that our intuition

of the other person may not be exactly what he or she is experiencing, yet experience the other's feelings, we are empathic.

(Chin et al., 1993, p. 42)

Descriptions of behaviors similar to the Western concept of sympathy are also embedded in Confucianism and Daoism: "Since the demonstration of Asian concept of empathy is to respond to the other person without asking them to verbalize explicitly their emotional state of being, a caring response to other people requires an intuitive awareness of their emotional state" (Chin et al., 1993, p. 46). Thus, the concept of sympathy, more than empathy, seems in line with the premises of the Hong Kong Chinese culture, for its emphasis on the receiver in communication rather than the speaker, and for its little emphasis on the use of speech and verbalization of thoughts and feelings. Intuition and ability to resonate with the other are particularly required of a person rather than objective listening or neutrality/indifference.

Being sympathetic with the other may be more functional for overcoming the impasse to put everything in words. Such a disposition may have developed as a response to the difficulty of naming feelings. Sympathy may be required of the counselor to help the client to speak out what s/he cannot express, or what s/he cannot even think.

It may be that in some Western cultures, clients may feel inclined to pursue a desire for knowledge (about themselves, about life, about their desires) more than simply solve problems of adaptation to the context. In Hong Kong Chinese culture, different values are promoted, and different concerns arise. Attention is not given to speech that transcends temporal, mundane issues (in search of the truth, for example); on the contrary, much attention is given to social interactions, and to relationships. A strong need to be understood and accepted is not necessarily a sign of immaturity, weak personality, or pathology; indeed, it has very practical reflections on everyday life, it is a social skill required by the context. It may therefore be that, in counseling, Hong Kong Chinese expect to be accepted and understood, rather than to gain some understanding of the origins of their distress, their symptoms, or knowledge about themselves and their desires, as may be the case for most Europeans or North Americans. Sympathy is this sense of being in resonance with the other. Empathy and sympathy also reflect another important issue characteristic of Chinese culture, which is reciprocity. Indeed, relations can be asymmetrical, but one is generally expected to receive and give something to the other. "Active empathy assumes an understanding and a demonstration of reciprocity" (Chin et al., 1993, p. 56).

What factors affect the reception of psychoanalysis?

Results from the PUNU

It is the first time that this questionnaire was used, so these findings cannot be compared with findings from another sample. Results from the Psychoanalysis

Table 4.11 Means, standard deviations and confidence intervals of the PUNU and CHKCC (N=217)

	Rank	Mean	SD	95% confidence interval of the difference Lower	Upper
Perceived Complexity of Psychoanalysis	1	4.09	0.71	3.99	4.19
Psychoanalytic Training	2	4.03	0.83	3.91	4.15
Eclecticism	3	4.00	0.70	3.91	4.09
Conflicts with Hong Kong Chinese Culture	4	3.49	0.76	3.38	3.59
Perceived Ineffectiveness of Psychoanalysis	5	3.20	0.79	3.09	3.31

Scores: Based on a 6-point Likert scale with anchors 1 = strongly disagree and 6 = strongly agree.

Use/Non-Use (PUNU) scale are shown in Table 4.11. This table should be interpreted in light of: (1) the scales' order; scales are listed by mean value, so as to assess the relative importance of the variables, and (2) the mean value and the confidence interval of each scale in respect to the theoretical mid-point (which in a 6-point Likert scale lies at 3.50).

Concerning the PUNU, Perceived Complexity of Psychoanalysis, Eclecticism, and Psychoanalytic Training have their confidence interval above the theoretical mid-point, whereas Perceived Ineffectiveness of Psychoanalysis lies completely below. Thus, results showed that among this sample, psychoanalysis is not perceived as less effective than other approaches: the majority of respondents reported that they do not hold the perception of psychoanalysis as an obsolete and inadequate method. Apparently, if they have received no or only minimal training in psychoanalysis, it is not because they are unwilling, or because they have biases against psychoanalysis; rather it is more likely due to a lack of local training opportunities in Hong Kong. Indeed, if such training were made available in Hong Kong, counselors might be interested. However, psychologists, social workers, and counselors reported that they consider psychoanalysis as a complex approach that takes a long time and requires significant involvement. Another issue against the reception of psychoanalysis is the professionals' attitude toward eclecticism; subgroup analyses have confirmed that eclecticism is common among all professionals, regardless of any other variables, showing that this is a culture-specific trait and not merely the result of a lack of training among counselors. Finally, here, professionals who had been in therapy (regardless of the therapeutic approach) reported statistically significant lower perceived ineffectiveness of psychoanalysis than respondents who had not been in therapy. Participants of 30 years old or younger reported a statistically significant higher interest in receiving psychoanalytic training, showing that interest in psychoanalytic training is stronger among new generations of counseling professionals.

Results from the CHKCC

The Conflicts with Hong Kong Chinese Culture (CHKCC) is the only scale that lies around the theoretical mid-point (from a low of 3.38 to a high of 3.59). Results showed, however, important subgroup differences: for social workers, the confidence interval lies completely above the theoretical mid-point of the CHKCC (in the Agree range), meaning that the great majority of social workers think that psychoanalysis is in conflict with Hong Kong Chinese values, whereas for psychologists and counselors it lies completely below (in the Disagree range), showing that they have the opposite opinion.

Intra- and inter-correlations among PUNU and CHKCC

A correlational study (Table 3.5) revealed that, among this sample, psychoanalytic training is correlated with perceived effectiveness of psychoanalysis, but not with other PUNU variables. This suggests that providing psychoanalytic training is likely to improve a counselor's understanding of psychoanalysis and their attitude toward it, but they will nevertheless continue to perceive psychoanalysis as a complex practice. Psychoanalytic training is not correlated with the counselors' attitude toward eclecticism; this might be interpreted as a confirmation that such an eclectic attitude is deeply rooted in the Hong Kong Chinese culture and may not change just as an effect of training. Finally, no association between psychoanalytic training and CHKCC was found, indicating that while the perception and understanding of a theory is mediated by some cultural values and assumptions, willingness to receive psychoanalytic training is not. Additionally, results showed that the more psychoanalysis is perceived as in conflict with Chinese cultural values, the more: (1) it is perceived as ineffective; and (2) counseling professionals will prefer a more eclectic approach. Conversely, a simpler and clearly defined approach may be perceived as more effective overall, requiring less time and involvement and thus potentially having less conflict with Hong Kong Chinese values. This confirmed that solution-oriented, brief, directive, and technical (eclectic) approaches may be preferred as a means to offset or avoid conflicts with certain cultural values.

What factors affect the use of psychoanalytic theory?

Use of psychoanalytic theory is predicted by previous history of therapy and academic major (a degree in social work being a suppressor and a degree in psychology or counseling a contributor) (Table 3.8). Interestingly, in this model, Conflicts with Hong Kong Chinese culture (CHKCC) resulted as statistically non-significant in relation to the use of psychoanalysis, suggesting that clients' resistance against psychoanalysis does not directly affect whether a clinician chooses to adopt psychoanalysis. Also the variable Psychoanalytic Training resulted as non-significant, but with a p value just above the cut-off point ($p = 0.07$), which makes interpretation inconclusive; the influence of psychoanalytic training over the use of psychoanalysis should be further examined. Finally, Perceived Ineffectiveness of Psychoanalysis resulted as non-significant as well. *These results suggest that diffusion of psychoanalytic theory may depend more on contingent conditions like the academic and professional training of the counseling professional as well as the working environment (or working culture) rather than inherent qualities of the theoretical approach itself.* For example, Zhang (2014) maintains that in mainland China, three therapeutic approaches are gaining great popularity: behaviorism, the Satir model, and sandplay therapy. In particular, he observed that the Satir model is increasing in popularity in China, although its influence has largely waned over the past three decades in the US, suggesting that reception of a model is not necessarily and not entirely correlated to its effectiveness or complexity, but rather to the personal encounter of the counseling professionals with that approach, and thus also to the activism of psychotherapists in proposing their school/approach (e.g. offering seminars and opportunities for personal psychotherapy and supervision).

What factors affect psychoanalytic and counseling dimensions in Hong Kong?

Referring to the results from multiple regression analyses (Table 3.8), we can say that:

1. Perceived Ineffectiveness of Psychoanalysis is associated with three variables: Use of the Psychoanalytic Theory, Restoration, and Directivity of the Cure; however, in this model, the results non-significant in all cases. This suggests that Perceived Ineffectiveness of Psychoanalysis is not a variable that might limit the development of psychoanalysis, at least not as much as other variables. Second, this also suggests that Perceived Ineffectiveness of Psychoanalysis might be moderated or mediated by some other variables in the model; for example, given the high correlation with the scale CHKCC, one hypothesis is that culture may at least partially explain whether psychoanalysis is perceived as effective or not; this hypothesis should be tested by future research. However, this is an important finding; today there is much debate about the effectiveness of psychoanalysis and this study offers a new perspective that might broaden the debate, showing that simply speaking of effectiveness might be a false or illusory problem. Finally, results show that among this sample the (in)effectiveness of psychoanalysis is not the main concern.
2. Perceived Complexity of Psychoanalysis is associated with two dimensions of counseling, namely Restoration and Directivity of the Cure, and is a predictor of the latter (CACWS). Interestingly, this variable is not a suppressor of any psychoanalytic dimension nor is it a suppressor of

Use of Psychoanalytic Theory, meaning that whether the counseling professionals perceive psychoanalysis as complex or not, this does not discourage them from learning and using it. Nevertheless, if they perceive psychoanalysis as a complex approach, they may orientate toward some counseling approach that they feel more in control of.

3. Eclecticism is a predictor for Transference, Focused Attention and Directivity of the Cure, whereas its contribution to Restoration is non-significant, in this model. Interestingly, Eclecticism is not a (either positive or negative) predictor of any psychoanalytic variable; this means that Eclecticism does orientate the clinicians' attitude toward counseling, but it is not a suppressor against the use of the psychoanalytic theory or psychoanalytical listening, among this sample.

4. Psychoanalytic Training is, unsurprisingly, a crucial factor in the understanding of the unconscious and transference. It is also important for the use of psychoanalytic theory, although in this model its evidence did not emerge clearly and further research is needed. Most important, in Hong Kong we should talk of the lack of psychoanalytic training, which today is one of the factors that really limits the development of psychoanalytic culture.

5. Social workers were shown to be more receptive to the unconscious than counselors and psychologists; this may reflect the fact that psychologists and counselors' conceptions of the unconscious is more similar to a cognitive unconscious than to unconscious as described in psychoanalysis (Kihlstrom, 1987, 2008). Or, as suggested by Xu et al. (2014), it may be that some Chinese psychiatrists and counseling professionals consider cultural issues as a kind of defense mechanism or distortion that should be overcome through analysis, whereas others see culture as primarily in unconscious life and inseparable from it. A different understanding of the unconscious might also explain why, at the same time, the variable Unconscious is strongly associated with Restoration for social workers, but not for psychologists/counselors. Finally, social workers are less likely than psychologists/counselors to adopt psychoanalytic theory in their practice. These findings might seem contradictory at first; however, it might be that even though social workers are receptive to the unconscious, they nevertheless prefer to adopt more directive and solution-oriented approaches because their role and work environment require them to do so.

6. History of therapy. Professionals who had been counseled had a listening disposition that was more psychoanalytically oriented: they reported a statistically higher ability to perceive and read transference, and a higher attitude to free floating attention, and at the same time remained less directive and concerned about defining what the therapeutic goals should be; this can be regarded as important data which underlines the centrality of receiving therapy (particularly for a counselor-to-be) as a way for experiencing and improving at least some dimensions of psychoanalytic

listening. Unsurprisingly, in this model, history of therapy is an important contributor to Use of the Psychoanalytic Theory, Transference and Free Floating Attention (and understandably not for its counterpart Focused Attention), and it is a suppressor of Directivity of the Cure. Thus, we can conclude that the lack of opportunities for receiving a personal psychoanalysis is one of the greatest limitations to the understanding and use of psychoanalytic theory, as well as the development of a psychoanalytic listening, in Hong Kong.

7. Combining Approaches is associated with Unconscious, Free Floating Attention and Restoration. As mentioned before, the combinatorial partially explains the functioning of free floating attention. Various geniuses seem to confirm this finding when reflecting on how they achieved their discoveries. Einstein named this combinatorial art as combinatory play: "taken from a psychological viewpoint, this *combinatory play* seems to be the essential feature in productive thought – before there is any connection with logical construction" (in Mednick, 1962, p. 220, italics added). In 1920, speaking of the collage process, Andre Breton wrote that it is "marvelous capacity to grasp two mutually distant realities without going beyond the field of our experience and to draw a spark from the juxtaposition." (in Mednick, 1962, p. 220). The famous mathematician Henri Poincaré (1913) reported a meaningful episode: "every day I seated myself at my work table, stayed an hour or two, tried a great number of combinations and reached no results. One evening, contrary to my custom, I drank black coffee and could not sleep. Ideas rose in crowds; I felt them collide until pairs interlocked, so to speak, making a stable *combination*. By the next morning [...] I had only to write out the results, which took but a few hours." Interestingly, Poincaré here seems to equate the process of discovery or invention to a rather effortless process of *listening*, in which all he has to do is to loose and shift the focus, lose some belief and simply receive the results. In fact, he adds that "facts worthy of being studied [...] are those which reveal to us unsuspected kinship between other facts, long known, but wrongly believed to be strangers to one another. Among chosen combinations the most fertile will often be those formed of elements drawn from domains which are far apart" (p. 387).

It is possible that a tendency to consider various elements in combination is embedded in the Hong Kong Chinese culture. Contrary to Western culture, which is grounded on non-contradictory logic and linear reasoning, Chinese culture is not averse to paradoxes and contradictions; in fact, participants to this study reported to normally combine more than one approach. This combinatorial attitude seems to be closer to the logic of *vel* (this AND that) than *aut-aut* (this OR that), and thus it might be closer to the logic of the unconscious and the psychoanalytic listening.

The variable Combining Approaches is also a predictor for Restoration, which might seem in contrast with free floating attention; however, this might suggest that combining various approaches is intended not simply as a way of finding new links and creative solutions in a specific moment, but also as a method for achieving more conclusive solutions. This *combinatorial* is what potentially opens up new understandings (by producing new associations), and is likely also what is at the base of *eclecticism*. However, the latter is most likely an attempt to systematize the association (which works in a specific moment) making it a norm, or a rule. In fact, results from this study (Table 3.8) show that Combining Approaches is a predictor of Free Floating Attention, meaning that listening and understanding the other possible meanings requires *association*, and thus listening proceeds by *two*, whereas instead (and unsurprisingly), Eclecticism is not a contributor to Free Floating Attention. Thus, whereas the combinatorial represents the intuition, invention, creativity, and thus is effective because it creates a *new* link between distant things (thus, it belongs to a symbolic registry, as it is a new saying, a new *formulation*), eclecticism is already a shift to the imaginary registry in that a rule or a technique is imagined governing the relation (regression analysis shows that Eclecticism is a predictor of Focused Attention) or the therapy (imagining that one could impose a direction to the cure; Eclecticism is also a predictor of Directivity of the Cure, see Table 3.8). However, a combination or association cannot be reified or imagined as a rule, or, literally, it is no longer an invention. Eclecticism is grounded on the belief that the combination or association could be valid in general, as if we could substitute the free associations of signifiers with the combination of therapeutic techniques or strategies, in an attempt to hypostatize or reify that free association *before* things are said. Potentially, Hong Kong Chinese culture is close to a hovering-attention listening style, given this strong tendency toward the combinatorial; however, the combinatorial develops too quickly into eclecticism, which hinders psychoanalytic listening. It is on this thin line that the question of listening in the Hong Kong Chinese culture is played out: between the combinatorial (which operates in the symbolic registry and is open to creativity and thus to free floating attention) and eclecticism (which operates in the imaginary registry and is the representation of psychotherapeutic intervention, thus focused attention and direction imposed on the counseling process).

8. Religion. No significant differences in any subscale were reported when the sample was divided by religion. Specifically, this sample was dichotomized into Christians and non-religious, as only these groups were in statistically relevant numbers. The percentage of Christians among participants (about 50 percent) is five times the average percentage among Hong Kong society. Interestingly, a research study among counseling

professionals in Singapore, where the predominant religious affiliations are Buddhism and Daoism, showed that a majority of practitioners indicated affiliation with Christianity (Foo, 2007), which apparently confirms the association between Christian values and the helping profession. In this study, one hypothesis was that professionals who are Christians would score significantly differently from non-religious counselors in the PACWS, given the different disposition toward speech in Christianity and in Chinese culture; however, Christians and atheists differed on no PACWS subscale. This result may suggest that: (a) Chinese culture is dominant over Christian values; (b) culture in general is more than a set of values, and represents a more complex and partially unconscious way of thinking (or cultivating); and (c) adhesion to a religion (Christianity) and its values may occur on a more superficial level than culture, and it does not necessarily produce any significant change in one's culture. Finally, it may also be that Chinese culture is a mediator or a moderator for the understanding of religion, which would explain various forms of syncretism mentioned before, in Chapter 1 (page 34). This hypothesis should be tested in future studies.

The impact of culture on the understanding of psychoanalysis

It is difficult to assess whether a culture can really hinder the development of a theory or not. Results show a complex picture that should be analyzed carefully. According to the literature, the impact of Chinese culture and Chinese values contraindicating psychoanalysis was expected to be perceived as strong by local professionals but, surprisingly, results from the CHKCC (Table 4.11 and subsequent subgroup analysis) showed that this was true only for social workers; psychologists and counselors showed an opposite opinion.

Chinese culture vs Hong Kong values

The CHKCC scale is composed of nine items; some refer to features of Chinese culture, others more specifically refer to the Hong Kong culture and lifestyle. If we separate these nine items on two dimensions we may gain a more detailed picture of the impact of culture on counseling as it is in Hong Kong. On the first scale we group the items referring to Chinese culture at large; on the second scale we group the items referring to Hong Kong and local clients (see Table 4.12).

As expected, correlation between the Conflicts with Chinese Culture (CC) and Conflicts with Hong Kong Culture (HKC) scales is high ($r = 0.74$, $p < 0.001$), showing great affinity between the two cultures. If we look at the mean values (Table 4.12), the CC scores about the theoretical mid-point, whereas the HKC scores completely below; this mean that while respondents have different opinions about the influence

Table 4.12 Descriptive statistical properties of the Chinese Culture and Hong Kong Culture scales (N=217)

Scale items	Cronbach's alpha (α)	M	SD	Skewness	Kurtosis	95% confidence interval of the mean Lower	95% confidence interval of the mean Higher
Conflicts with Chinese Culture (CC)							
Overall scale statistics	0.81	3.58	0.83	0.17	0.15	3.46	3.69
1. Chinese culture does not welcome recognizing aggressive feelings		3.96	1.09	−0.33	−0.10		
2. Chinese culture does not welcome recognizing inner desires and sexuality		3.86	1.15	−0.05	−0.46		
3. Chinese culture does not welcome talking about emotions		3.45	1.19	0.03	−0.58		
4. Psychoanalysis is too individualistic to work in Chinese society		3.36	1.01	0.14	0.08		
5. Psychoanalysis conflicts with Chinese values		3.28	1.08	0.21	−0.01		
Conflicts with Hong Kong Chinese Culture (HKC)							
Overall scale statistics	0.73	3.36	0.79	0.17	0.45	3.25	3.47
1. My clients may not be interested in speculative argumentations		3.42	0.90	0.05	0.68		
2. My clients do not want to investigate their inner desires		3.41	1.03	0.10	−0.18		
3. Hong Kong people don't want to engage in in-depth counseling		3.37	1.22	0.13	−0.37		
4. Hong Kong people are little interested in pursuing knowledge about themselves		3.18	1.08	0.18	−0.37		

Scores based on a 6-point Likert scale with anchors 1 = strongly disagree and 6 = strongly agree.

of Chinese culture against the practice of psychoanalysis, they are generally more optimistic when asked about Hong Kong values; according to the participants, Hong Kong clients should not be unwilling to undergo psychoanalysis. However, this is just what respondents explicitly think; when we look at the correlations among variables, we get a different picture. For instance, the HKC showed a stronger association with the variable Unconscious ($r = 0.32$, $p < 0.001$) than there is between CC and Unconscious ($r = 0.26$, $p < 0.001$). This slightly stronger association between HKC and interpretation of the unconscious suggests that Hong Kong values and lifestyle are perceived as being more repressive than traditional Chinese values, thus leading counseling professionals to pay more attention to the unconscious.

Interestingly, the HKC also shows a statistically significant negative correlation with Focused Attention ($r = -0.20$, $p < 0.004$), meaning that the counselor's active listening and the client's resistance to therapy (as understood by counseling professional) affect each other; in contrast, the CC is not significantly correlated with Focused Attention, suggesting that traditional Chinese values are perceived as not being directly affected by the therapist's active participation in counseling.

As shown in the multiple regression analysis (Table 3.8), the use of psychoanalysis is predicted by the variables Perceived Ineffectiveness of Psychoanalysis (suppressor) and Major (could be either a contributor or a suppressor). Most important, what has clearly emerged from this model is that the variable CHKCC is non-significant (it can be accounted for neither as a contributor nor a suppressor to the Use/Non-Use of Psychoanalytic Theory), meaning that the norms and restrictions against expression and disclosure determined by local culture and lifestyle do not affect the use/non-use of psychoanalysis among counselors in this sample.

Finally, here, it has to be noted that the CHKCC is accounted for as a predictor for Unconscious (PACWS), Restoration and Focused Attention (CACWS) (Table 3.8). This means that, altogether, the local culture has no great impact *against* the understanding of psychoanalysis (as reflected by the effects on the three dimensions of the PACWS); however, it does influences how counseling is understood and practiced (as reflected by the CACWS). Furthermore, culture can also mediate and then explain the effects between other variables, meaning that it can affect both directly and indirectly the reception of psychoanalysis and counseling.

In fact, culture and values do not simply filter the content of a message, *what* we listen to. At a deeper level, they influence *how* we listen and understand. So, within the broad concept of culture, one could also take into account the variable Eclecticism, which indeed is also highly correlated to CHKCC in this sample. Specifically, the variable Eclecticism was shown to be a predictor for Transference, Focused Attention and Directivity of the Cure; somehow, this could be interpreted as an indirect effect of culture on the understanding of counseling and psychoanalysis.

Direct and indirect effects of culture

The CHKCC can (directly) assess only what respondents think *about* culture (their opinion), and not the effect of culture on their counseling style. Thus, because the CHKCC was correlated with the PUNU subscales Solution-Oriented Approach, Perceived Ineffectiveness of Psychoanalysis, Perceived Complexity of Psychoanalysis, and Eclecticism, this suggests that culture (indirectly) influences the counselors' theoretical orientation and how they understand psychoanalysis. Simply considering the variable CHKCC, the impact of culture is at least fourfold: (a) it may contribute to the counselors' psychoanalytic attitudes (as measured by PACWS), fostering one or more components (unconscious, transference and/or free floating attention); (b) it may enhance or suppress one or more counseling dimensions (as measured by CACWS), which in turn might determine a greater/lesser distance from psychoanalysis; (c) it may promote values and beliefs about psychoanalysis among counseling professionals (as measured by the CHKCC); these beliefs may explicitly affect the reception of psychoanalysis; (d) it may indirectly influence how counselors perceive psychoanalysis (as shown by the inter-correlations between PUNU and CHKCC); for example, culture may mediate or moderate the clinicians' perception of psychoanalysis as an ineffective and/or complex method).

Results from this study show that psychoanalysis could be received in this context. The impact of (a) and (c) against psychoanalysis is limited, or even positive; however, culture seems to enhance a counseling attitude more than psychoanalytic listening. Multiple regression analysis showed that CHKCC is not a suppressor against the use of psychoanalytic theory, meaning that concern for cultural issues does not significantly influence the application of psychoanalysis among these participants.

These results show that culture is a broad concept; the CHKCC reflects a set of values and beliefs largely shared in Hong Kong. Similarly, professional training might reflect a kind of culture as well, precisely a *working culture* embedded among a group of professionals who work in a similar context. Results from this study show that social workers have a rather different attitude toward clinical work than psychologists and counselors, and that this reflects on the use/non-use of psychoanalysis (maybe unsurprisingly, in Hong Kong social workers largely outnumber psychologists and counselors; this may already reflect a particular inclination of the local culture). Thus, we should expand our concept of culture and, for example, we could develop a specific scale for assessing the effects of the clinicians' professional training (working culture) on the understanding and reception of psychoanalysis.

Indigenization

Some scholars maintain that Chinese therapists need to undergo a "bentuhua" process by intentionally embracing therapeutic models that are more congruent with Chinese cultural sensibilities and by recasting them through the Chinese cultural repertoire (see, for example, Zhang, 2014). Bentuhua is a process of fitting that can be roughly translated into English as "localization," "indigenization," or "culturing." However, this study revealed that this "acculturation" process occurs in any case, regardless of the intention of the therapist. As culture is ultimately a product of the unconscious, then the so-called acculturation or indigenization process occurs unconsciously, it is what mediates the process of understanding of (any) theory; further processes of adaptation are already redundant, being a sort of meta-language or the reification of a "lapsus," the original (mis) understanding implied in any translation.

Psychoanalysis: groundbreaking for the West but not for the Chinese?

Psychoanalysis could probably not be invented in a Chinese context. Chinese thought has shown some indifference toward aspects emphasized by psychoanalysis, such as: relevance of speech, questioning, abstraction, invention, curiosity, otherness, originality, analytic mind, creativity. However, this study shows that Hong Kong Chinese counselors have some interest in psychoanalysis, and they would pursue further training, if it were possible.

This study has also pointed out that European and American cultures are more likely speaking oriented, while Hong Kong Chinese culture is more listening oriented. This has important consequences for the practice of psychoanalysis (and counseling). Indeed, this study has also attempted to redefine psychoanalysis in terms of listening. This is quite the opposite of the common idea of psychoanalysis as a "talking cure," as it was named by Anna O., one of the first patients in psychoanalysis (Launer, 2005).

Indeed, it is argued that psychoanalysis has had a deep impact on Western societies precisely because they had (have) some lack in listening. In contrast, it is proposed that it would not have been so effective in Chinese culture, where indeed a (different) listening disposition was already cultivated.

However, particularly when referring to the Western discourse, psychoanalysis can be described as a different listening disposition, a listening that goes beyond the manifest meaning of what is verbalized. *The very concept of resistance, for instance, is not a resistance to speaking but a resistance to listening.* The same symptom is theorized by psychoanalysis as something that urges for a different understanding, a different reading, and a different listening. Only at the very beginning of his career did Freud describe catharsis as the therapeutic method for letting patients experience and express feelings that were repressed, and this was when Freud still used hypnosis for treating his patients; when he adopted the method of free association, he also operated a shift from talking (to the patient) to listening (to the unconscious).

Obviously, psychoanalysis is also a talking cure, but it shows that *the condition for talking is first of all that there is a listening.*

Some emphasis on listening was already present in Chinese culture. Clearly, Chinese thought has never met the psychoanalytic unconscious, so listening has another nuance; it is *listening to the other* (literally, the other persons), and *not to the Other* (finally, the unconscious). It is a very different listening. However, psychoanalysis probably did not introduce anything groundbreaking for Chinese thought, or at least not as fascinating to the Chinese societies, which were pursuing different ideals (i.e. how to live in harmony rather than how to gain knowledge), and so was discarded. Psychoanalysis is therefore probably more effective within the discourse where it originated.

Participants scored relatively high on Perceived Complexity of Psychoanalysis (see Table 4.11), meaning that it is a theory difficult to understand. However, it is suggested that a major limitation for the understanding and use of psychoanalysis in Hong Kong is a scarce propensity to rearticulate the questions and gain further knowledge, as highlighted by the relatively low scores on use of the unconscious (see Table 4.10). Whereas, on the one hand, respondents were shown to be attentive to others, to be receptive, and to be able to read others' feelings, on the other hand, they showed little propensity to investigate the clients' unconscious fantasies and beliefs or their dreams. The unconscious is not just one component of the psychoanalytic practice, it is the cornerstone of psychoanalysis, and listening to the unconscious represents at the same time the means by which psychoanalysis is continuously reinvented; it is the way a new saying is achieved, as well as the way a new theory is produced. Psychoanalytic practice is not just the application of a psychoanalytic theory obtained in laboratory. On the contrary, it is probably not possible to distinguish the moment of the practice from the moment of the theory: the two moments get along together, one cannot exist without the other. The very psychoanalytic interpretation, as well as the clinical case, exists as a continuous invention, or reformulation, by the clinician. Listening to the unconscious is what keeps the question open, meaning that no answer will ever be definitive; and not everything can be explained. But what has emerged from this study is a Hong Kong Chinese culture as flattened on a horizontal, relational level, with a perception of something unconscious, but without the term to name it, and thus with little openness and little emphasis on speech or any narrative dimension.

However, this study has registered at least an openness to psychoanalytic theory and a significant interest to engage with it. As long as there is some *transference*, some psychoanalysis is possible. So, there are no reasons to think that some psychoanalytical effects should not be possible in Hong Kong as well. Thus, it is hoped that such an attitude of opening toward psychoanalysis continues, so that psychoanalysis can still be invented (and not just taught, or exported) again and again.

Different reception of psychoanalysis between Hong Kong, mainland China, and Taiwan

Psychoanalytic training

Psychoanalysis is grounded on a tripartite system: (1) theoretical seminars; (2) personal (training or didactic) analysis; and (3) clinical supervision. While other counseling approaches rely primarily on academic teaching, transmission of psychoanalysis may be greatly impaired if any of the three aforementioned pillars is missing. First, the function of the seminars is to provide candidates with the psychoanalytic knowledge toolkit; however, as this study shows, the lack of opportunities for psychoanalytic training in Hong Kong is a serious limit to the understanding of psychoanalysis. Second, the notion that an aspiring analyst should first be required to be analyzed was advanced in 1918, at the Fifth International Psychoanalytic Association Congress. Two years later, "didactic" analysis became the training standard, mandated at the first psychoanalytic institute in Berlin (Wallerstein, 2010). The functions of this training – or didactic – analysis are: (a) to analyze the internal conflicts, blind spots, and potential neurotic problems of the candidate; (b) to experience the therapeutic force of the method, particularly transference, which is the "engine" of the therapy; and, (c) to experience how a therapeutic setting is established and maintained, how feelings are tended to, and how latent materials are interpreted. As emerged from this study, respondents who had been in therapy reported a more favorable disposition toward psychoanalysis, indicating that psychoanalytic teaching can enhance the perceived effectiveness of psychoanalysis, but a personal therapy is most likely to lower the perception of psychoanalysis as a complex method. This is important, as it underlines the centrality of receiving therapy (particularly for a counselor-to-be) as a way to understand the therapeutic process. A personal analysis is fundamental in psychoanalysis for becoming a psychoanalyst, while it is not always mandatory in other psychotherapeutic or counseling orientations. Third, psychoanalytic supervision is deemed essential as: (a) it provides an understanding of psychoanalysis in action; and (b) is an opportunity for an in-depth analysis of the candidate's own analytical work (Zachrisson, 2011). The lack of psychoanalytic supervision is then another serious obstacle to the reception and understanding of psychoanalysis in Hong Kong.

Psychoanalytic training in Hong Kong, mainland China, and Taiwan

Psychoanalysis has raised some interest in Taiwan and mainland China, where it nowadays is increasingly drawing the attention of both clinicians and intellectuals, but it remains largely unknown in Hong Kong. Although originally coming from the same culture, in the last century, Hong Kong, mainland China, and Taiwan have undergone very different historical trajectories. The recent history of Hong Kong is both more stable and less traumatizing than that of mainland China and Taiwan (Jaffe, 2011).

Since the end of the Cultural Revolution, mainland China has undergone probably the most remarkable period of reform and open policies in its history (Zhong, 2011; Y. Liu, 2013); the rigidly planned economy collapsed and also the one-child policy was implemented. Society had not yet recovered from the wounds and traumas of the Cultural Revolution (Plänkers, 2011) when it was once again overturned by deep and large-scale economic and social changes. Taiwan, too, which was a Japanese colony before being occupied by the Kuomintang, has not yet recovered from a recent history of invasion, occupation, war, suppression, separation, and loss (Roy, 2003). It is likely that traumatic historical events, rapid changes in society, and crisis open up to psychoanalysis more than stability and conservatism (Makari, 2008).

These different heritages have (directly and/or indirectly) influenced how psychoanalytic and counseling training has been received within these three contexts. In particular, four elements emerge: (1) Hong Kong has built a stronger connection with Western academics; therefore many counseling approaches have been imported, but not psychoanalysis; (2) in mainland China, psychoanalysis has had a stronger reception, after having been culturally isolated for many years; (3) psychoanalysis in mainland China and in Taiwan has been received by a population of mental health professionals very different from those in Hong Kong; and (4) Western psychoanalysts have been very active in promoting psychoanalysis in mainland China, but not in Hong Kong.

The rise of counseling and psychoanalytic training

Hong Kong was for many years a British colony, and has developed an inclination, an admiration, almost a fascination for the cultures of English-speaking countries (Tsang, 2004). Many professionals offering and teaching counseling today in Hong Kong were trained abroad, in such places as the United States, Canada, Europe, and Australia (Leung et al., 2007). These professionals have therefore "imported" to Hong Kong the theories and knowledge they have acquired during their training abroad. Since we are referring mainly to English-speaking countries, such theories would first of all be behavioral therapy, cognitive psychology, person-centered (Rogerian) therapy, narrative therapy, positive psychology, and brief therapy, as these are in the academic mainstream. It is unsurprising, then, that these orientations and those derived from them (and not psychoanalysis, which is not popular in academic departments) are now the most known and practiced in Hong Kong. In contrast, the reception of psychoanalysis in China (which began with the Sino-German course in the late 1990s, as mentioned in the first chapter) occurs within a more general rise of interest in psychology books, counseling theories, psychological idioms, psychometric methods, and training in psychotherapy: a "psycho-boom," as it has been called by

Kleinman (2011), which started from the early 2000s. Qian and colleagues observe that popular demands for psychological help have been increasing steadily among the urban middle classes since the 1990s due to profound socioeconomic transformations and uncertainty (Qian et al., 2002). Although some (J. Yang, 2013) observe that this sudden emphasis on counseling actually simply promotes a cultivation of "fake happiness" that is functional to a political project, as do several television counseling programs, Kleinman (2011) thinks that it represents a shift in mentality, because in the past, talking about the self would have been regarded as selfish and egocentric, whereas today many people learn to appreciate the psychological dimensions of experience. Huang (2015) observed that, at least for some time, the psycho-boom used to be dominated by psychoanalysis, and that many celebrity therapists and practitioners identified themselves with this orientation. Psychoanalysis became very popular, even though the understanding of it among counselors is questionable because training mainly exists in the form of short-term teaching, which is clearly inadequate for psychoanalysis. In fact, a major limit of the psycho-boom is that psychotherapy became a sort of popular movement. A multitude of training and social activities were suddenly promoted; however, the quality standards were normally quite low (Huang, 2015). In most cases, the entry requirements for the training courses (no longer exclusive to academics and hospitals, but delivered by private companies) were lowered so as to accommodate more trainees. For example, it is estimated that the state-sponsored counselor program that began in the early 2000s (administered by the Ministry of Labour and Social Securities) have certified about 600,000 counselors by the end of 2014 (Huang, 2015).

Different mental health professionals' reception of psychoanalysis

Psychoanalysis in Hong Kong has been received differently among various groups of mental health professionals. Social workers from this sample reported preferring a more directive and solution-oriented approach than did psychologists and counselors; they are less likely than psychologists and counselors to have had their own therapy, and are more receptive to the unconscious, but at the same time, they are less receptive to the use of psychoanalytic theory than are psychologists and counselors, and perceive psychoanalysis as more in conflict with local cultural values. However, it is not clear what can explain this opposing attitude toward psychoanalysis.

Altogether, participants in this study reported a relatively low level of personal history of therapy, whereas, for example, approximately 80 percent of therapists in European countries report having at least one experience in personal therapy (Orlinsky, Rønnestad, Willutzki, Wiseman, & Botermans, 2005). Social workers are frequently the category among counseling professionals that is less likely to receive a personal therapy. For example, in the US, Norman and Rosvall (1994) found that psychologists were the most likely to seek therapy, followed by marriage therapists and social workers. In South

Korea, practitioners with a degree in counseling reported a personal therapy in the 69.8 percent of cases, followed by psychologists (48.6 percent), psychiatrists (32.1 percent), and social workers (25.0 percent) (Bae et al., 2003). Thus, the fact that the great majority of the counseling population in Hong Kong is composed of social workers (the less likely to receive therapy) might indeed be an obstacle to the development of psychoanalysis, when compared to other countries.

When examining the training received, the population served, and the work settings of the two subgroups, some differences emerge. For instance, the majority of psychologists and counselors reported that they had received training at the Chinese University of Hong Kong and at the University of Hong Kong, whereas social workers were primarily trained at the City University of Hong Kong and at the Hong Kong Polytechnic University. Frequencies in the orientation of various approaches did not differ greatly among the two groups, except that psychoanalysis and person-centered approaches were more common among psychologists and counselors (17 percent and 60 percent respectively) than social workers (8 percent and 40 percent). The large majority of social workers from this sample (89 percent) reported working for NGOs, twice the percentage of psychologists and counselors (44 percent); in contrast, a higher number of psychologists (35 percent) than social workers (1 percent) worked for the Social Welfare Department. Finally, here, psychologists and counselors reported a higher incidence of private practice (19 percent) than did social workers (6 percent). Concerning the target population, 82 percent of psychologists and counselors reported working with adult clients whereas only 54 percent of social workers did so; by contrast, the latter group reported a higher percentage of clients among the elderly (31 percent vs 18 percent). Both groups reported an equal distribution of children (42 percent) and youths (52 percent). Almost all respondents work with individuals (94 percent for both groups), but psychologists work more with couples (58 percent) than do social workers do (38 percent). Both sets of professionals treat families and groups with similar frequencies. Lastly, when examining the incidence of variables such as number of clients, years of working experience, or religion no significant differences among the groups were found.

Research from Yip (2002) has shown that most social workers in psychiatric services in Hong Kong are concerned with patients' immediate problems and with providing them with concrete solutions. Basically, social workers "largely give advice and guidance to their patients rather than performing counseling" (Yip, p. 39). They lack specialized training and skills in in-depth counseling, and although they are supported by their agencies, they receive insufficient theoretical backup from their colleagues and their supervisors (Yip, 2002). Although some of them might mention some psychotherapeutic approach as being relevant to their practice, or they even claim to be a psychotherapist, Yip (2004) describes social workers as not having sufficient knowledge, understanding, and experience in carrying out psychotherapy, which puts their practice at risk of being labeled superficial. This study has revealed that, among social workers, cultural values that may affect the clients' attitude toward expressing, and their preferences for counseling are associated with the understanding of the unconscious (whereas such association does not occur among psychologists/counselors); however, at the same time being a social worker was a suppressor against the use of the psychoanalytic theory (whereas being a psychologist/counselor was a contributor). This suggests that the association between CHKCC and the unconscious can be understood in two ways: (1) the higher the conflicts between Hong Kong Chinese culture and psychoanalysis, the higher the understanding of the unconscious (CHKCC is the independent variable); and (2) the higher the interpretation of the unconscious, the higher the resistance toward psychoanalysis among local clients (unconscious is the independent variable). Both may be true. For instance, we may say that the unconscious was "discovered" in a cultural and historical context where moral repression was rather strong (but, more generally we become aware of an unconscious conflict whenever we perceive that something is being repressed), and at the same time, we may say that interpreting the unconscious may cause a higher resistance. However, why this association between CHKCC and the unconscious exists among social workers but not among psychologists/counselors is difficult to say. One reason may be that psychologists and counselors share a conception of the unconscious that is more similar to a medical unconscious than a psychoanalytic unconscious: this may partially explain the difference between the two groups of participants concerning the understanding of the unconscious. On the other hand, as regards the use/non-use of psychoanalytic theory, it may be that social workers more than psychologists/counselors prefer to rely on some counseling techniques that allow them to *respond* more effectively to their clients' needs; this is supported by the strong association between the variables Unconscious and Restoration among this sample, and particularly for what concerns social workers (Table 3.6). Social workers may be in a good position to *understand* the unconscious and the motives behind their clients' resistances and preferences, but then they may think that their role requires them to operate on a more practical level (for example, giving instructions and advice to their clients).

In this study, the ranking of the subscales does not vary among social workers, counselors, and psychologists. However, results from this study showed that social workers: (1) use psychoanalysis less than psychologists and counselors; (2) perceive psychoanalysis as in conflict with local culture; (3) are less likely than psychologists and counselors to be in therapy; and, (4) are more receptive of the unconscious. Social workers may be less interested than other clinicians to practice psychoanalysis because psychoanalysis is an elective method for working with individuals (although it has application also with children, couples, and at times even families), in a controlled setting; in contrast, social workers from this sample mainly operate in nonstandard settings (at least from a strict psychoanalytic perspective), and might be required to pursue rather practical goals in limited time. For these reasons it might also be hard for psychoanalysis to be well received where counseling is delivered mainly by social workers; nevertheless, this study also suggests that psychoanalysis will be better received as the standards of counseling education and training improve, and if more psychoanalytic ideas are introduced into training. Contrary to the situation in Hong Kong, psychiatrists, neurologists, general practitioners, and psychologists in mainland China generally practice counseling in clinical settings (Shi, Sang, Li, Zhou, & Wang, 2005). Thus, psychoanalysis in China has been received by a very different population of mental health professionals from that in Hong Kong (Varvin & Gerlach, 2014; Xu et al., 2014; Y. Liu, 2013). In the last twenty years, the German–Chinese Academy for Psychotherapy, the Sino-Norway Continuous Training Program for Psychodynamic Psychotherapy and the China American Psychoanalytic Association have mainly been training Chinese psychiatrists and psychologists (mainly from hospitals and universities) in cities like Shanghai, Beijing, Guangzhou, Kunming, Wuhan, and Chengdu. Furthermore, the training was offered mainly at institutions like the Anding Hospital (Beijing), the Shanghai Mental Health Center (Shanghai), and the Tongji Medical University (Wuhan). Yang (2011) observes that among the first 90 participants in the Sino-Norway Training program, 28 percent came from college and universities, 16 percent from general hospitals, 42 percent from psychiatric hospitals, and only a few from private counseling centers (9 percent) or other organizations (5 percent). Li (2014) has conducted a research study among about three hundred psychodynamic psychotherapists in mainland China and found that the mean age was around 38, and they were mostly females (74 percent); one third of them had a medical background, whereas social workers accounted for only 11 percent of the sample. Interestingly, the majority of the participants (65 percent) reported that a personal therapy is essential and should be required for all therapists; however, only 42 percent were currently in therapy, and 35 percent only had personal therapy in the past.

Zhang (2014) observes that there are three main groups of counseling professionals in China: (1) the academy-based (*xueyuan pai*): university psychology professors with mainly a theoretical background; (2) the hospital-based (*yiyuanpai*): psychiatrists who focus on drug treatment and engage only in brief talk therapy; and (3) the society-based (*shehui pai*): private counselors who come out of the short-term certification programs. Remarkably, the first two groups are relatively small in number and have strong institutional support, which make them "elitist" compared to others. The third group is the largest in terms of "licensed" counselors (i.e. over 100,000); however, for various reasons, only 15 percent actually open a private practice after getting their certification. This means that psychoanalysis in mainland China was received by clinicians with a relatively high academic and professional profile (likely, clinicians from the first two groups); this might have been strategic to the penetration of psychoanalysis in China. In Taiwan, too, psychoanalysis has been received mainly by psychiatrists and academics (C. Liu, 2013). Thus, it is likely that in these settings psychoanalysis has reached a different audience. It is not clear to what extent such differences in underlying mental health training and practice have influenced the reception of psychoanalysis in Hong Kong.

The desire of the analysts

Since the beginning of the 1980s, Western psychoanalysts have been very active (often as volunteers) in promoting psychoanalysis in China, organizing conferences, training programs, study groups, and visiting the country several times a year. At present, psychoanalytic training in mainland China is conducted by a few recognized and well-established organizations. Instead, training in Hong Kong is offered much more occasionally by professionals acting individually.

Teaching under the auspices of a credited association has a radically different impact. To students, it might guarantee more continuity in education and it might give the impression of more authority and professionalism. To professionals, it can guarantee more audience and can allow them to work directly with institutions. This kind of activism (which has never affected Hong Kong) is remarkable, and it has largely contributed to the reception of psychoanalysis in China. Nevertheless, it does not go without consequences. For example, it was observed that the Chinese psychoanalytic associations that have been set up have not developed any independent club life, and this has been interpreted as a consequence of a lack of independent thinking in China (Plänkers, 2011). This might be partially true, and this "resistance" could be simply interpreted as a minor obstacle on the pathway to the penetration of psychoanalysis in China, perhaps due to some aspects of the Chinese culture. Or instead, this "small detail" could allow for a different understanding of the premises that guide how psychoanalysis is being exported to or received in China. Namely, this detail is informative not only of the transfer of psychoanalysis to China, but is also important because it is informative of the transference of (Western and Chinese) psychoanalysts. Thus, rather than considerations of cultural differences, which could be biased by a Western perspective, it is suggested that two other issues should be considered to explain this apparent passivity expressed by the Chinese: (1) the reasons why psychoanalysis today is appealing to the Chinese are largely ignored, and may be different from the reasons that appealed to Western psychoanalysts in different contexts and ages; (2) the passive role of the Chinese might be a consequence of too much activism in their Western counterparts.

On the one hand, the myth of *the* Chinese learner as passive has been questioned (Mok et al., 2008; Watkins & Biggs, 2001); rather than a lack or a deficiency of Chinese culture, it may simply be that Chinese professionals have different reasons for becoming psychoanalysts (perhaps it is a better professional career, or that being a psychoanalyst is more prestigious) that are not necessary to the development and the diffusion of psychoanalysis. Or, because they might perceive psychoanalysis as a Western theory, they might not yet feel ready to make their contributions and instead might expect the Western "experts" to give them direction. These questions should be further investigated and are revealing of a surprising gap in the literature.

On the other hand, probably the most significant questions for Western psychoanalysts (also ignored by literature) are: why is China fascinating? What has led Western psychoanalytic organizations to mainland China but not to Hong Kong? Where is the desire of the analyst? Snyder (in Osnos, 2010) observes that there is much enthusiasm about psychoanalysis in China, and that the Chinese have a passion for psychoanalysis the way people were in love with it in New York during the 1950s and 60s. She also reports that many Americans conducting analyses in China are partly retired, and the work with the Chinese patients allows them to prolong their working lives (Snyder, 2009). According to Osnos (2010), it is fascinating for Western psychoanalysts to teach in China where they are considered experts, while their profession is under attack at home (Scull, 2011), so it is likely that they find much more respectful and less critical disciples in China. Nowadays, many psychoanalysts too have been fascinated by what they perceive as a new frontier for psychoanalysis in China: a challenge, but likely a place to colonize as well. Instead, it is possible that Hong Kong does not occupy the same place in the Western imagination, as it may be perceived as not culturally distant and mysterious enough. These motivations are legitimate and cannot be ignored. Specifically, do these premises support the idea that the Chinese should become active and independent? An American analyst and ex-trainer in China is critical toward what he calls "expansive programs" that likely cover "colonialist impulses," and warns us against the perils of a "psychoanalytic evangelism" (Saporta, 2011). Namely, if the goal is only to export psychoanalysis (Schlösser, 2009) and teaching to the Chinese, cultural differences might be an obstacle to such a mission, and in particular large organizations will tend to neglect it rather than acknowledge it (Saporta, 2011).

Historically, Europeans and North Americans have been fascinated by China for centuries. The first to come to Macao and China were Father Alessandro Valignano and Matteo Ricci, Jesuits, 400 years ago. They came with the intention of evangelizing the country, but they soon realized that they needed a much more culturally sensitive approach (Busiol, 2013). The writings they left us with are the first accounts of cultural differences between East and West, and are memorable considerations that sound very up to date for psychoanalysts coming to China today. More recently, an anthropologist like Arthur Kleinman has found that "otherness" to Western culture among clinicians in China and Taiwan has helped them to question and rethink Western psychiatry. His research on depression, somatization, expression of pain, and mental health has shown that what was generally accepted as universal is probably not.

It seems that psychoanalysis is simply going from the West to China (a one-way transfer of knowledge), regardless of cultural differences, and regardless of reflections on what this might imply for psychoanalysis itself. But can psychoanalysis develop from encounters with Chinese thought? Can this become a chance for rethinking psychoanalysis? I argue that this is the chance for psychoanalysis to develop. On the contrary, to simply wonder how to "export" psychoanalysis is not very farsighted, and perhaps after some initial enthusiasm, psychoanalysis will be criticized and eventually rejected in China.

Note

1 These results can be compared with the profile of psychotherapists in American, European, and other Asian countries as reported at the end of the first chapter.

5 Why the (Freudian) unconscious was not discovered in China
Other and desire in Hong Kong

> There are so many more people who believe in the miracles of the Blessed Virgin than in the existence of the unconscious.
> Freud, *New Introductory Lecturers on Psychoanalysis*

Apparently, Chinese thought has not theorized anything like the Freudian unconscious. How was this possible? And is it possible that today the unconscious remains largely marginal in Hong Kong? The Freudian invention was inextricably tied to Western discourse, and it was somehow anticipated by philosophers such as Nietzsche and Schopenhauer. Then, one might ask: could it ever have been possible to "discover" the unconscious out of Western discourse?

The (Freudian) unconscious

This concept was likely being used by others before Freud, but always in a phenomenological, descriptive manner. Freud came to imagine and describe what we now know as the unconscious in particular through the study of dreams, neuroses, and all those elements of the psychopathology of everyday life: oversights, blunders, lapses, omission. The discovery (or invention) of the unconscious represented the beginning of psychoanalysis. For Freud the *psyche* was not a unified entity coincident with the consciousness of the person; on the contrary, the "I" represented just a small part of it.

Freud proposed a twofold model of the unconscious. The first is called the topographic model of the mind, which consisted of: conscious (Cs), preconscious (Pcs), and unconscious (Ucs). In this model, unconscious was a *noun* referring to a specific unit. The three instances were qualitatively different and governed by very different principles, and because the unconscious was not just a second conscience, Freud made clear that the term "subconscious" should be rejected. The principle organizing the psychic materials between the different instances was repression, which answered to the simple principle of the avoidance of unpleasure. Thus, in this model, the unconscious was equated with the repressed. However, with the structural model from 1923, the psyche was divided into Id, ego, and superego, with a tripartite form which did not simply overlap the previous one; clinical experience had shown Freud that there was not simply the repressed unconscious on one hand, and the ego with the preconscious on the other. Though the Id was described as being in large part unconscious, the ego and the superego were partially conscious and partially unconscious. Unconscious thus became an *adjective*.

How did Freud intend to give voice to the unconscious? Through what he described as the main technique of psychoanalysis: free association. This is the Freudian invention: that the answer could come from the patient, even though the patient him/herself had no idea s/he possessed this knowledge. Freud's hypothesis was that what is repressed is not erased but still present on another level, and that it is possible to access it. For Freud the unconscious is not simply what we forgot, or repressed, or what we do not know: it is also what we *do not know we know*.

Individualism and collectivism

The cultural variation between most Western and Chinese societies is normally described in terms of individualism and collectivism (Liu & Rau, 2012; Yang et al., 2011). In particular, the "self" of Westerners is often described as "independent," as opposed to the self of the Chinese, which is more "collective" or "interdependent":

> Self in the Confucian sense is defined by a person's surrounding relations, which often are derived from kinship network and supported by cultural values such as filial piety, loyalty, dignity. Given that, the Chinese self traditionally involves multiple layers of relations with others, a person in this relational network tends to be sensitive to his or her position as being above, below or equal to others.
>
> (Gao, 1996, p. 83)

It is possible to say the notion of *self* has two rather opposite meanings: whereas in Europe and America, the self is better described by the peculiarities of the individual and the *differences* from the group, in Chinese cultures, the self is described in terms of *similarities* and *relations* to the group:

> The other-orientation thus is the key to an interdependent self. Congruous with the notion of an interdependent self, the Chinese self also needs to be recognized, defined, and completed by others. The self's orientation to others' needs, wishes, and expectations is essential to the development of the Chinese self.
>
> (Gao, 1996, p. 84)

And what is the *collective*: the society as a whole, the family, the group of friends, or the co-workers? In Hong Kong, it has been described in terms of "utilitarian familism," and is thus a well-defined group and not the entire society; in mainland China, instead, the collective is more likely represented by the "working units" (which were introduced so as to weaken the power of families, see, for example, Y. Yang, 2013).

Hall and Ames (1998) observed that various scholars have erroneously described the Chinese as *selfless*. In their opinion, this is mainly due to the misapplication of the Western understanding of "self" (in terms of rational consciousness, physiological reduction, volitional activity, and organic functioning) to the Chinese. However, the idea of the self is not completely foreign to Chinese thought; for example, one of the most known passages from Zhuangzi says:

> Once upon a time, I, Chuang Chou, dreamt I was a butterfly, fluttering hither and thither, to all intents and purposes a butterfly. I was conscious only of my happiness as a butterfly, unaware that I was Chou. Soon I awaked, and there I was, veritably myself again. Now I do not know whether I was then a man dreaming I was a butterfly, or whether I am now a butterfly, dreaming that I am a man.
> (Lin, 1948, p. 238)

So, not only is the sense of self not foreign to the Chinese, but actually it might even be enhanced by this societal structure. Pye (1992), for example, describes two kinds of self in Chinese culture: "The Chinese sense of identity comes from the notion of the greater self (*da wo*), and from the necessity of sacrificing the smaller self (*xiao wo*) to fulfill the greater self" (pp. 59–60). To be self*less* then requires that a self exists first. The small self can be sacrificed for the big self, but what remains central is the notion of self, understood differently from that in the West. In Chinese society, one can sacrifice for one's clan, one can devote oneself to one's group, and one day one will also benefit from this system of mutual obligation. Thus, the group might apparently overcome the individual, but ultimately the individual is protected by the group. Everyone contributes to making the group, and the group will sustain each one. For example, within groups the hierarchy is quite strong, which means each individual occupies a clear position. So, the collective or interdependent self might actually be just a different strategy for preserving the individual rather than being in opposition to it. Not very surprisingly, for example, the collective and interdependent Chinese families are now facing the recent phenomenon of the spoilt only child, who they call "little emperor" or "little princess": an exaltation of the self.

Individualism and collectivism as different strategies for avoiding the unconscious

According to Saporta (2014), the self and the world are not two separate entities in Chinese culture, as the self arises within the world; in Western tradition, however, the conception of self is seen as set apart from and actively entering into the world. We normally call an *individual* a person seen as detached from the group, thinking that the singular one is the smallest (thus indivisible) particle. However, after Freud we have learnt that there is nothing like one because "the ego is not master in his own home."

In Latin, the term *individuum* means "an atom, indivisible particle." However, Freud (and Lacan) showed that: (1) speech comes first, meaning it is original and antecedent to the subject; and (2) speech (and not language, understood as natural language) comes from the place of the Other (we could say that the mother tongue is the tongue of the mother). Thus, first of all, the Freudian invention, the unconscious, shows that nothing like an individual really exists, because nothing is indivisible; if speech comes first, the so-called subject or self is built only secondarily and in the field of the Other, which pre-exists the self. Second, if speech comes first, the distinction between individual and collective is also not original. It is illusory, meaning that the individual and the group are not necessarily in opposition, as it is normally understood.

The unconscious is neither inside (monism) nor outside (collective) nor in between (interpersonal); it is not just made up of memories, meaning it is not just past, but it anticipates the future; the unconscious is not already there, pre-existing (to me, the idea of the collective unconscious is the reification of speech, meaning that the unconscious is not intended as the effect of a singular act of speech, but instead as the product of a universal and common language of shared meanings, archetypes). More likely, I understand the Freudian unconscious as an *effect* of speech, and as such, it goes beyond the spatial and temporal categories (space and time are also not original and cannot be measured if not as effects of speech), and it goes beyond the individual and the collective. Freud elaborated two main models of the psyche, and in both cases he described the psyche as divided into different instances, out of control of the individual. Individuality is the indivisible mind; thus it is equated with the conscious mind. Philosophy, psychology, and related disciplines focus on the study of thought, of the conscious mind, of the "I" (they do not theorize the unconscious, so they label the formations of the unconscious as "irrational," "disorders," "dysfunctions," or "illogical"), but this is clearly not the case of psychoanalysis. Individualism might be an ideal of Western discourse, but it is not a pillar of Freudian psychoanalysis. Not even the ego can represent individuality, because it is partially unconscious, and because it is also not master of what it speaks; the ego too originates in the field of the Other, and as such is not original; it is literally spoken to rather than being the expression of an individual. Further, the signifier continuously reveals its multitude of possible significations, meaning that there is nothing like an original unity. The Freudian "subject" is already a divided subject because it is made of language, because it is an effect of speech. If we can find something like the Freudian unconscious, it is because the "individual" is an ideal; indeed, we all are inhabited by language, thus by the unconscious, thus, by a radical and inexhaustible otherness.

There is not much else that we can do other than speaking and listening to what we happen to say, or better attending to what "is being said" (by the unconscious). The experience of psychoanalysis shows that the old saying "think first speak later" is impossible. On the contrary, we can only speak first (which does not necessarily imply a verbalization; the thought too is made of speech) and then listen to "what comes to mind." It seems paradoxical, at first, as we normally think that we are the author of our speech. We normally assume that we know what we are saying; however, in the moment we open our mouth we are spectators of what we say. Indeed, many times we are surprised at what comes to our mouth (or simply to our mind). Essential, here, is that we cannot avoid speech (in any case, even if we do not verbalize to others, even if it remains a thought); speech comes first and there is no way for us to know anything without putting it into words. Even when we are alone, we cannot avoid it; we can only try to listen to what is being said (meaning that the subject is impersonal) and then start from there, from the signifiers that are being used. *This is, by the way, the only condition that makes psychoanalysis possible.* And we should listen to the signifiers that are used, as these reveal the division of the subject; these reveal that there is something that goes beyond what we intended to say. (When the psychoanalyst points out some specific signifiers said by a client, the latter will often try to make clear by saying, "What I wanted to say is that... blah, blah, blah...." This is the imaginary indivisible subject).

Both individualism and collectivism aim at avoiding or controlling the unconscious. Individualism is the triumph of the "I" and the will: "I do what I want." It is the ideal of being self-sufficient. It is the ideal of making "one" with oneself. Collectivism is the triumph of renunciation and control of one's own drives in favor of the group. It is the ideal of making "one" with the group. However, Freud described collective phenomena as not necessarily qualitatively different from individual phenomena. In this sense, the very success of Confucianism in Chinese society can also be read as a defense of the unconscious, where a rigid social structure and a hierarchical organization prevent and contain the effects that could arise through free expression of the unconscious. This is the sacrifice of the (small) self of each one, for the sake of the (big) self of the group; however, the idea of the self has simply shifted to a different level.

Similarly, the ideal of individualism can also be understood as a defense against the unconscious or an attempt to submit the unconscious to the ego. *Psychoanalysis goes beyond both individualism and collectivism,* as it invites us to pay attention to our own speech and investigate our unconscious desire rather than focusing on the conscious will. I find myself puzzled when I hear some scholar (or even some psychoanalyst) saying that psychoanalysis conflicts with a collective culture but not with an individual culture: psychoanalysis conflicts with both collectivism and individualism, and this is the reason why, even in Western countries, there is a profusion of psychotherapies, new age practices, wellbeing disciplines, and so on that focus on "liberating" the ego and taking control of one's own life. Here, psychoanalysis goes in a different direction. Psychoanalysis conflicts with any conception of the "indivisible," whether it is at the level of the single person (so-called individualism) or the group (so-called collectivism); instead, psychoanalysis shows that the *difference* introduced by the signifier is original (for example because there is an irreducible distance between what we say and what we wanted to say), and thus the Two (and not the One, not the unity) is original.

Lin (2014) wrote that "Confucianism [...] can be distilled into two words: 'faithfulness' and 'forbearance.' They mean that one has to be oneself, but meanwhile, one must think of others." (p. 57). Paraphrasing Lacan, we could instead say that in psychoanalysis *one authorizes oneself only by oneself, but not without the Other*. What does this mean? Here the self of "oneself" is not the ego; it has nothing to do with autonomy. It is not the "oneself" that must be (for example) respectful of others; the Other (with capital letter) does not indicate the other persons. It means that one cannot neglect the unconscious, and thus authorization cannot come either from *myself* alone (as an autonomous decision, taken by the ego) or from *others*: one can authorize oneself only by recognizing and accepting a desire that comes from the Other: a *call*, or a *vocation*. Not neglecting the Other means encountering solitude, because one can be responsible for one's speech only. There is an irreducible gap with the Other; what we can do is only trying to articulate the unconscious desire; others cannot provide answers or guarantees for our unconscious desire. Independence or interdependence may be two strategies for representing the Other as others; in fact, they easily lead to isolation or, conversely to fear of being alone. Instead, solitude is the only condition for some encounter to happen, because the "right" encounter (the "coincidence") happens as an effect of speech: this is the miracle.

Faithfulness is also important in psychoanalysis, but that "faith" in psychoanalysis is intended as faith in speech, or faith in the unconscious, or faithfulness to the unconscious desire (ethics) and not just as faith in myself (as individualism would suggest) or faith in the group (as collectivism seems to imply). Thus, psychoanalysis does not promote individualism, intending to "do what you want," but instead it encourages recognizing and having care of speech, not neglecting the Other. Lacan (2006) recalled a saying that goes: "The prince who thinks he is in fact a prince is just as mad as the beggar who imagines himself one" (p. 139); this means that there cannot be a prince or king without the Other, and thus in consequence of a position in discourse. Thus, no one can neglect the Other, thinking, for example, to be self-sufficient (this does not work for any one, be it a person, or a group, or even a nation, as we see today). On the other hand, being in a group does not guarantee that there is care of speech. Most groups do not simply function by free association; instead, they are grounded on some basic assumptions and they require their members to adhere to a more or less explicit group code. Well-established groups tend to foster unanimity, cohesion, and conformity to a discourse; they give their members a sense of identity and promote identification to an ideal or a leader; and they have a strong hierarchy. Furthermore, they tend to minimize the perception of differences between in-group members while exaggerating the differences with the outside, so as to enhance group distinctiveness. We can see these regulatory mechanisms adopted by groups as aiming at controlling the original difference introduced by speech (in speaking we can experience that there are not shared meanings and that misunderstanding is structural and unavoidable), and thus as an attempt to reify the relation and norm the association. Thus, collectivism does not encourage open-ended questioning and conversation, because for the sake of the group, misunderstanding must be avoided; there is no room for the lapse. Just as with individualism, collectivism too aims at monologue and the exclusion of the Other. (What does not conform is disturbing; it is not perceived as a resource. Thus it can only be tolerated or repressed.) Or, we could say that collectivism poses itself as an Other that is not barred, meaning a real and complete Other, and this prevents an individual from accessing the unconscious.

The subject: highway to the Other

Could it have been possible to invent the Freudian unconscious out of Western discourse? Probably not, and probably this is one reason why still, today, it is apparently not successful in Hong Kong.

One hypothesis is that the Chinese thought has not theorized anything similar to the Freudian unconscious because it has not developed a conception of the *subject* similar to the Western one. Jullien (2004) suggests that Western thought could conceive a subject of action by isolating human personality from a situation. In fact, among the most notorious characters of Western heroes we have the solitary figures of the explorer, the adventurer, the conquistador, the cowboy, the seducer; all characters with a strong curiosity, will, perseverance, and desire. Conversely, the Chinese ideal was that of non-action, meaning to slip into the world without interfering with the world's proceedings. Thus, it may be that only by imagining an individual of free will (some say "subject of free will," but this sounds already paradoxical, because the idea of being a subject contrasts with the idea of a completely independent free will) could it have been possible to see its limitation and inconsistencies. Only by first assuming the idea of a being fully master of his actions has it been possible to discover the unconscious. For example, "person" in Western societies normally indicates an individual as a separate entity, and "personality" describes his/her attributes; instead, in Chinese 人 "*Ren*" (person) includes the individual and his/her societal and cultural environment, meaning that the concept of Ren "puts the emphasis on interpersonal transaction. It does not consider the individual psyche's deep cores of complexes and anxieties. Instead it sees the nature of the individual's external behavior in terms of how it fits or fails to fit the interpersonal standards of the society and culture" (Hsu, 1971, p. 29). Unsurprisingly then, most personality scales have been developed in the West and not in China.

The philosophical concept of subject has had some fundamental consequences at societal and political level (becoming autonomous subjects means that there are no longer masters and slaves, but individuals with the same rights and dignity); but the subject, as theorized within the Western discourse, is probably one of the greatest sources of confusion and an origin of problems.

Probably, Chinese thought has not had the chance to theorize a radical "otherness." Chinese thought has developed around the concept of society or group, meaning that, in Chinese thought, the Other is in the flesh. But in the Western tradition, this otherness has been more radical, something that could not be represented. As Hansen (1992) suggested, the difference between China and the West is that the first put the subject in the world, and the second put it in the mind. What does this imply? In Chinese tradition, the individual has to face the rules and the law of humans (society, the group); conversely, in the West, the person is not necessarily in relation to many others, but s/he is in relation to something radical, absolute, something "inward."

The transcendent and the relational

Another consequence of the emphasis placed by Confucianism on the relational dimension is that there are few elements of transcendence in Chinese culture, particularly in Hong Kong, whereas, thanks to Christianity, transcendence has been significant in Western culture: "When Confucians were contemplating the ontology of the universe, they did not conceive a transcendent creator as Christians did" (Hwang, 2009, p. 936). The idea of a transcendent creator matches well with the concept of the subject, the two go together. Further, if there is a transcendent creator, and if all people are created equal before God, as said in the Bible, then all people experience and share the same finitude toward life. For example, for each person there is something that goes beyond the registry of comprehension, there is a part of mystery that we cannot access; all people are equal when facing this absolute, and each person is confronted with his/her own solitude. One implication is that if all people are equal before God, then no one person can access a universal knowledge, and no one can have the answer for others. All people necessarily have to refer to this radical otherness. Thus, one of the main issues is how to address a question to God, so that God can answer? In Christianity, the question became more important than the answer, because God has oftentimes proved to answer in rather mysterious ways, if answer at all. Thus, this care for the question is the care for one's own speech.

Understandably, this is rather different in a Chinese context, where relationships are regulated by strong hierarchy (because of the lack of a transcendent creator), and people address demands to their significant others like parents, teachers, ministers and expect clear answers from them. In Hong Kong Chinese culture, one is confronted with many, but unlikely with a transcendent otherness. This may explain why, generally, the Hong Kong Chinese have little tolerance for ambiguity (despite the fact that the Chinese language can be more ambiguous than English, for example), or we might say for mystery, and expect the expert to really have an answer on anything. Admitting that one might not know something, if one is supposed to know, for example because one is the teacher, is hardly tolerated in a Chinese context.

Western tradition placed this (big) Other on a transcendent level, which has led to emphasizing dimensions of speech like the prayer, the invocation, and, most important, the question; in contrast, Hong Kong Chinese thought located this otherness in an external reality, finding many small others, thus emphasizing a demand or request of the other, thus authority rather than speech, and the answer rather than analysis and introspection.

The desire is the desire of the Other

Lacan used to say that the desire is the desire of the Other. We could understand this in a few ways: the desire originates in the field of the Other, thus it has to do with the unconscious and is different from the will. Desire comprises the two dimensions of desiring and being desired; it is desire from the Other and desire for the Other. The desire, and not the object, is original (desire has no specific object; or, desire is desire for something else). Thus, one's desire might rely on how strongly the other desires; for example, one has to be desired first so as to desire. Or, recognizing the fact that the other desires (even when his/her desire is addressed to another object) might enhance one's desire (both for the other and for the object of his/her desire). Thus, the desire of the Other names the object of desire and opens up to the "recognition" of one's desire (it might be experienced as a recognition, although it is more likely a creation). Thus, this formulation of the "desire of the Other" suggests that being desired and desiring are strictly associated and influence each other.

As in several Asian cultures, so also in Hong Kong, expressions of desire are not always encouraged. For example, in Hong Kong Chinese culture, manifestations of desire should be limited and public expressions of desire may bring shame. However, and maybe in consequence of this, the desire of the Other is particularly important. The other is expected to be desiring, and his/her desire has to be strong, continuous, and reliable, without uncertainties or intermittences. Just as if only the other is called to define what is desirable, it could only be possible to desire what the other desires or where its desire is oriented. I interpret this to mean the fascination that Hong Kong feels for the West, or those countries that more easily occupy the position of the Other. The Other can be extremely fascinating; everything that comes from the Other is attractive. Then, the more the Other is repressed, the more it emerges; and the desire is represented and projected all over objects, goods, and idealized lifestyles. Again, this seems to reflect a general tendency of being in the position of receiving rather than expressing or voicing out. This reflects once more a tendency toward being very sensible and perceptive of what comes from the other, because one is less experienced in naming one's own desire. Then, it is not surprising that a concept of the unconscious is missing in Hong Kong, but this does not mean that the unconscious does not produce its effects.

The power of thought and the unconscious

Starting with Greek philosophy, European thought has focused heavily on thought and the power of reasoning. In contrast, Asian cultures developed techniques and meditation practices, which appear to aim at diluting, diverting, containing, and quieting thought:

> The Chinese *xin* is not so much an arousing factor as a stabilizing medium. A premodern exegesis of the term *qing*, which means "emotions" or "affect" equates it with *jing*: "quietude." The modern sage Liang Shuming says: The human mind-heart (*xin*) is capable of quietude; what is contrary to quietude is emotional impulse. Emotional impulse is a state of the body (*shen*).
>
> (Sun, 1991)

Psychoanalysis is different from both traditions; it does not neglect the power of thinking (cognition), yet it does not encourage the pursuit of emptiness or quietude. Psychoanalysis aims at a different listening, as to listen differently to what is being said, meaning that both reasoning and emotions and affects are *effects* of speech. Thus, psychoanalysis does not confirm or disconfirm what is being said; instead, it takes it by the letter, so as to understand where it comes from; it operates a subversion of the utterance, of the statement, to retrace the singularity of each one in his/her saying.

The Other is at the same time inside and outside. It opens to the infinite: time and space are no longer the traditional categories. The unconscious is timeless, and it cannot be confined in a given space. It is not in me, or in you, or between us. It is collective in the way it concerns everyone. It is a radically other dimension, which cannot be inscribed in any philosophical category. It is not simply the non-conscious (*wu yishi* 无意识), it is not just a void (*zhōng kong* 中空), and is not simply what lies under the conscious, not simply what we are not aware of (*chim yee sik* 潜意识, subconscious). The unconscious is not just the opposite of the conscious. It is not just its negative. The Freudian unconscious is also different from the various conceptions of consciousness which have emerged in Buddhism. Indeed, it is not a storage site. The contents of the unconscious can never be spoken out completely because being an effect of speech, the unconscious is continuously at work.

Meditation and the idea of healing the thought

In the Greek-Christian tradition, thought has mostly been considered the way to knowledge and truth. In particular, from Plato on, men thought that posing radical questions was a sign of the level to which a civilization had advanced. The intellect became then the main instance for investigating the world, and argumentation the basis for speculation. This is probably not the same way taken by Buddhism, Daoism, and Confucianism, which instead underlined the uselessness of any question for knowing the world. Most Western thought has insisted on the search for truth, universal or singular as it can be defined. And still, even facing the inconsistency of any explanation, the question was insisted upon as the means for accessing, or we could say, for inventing, the world:

> The way and the truth: in the West, truth is a knowledge of what is real and what that represents: reality. For the Chinese, knowledge is not abstract, but concrete, it is not representational, but performative and participatory, it is not discursive, but is, as a knowledge of the way, a kind of know-how.
> (Hall & Ames, 1998, p. 104)

While in Europe, thought has been radicalized (not only by Descartes: "I think, therefore I am"), and turned into creative thinking, critical thinking, absolute thinking, weak thinking, etc., China has met this development with silence and meditation. In particular, the Chinese way has never been extreme, radical, absolute, but rather median: China (*Zhong Guo*, 中国, the Middle Country), the median void (*zhong kong*, 中空), and the middle way (中庸 *Zhong Yong*).

While the West focused on rhetoric and logic as premises for the correct and effective art of argumentation and practice of speech, meditation seems rather to assume that no answer can be found through the formulation of a question and reasoning. Psychoanalysis has revealed the imaginary status of the subject and suggested that the subject is at least divided; instead, meditation practices generally seem to remark on the illusory status of any subject of knowledge, which should be overcome by pursuing the void, or the emptiness, described as something that can neutralize or moderate the various drives. Whereas Western philosophies have mostly focused on how to realize oneself or *fulfill* one's desires, Chinese culture has in most cases indicated ways for *emptying* the mind. Psychoanalysis instead does not suggest simply following the imaginary representations of the subject and its will; at the same time, it does not simply neglect it as purely illusory. For psychoanalysis there is nothing to fulfill or to empty, but an unconscious desire to analyze.

Opening

As has emerged from this study, there is little interest in exploring the unconscious in this context. Perhaps, what belongs to the unconscious is considered as something imaginary, and thus less important or even not real. This might be confirmed by the tendency to focus on practical and concrete things. Furthermore, Hong Kong Chinese culture is action oriented, and seems to interpret behavior as just a consequence of one's will.

In this study, several items were developed so as to understand the counselor's ability to reformulate what the client's discourse implies in a way that may open up new questions; the ability to move from the manifest meaning to another meaning; it is the ability to go beyond what is being said; to shift attention from single facts to broader questions. Such items include: "I intervene in a way that may sound enigmatic to the client," "After counseling, clients have more questions," "Most of the client's material is unconscious," "In most cases the client does not realize the ambiguity of his/her words." The results for these items were significantly correlated and initially they were grouped on a scale named Opening (Cronbach's alpha 0.65; the scale was later discarded because factor analysis showed that items had multiple loadings). Results showed that participants scored below the theoretical midpoint on this scale, meaning in the Disagree range. In my interpretation, this showed little openness to the unknown and little curiosity for the unconscious. In fact, Opening was strongly correlated with the three other psychoanalytic dimensions, particularly with Unconscious ($r = 0.61$, $p < 0.001$), and negatively associated with the other counseling dimensions, particularly Focused Attention ($r = -0.38$, $p < 0.001$). Interestingly enough, Opening was also strongly associated with Conflicts with Hong Kong Chinese Culture (CHKCC) ($r = 0.42$, $p < 0.001$). On the one hand, if we assume the CHKCC to be the independent variable, results might suggest that Opening is one way of responding so as to avoid direct confrontation; on the other hand, if we assume Opening to be the independent variable, this might suggest that emphasizing questions rather than answers and maintaining ambiguity and/or an enigmatic attitude in speaking greatly conflicts with the Hong Kong Chinese culture.

Interestingly, among the psychology literature, cross-cultural research on personality factors showed that on the five-factor model, Openness to Experience, or simply Openness, is the most controversial and has the weakest psychometric properties in non-Western contexts (the other four factors being: Neuroticism, Extraversion, Conscientiousness, and Agreeableness) (for a review, see Cheung et al., 2008). In particular, lexical studies suggested that, in Europe, the factor Openness could be labeled more as Intellect, Creativity, or Imagination, whereas in Chinese culture, the factors that might be closer to Openness were Expressiveness–Conservatism, or Conforming versus Nonconforming. Cheung and colleagues (2008) observed that openness in a Chinese context does refer much to cognitive or intellectual characteristics such as the openness to ideas and interests found in Western-based studies, but more likely to relationships to other people, in conjunction with extraversion and leadership characteristics. This is very much in line with findings from this research and suggests once more that European and American cultures value more the intellectual abilities that might lead to knowledge, discovery, and invention, whereas Chinese culture emphasizes more the relational level.

We have other examples of this. In a class situation, Chinese and Westerners tend to show a very different attitude toward learning and stimulated thinking. In a previous study, Tan (2007) reported that Chinese teachers normally "regarded questioning as a means of checking students' understanding of the texts that form the basis of the lesson, making sure if they had already mastered what they were supposed to learn" (p. 93), whereas instead foreign teachers would usually lead the students to explore the question in depth, asking how they arrived at the answer, and requiring a justification for the answer. My experience teaching psychology at a university in Hong Kong is similar. Not only is the interaction different, but more specifically, the very quality of questions posed is different and serves different goals. Students I taught were quite surprised by the kind of open-ended questions that I posed to them; today I would not be surprised to find out that some of them might have misunderstood my attempt to involve them in a conversation by asking their opinion as a lack of knowledge on my part. In fact, Chinese teachers tend to play the "expert" and normally in class "most questions focused on the background knowledge, content, structure and language of the material used, to elicit answers the teacher already knew and expected. Higher cognitive questions requiring learners to compare, contrast, persuade, determine cause and effect, to develop their thinking were rarely asked" (Tan, 2007, p. 92).

The Hong Kong Chinese attitude toward posing questions is largely different, if not the opposite, to that in psychoanalysis. In psychoanalysis, the use of questioning does not aim at eliciting answers that the psychoanalyst already knows; as every case is different, even an experienced analyst cannot know all the issues of the analysand. Questioning is therefore not simply employed to guide the analysand to a predetermined destination (this would be *maieutics*, which is closer to pedagogy than to psychoanalysis). The use of questioning in psychoanalysis aims at eliciting a production of knowledge from the unconscious; it is not a questioning between the psychoanalyst and the analysand. Questioning is directed to the unconscious; it is not one interrogating the other. Questioning, in psychoanalysis, is grounded on the assumption that most of what the client says comes from the unconscious, and as such, the client does not know the answer yet. The aims of posing a question, in psychoanalysis, are then not simply to obtain an answer or to "discover" the cause of a symptom or a repressed memory, etc.

The very act of questioning is more important than the answer itself. The question can provoke a change when it remains an open-ended question, when it continues to operate against a background (not just in a session, but between sessions as well), when it produces further associations of memories and thoughts, meaning when it continues to question the subject. However, what is interesting here is that this very process of questioning, which is at the core of psychoanalysis, is likely not universal, meaning that questioning might be a feature of some cultures and some people more than others who do not find posing questions so beneficial.

Western literature generally suggests that curiosity is what supports a process of gaining knowledge, and thus questioning and openness. Some recent experimental results seem to show that acquisition of knowledge is emotionally pleasing and that satisfaction of curiosity through acquiring knowledge brings pleasure (Perlovsky, Bonniot-Cabanac, & Cabanac, 2010). However, it is unclear whether this kind of *intellectual* curiosity is universal or culture specific; it may be that Western literature is biased. For example, one psychoanalyst who has extensively taught psychoanalysis in China has observed that "the lack of curiosity about oneself is deeply rooted in Chinese culture" (Haag, 2014, p. 28). Generally speaking, I cannot deny this observation. Whether Chinese culture hindered the development of curiosity or not is also debated among historians of science (Elvin, 2014). It is likely too simplistic, however, to maintain that one culture is averse to curiosity in any form; instead, it may be that curiosity can be expressed only in given conditions. For instance, Chinese culture emphasizes conformity, interdependence with significant others, and obedience; thus, given this background, it may be that Chinese culture implicitly reinforces comparison to (thus, curiosity for) others rather than cultivation for oneself. Interestingly, a research study from Hong Kong (Ye, Ng, Yim, & Wang, 2015) found that, among local university students, curiosity was positively associated with interest in others, empathy with others' feelings and concern for others' wellbeing; however, previous research in Western samples did not find this correlation, and the authors have interpreted these results to suggest that in Hong Kong Chinese culture, curiosity refers not only to ideas and interests but most importantly to social relationships with other people. Or, we can say that posing questions leads to more openness.

Posing questions can lead to more openness?

Posing questions in psychoanalysis is an effective way to investigate unconscious fantasies and beliefs; a way to subvert the meaning supposed by the analysand, deconstruct it, and open him/her to new possibilities. But, can this approach be universally valid, regardless of the culture? Western psychologists described posing questions as one powerful way to stimulate curiosity. For example "the posing of a question or presentation of a riddle or puzzle confronts the individual directly with missing information and is therefore perhaps the most straightforward curiosity inducer. Berlyne referred to curiosity-inducing questions as 'thematic probes'" (p. 91). Indeed, posing questions can induce investigation into a phenomenon; can induce one to think critically; and it can literally induce higher listening; Haroutunian-Gordon (2007) even states that listening always involves questioning. However, this may be limited to Western cultures descending from the Greek-Christian tradition. By contrast, Chinese thinking, as philosopher Hajime Nakamura notes, reflected a genius for practicality, not a penchant for scientific theory and investigation. And as philosopher and sinologist Donald Munro has written, "In Confucianism there was no thought of *knowing* that did not entail some consequence for action" (Haroutunian-Gordon, 2007, p. 8).

An attitude toward opening is associated with higher curiosity, suggesting that expressing and elaborating questions and curiosity enhance each other. In English, the etymology of a "question" generally refers to a doubt about the truth or validity of something; it can be a proposition; it generally implies discussion, consideration, conversation, speech, and talk. The very act of questioning is an act of challenging, wondering, and doubting; it shows curiosity. A question may call for a reply, but not for an answer. An answer is instead asked. Similarly, demanding, requesting, or claiming also always specifies an object. The question can be addressed to someone (meaning that that question is taken in a transference), but is not a question of something specific: that would be a demand, or a request. So, the question already reflects a particular disposition toward speech; the question emphasizes the narrative dimension; the question is potentially unending, and is continuously reformulated, rearticulated. By contrast, requests are always caught in a series, one after another. So, is listening possible without questioning? According to the results from this study, listening is important in the Chinese context; however, a question is not always fully articulated. Curiosity, investigation, opening, and questioning are relatively weak dimensions in Hong Kong. It is suggested that in Hong Kong Chinese culture, making requests, asking, and demanding are more likely to represent the standard. This is not surprising, and is in line with a culture that is very much oriented to a dyadic, relational level, where mutuality and reciprocity are emphasized and even rewarded.

Curiosity

Nisbett (2003, p. 4), commenting about the Greeks, writes

> as striking as the Greeks' freedom and individuality is their sense of curiosity about the world. Aristotle thought that curiosity was the uniquely defining property of human beings. St. Luke said of the Athenians of a later era: "They spend their time in nothing else but to tell or to hear some new thing." The Greeks, far more than their contemporaries, speculated about the nature of the world they found themselves in and created models of it. [...] Only the Greeks attempted to explain their observations in terms of underlying principles. Exploring these principles was a source of pleasure for the Greeks. Our word "school" comes from the Greek *schole*, meaning "leisure." Leisure meant for the Greeks, among other things, the freedom to pursue knowledge.

Loewenstein (1994) conducted a review of the concept of curiosity in Western thought, particularly in philosophy, psychology, and social sciences, and found that, traditionally, the pedagogical literature encourages teachers to stimulate curiosity, which "has also been cited as a major impetus behind scientific discovery, possibly eclipsing even the drive for economic gain" (p. 75). Curiosity was mentioned by Aristotle, Cicero, St. Augustine, Hume, Kant, Feuerbach, and of course Freud, for whom it derived from the sex drive, as sexual curiosity can be sublimated into a curiosity about the world. Behavioral psychologists started to refer to "exploratory behavior" as a meaning for curiosity, where exploratory behavior was normally considered a major determinant for the development of intelligence. Piaget thought that "curiosity reflects a natural human tendency to try to make sense of the world." However, this might be a wrong assumption. In fact, measuring curiosity has always been "a task that has proven to be extraordinarily difficult. Attempts to cross-validate curiosity scales have typically produced low intercorrelations, and efforts to correlate scales with behavior or with individual characteristics such as age, gender, and IQ have produced contradictory findings" (Loewenstein, 1994, p. 76).

Curiosity and paradoxes

As mentioned before, Western cultures are typically described as linear cultures, meaning that they largely rely on Aristotelian logical thinking. Such cultures consider reasoning and Aristotelian logic as the correct form of thinking. As a consequence, a paradox is generally thought-provoking, as it indicates an error or at least a wrong assumption in the discourse. The paradox (which etymologically is a statement contrary to common belief or expectation) can then function as a stimulus for activating curiosity in a Western mind. The paradox, while it shows the inconsistency of a reasoning, might open up to something new, something unthought. However, Chinese thinking is grounded on different premises, which lead to a very different disposition toward the paradox. Chen (2002) suggests that Chinese culture found a way of "transcending" paradox. The paradox is not necessarily as thought-provoking for the Chinese as it can be for Westerners, because Chinese culture has a different attitude toward contradictions, and does not require one to solve or to overcome the paradox. According to Chen (2002, p. 183):

> Confucian philosophy recommends *zhong he*, a concept based on middle way thinking (literally, "middle way," *zhong*, and "harmony," *he*) as the key to obtaining prosperity: "If *zhong* he is reached," writes Confucius in the Book of Means, "heaven and earth will be in place, and all things will grow." In this view, a system is harmonious only when it has achieved a balance between paradoxical tendencies.

Thus, it might be that the paradox does not have the same power to stimulate curiosity in the Chinese mind and thus find new ways for reorganizing or gaining new knowledge, or for coming to a new saying, a new formulation.

How curiosity developed in some cultures and not in others

According to Nisbett (2003), the Greeks developed great curiosity because of their geographical location. At that time, they were at the crossroads of the world, which brought them continuously in contact with different people who expressed very distant attitudes, beliefs, and thoughts. The richness of such experiences, introduced by the diversity of people met, brought some contradictions to the Greeks; at that point, they developed the use of logic and reasoning to overcome such contradictions and make sense of what they were listening to. In contrast, nothing similar ever happened in China, where most of the people have never encountered any foreigners. When, in the fifteenth century, the expedition of the Grand Eunuch came back from Southeast Asia, the Middle East and Western Africa,

> the Chinese were quite uninterested in seeing anything that those societies might have produced or known about [...] This lack of curiosity was characteristic of China. The inhabitants of the Middle Kingdom (China's name for itself, meaning essentially "the center of the world") had little interest in the tales brought to them by foreigners. Moreover, there has never been a strong interest in knowledge for its own sake in China. Even modern Chinese philosophers have always been far more interested in the pragmatic application of knowledge than with abstract theorizing for its own sake.
>
> (Nisbett, 2003, p. 40)

We can say that curiosity is intimately associated with exploration, be it exploration of an external territory or country or the exploration of our thoughts. A journey, if it is intended as a discovery of the unknown, is inevitably guided by the unconscious; the unconscious is the only reliable *tour operator*. The unconscious prepares the destiny of our journey. Otherwise, what we have is tourism, intended as the "visit" (which derives from "to see, to observe or inspect," meaning that what works here is the look/gaze rather than the listening) to some universally recognized destinations. But tourism is the repression of the lapse (all must be scheduled, nothing can "go wrong"); it is the repression of the unconscious. Tourism is a strategy for avoiding an encounter with the Other (thus, the encounter with one's own saying, meaning that when we are in the journey the categories of the external and internal world no longer exist: it becomes impossible to make such a distinction) while preserving a representation of the other as different (tourists have no time for talking with the locals; they have only time for taking pictures that no one will ever look at). The metaphor of psychoanalysis as a journey is not new, but it seems to be still valid; the way a population travels might give us some hints on the attitude toward exploring the unconscious. Thus, it should not be surprising that traditionally Chinese people are known for visiting foreign countries in large organized groups (typically one day for each different city) but not as famous as explorers or adventurers.

Curiosity has a different place in Western and Hong Kong Chinese culture; particularly, without a conception of the Other, curiosity remains as curiosity for others (the group, the other persons; thus, gossip) rather than curiosity for life (for the transcendent, for the unconscious). This might also support the hypothesis that Chinese listening is not an interpretive listening but more likely an empathic/sympathetic listening. Finally, in this context, the openness of the speech at which psychoanalysis aims may result in a double-edged sword because posing questions might not be thought of as provoking as perceived in the West; on the contrary, it may be perceived as creating an unnecessary confusion, leading nowhere.

Psychoanalysis beyond Western discourse and Chinese thought

I did not come to Hong Kong with the intention to "export" psychoanalysis, although I have been interested to see whether psychoanalysis could be received in this context. This study has provided some answers. However, most importantly, this research journey has been for me the opportunity to rediscover my culture of origin (I had not been so aware of it until I came to Hong Kong) and reconsider psychoanalysis.

Facing culture's "others" is the chance for us to discover something more about our values, our assumptions, and the limitations of our thinking. It would be presumptuous, and theoretically wrong, if we really believed that we can describe "how the other culture really is," because reading another culture with our vocabulary leads inevitably to interpreting that culture as lacking something (compared to ours). It's the best way to fail any comprehension of any culture.

Facing Chinese thought has helped me to perceive clearly some limits of the Western discourse: the (ab)use of reasoning; the continuous need to define "the thing," in the attempt to master the object; the rather obsessive research of the Truth, as if a truth were possible out of speech (the so-called *objective* truth); the dogmatism (or fundamentalism) derived by a sometimes blind belief in reasoning; the belief in an external reality, and the supposition that knowledge is the key for accessing the world. Not surprisingly, indeed, Western discourse is often criticized, and today "Westernization" has generally a negative connotation. However, experiencing Chinese culture has helped me in reconsidering the strengths of Western discourse as well. For example, with the ancient Greeks and after Christianity in particular, Europeans have developed a unique attitude toward rhetoric, narration, and telling that probably is also what has opened it to the scientific method. This attention to the dimension of speech probably remains the biggest strength of the Western discourse, even though modernity seems to forget it at times. Today, particularly among social sciences more than "hard" sciences, a naive reductionism is emerging. Some imagine it being possible to isolate the dimension of speech from "facts." However, discovery and theorization may come only in consequence of curiosity, invention, creativity, and thus require narration and speech; they require the dream, and thus the work of the unconscious. Similarly, this lack in theorizing speech is the also greatest limit of Chinese thought.

Furthermore, this experience allowed me to reconsider psychoanalysis essentially in terms of listening. I consider listening as being more pragmatic and fruitful than identifying psychoanalysis with some concepts or school of thoughts. Operationalizing psychoanalysis in terms of listening has not only allowed me to do research in a context where psychoanalytic theory is almost absent, but it also allowed me to distinguish psychoanalysis from both Western discourse and Chinese thought. For example, results from this and other studies indicate that while European and American cultures are more speaking oriented, Chinese cultures are more listening oriented; this is an interesting finding, which opened to further speculations on why psychoanalysis was invented in Europe rather than China. However, Chinese cultures have never theorized anything like the Freudian unconscious, and so listening in such a context is very different from psychoanalytic listening. Then, we could say that *psychoanalysis is beyond both Western discourse and Chinese thought, because besides being grounded in a tradition of speech, it nevertheless emphasizes the dimension of listening as listening to the unconscious.*

Finally, the unconscious remains the most challenging term to define. There is not one univocal and unambiguous definition of the unconscious. Freud himself attempted more formulation, and after him, several psychoanalysts gave different interpretations, even though it is sometimes reduced to a philosophical or medical concept. Further, the difficulty in translating such a term into Chinese may be indicative of the difficulty in defining what the unconscious is, even after more than a hundred years of psychoanalysis. A question that might deserve further attention is: is it possible to reinvent a term for the unconscious in Chinese language? This question would imply asking how could we describe what the unconscious is without using the word unconscious. And then, how can we reformulate the unconscious, so that it may be perceived as more tangible, more pragmatic, and thus essential in both Chinese and Western cultures? Again, the encounter with a foreign culture may be the chance for reinventing and advancing psychoanalysis.

Glossary

Analysand   This term is used to replace the term "client." Derived from the gerund, this term indicates an ongoing process. In psychoanalysis, a client will address his/her speech to the analyst, because the analyst occupies the position of the Other. This means that ultimately the psychoanalyst is not the real addressee, although this misplacement can be fruitful. The analyst should be conscious of speaking from this position, not believing, for example, that s/he is *really* the expert and/or someone supposed to *respond* to the client's demand. By not answering, the client will have a chance to become the analysand of his/her own speech and investigate his/her relation with the Other. This implies that the analysand is not simply a patient "in need," or a client/"user" who passively *receives* service from an expert. The psychoanalytic journey proceeds if the client has the chance to cultivate a psychoanalytic listening and analyze his/her speech.

Brief therapy   This is described as a systematic process that focuses on obtaining a specific behavioral change in a short time. It is a solution-focused rather than problem-oriented approach, where the therapist is normally more proactive than in other psychotherapies. Various brief therapy approaches were developed by authors like Milton Erickson, Paul Watzlawick, and Giorgio Nardone, among others.

Confidence interval   estimated range of values which is likely to include the "true" value for a population. Confidence intervals are typically stated at the 95 percent confidence level, which means that the range of values has a 95 in a 100 chance of including the "true" value.

Confucius   also known as "Master Kong" (Chinese: 孔子 *Kǒng Zǐ*) lived between 551 and 479 BC. He is the most influential thinker in Chinese history, comparable to Socrates in the West. He was also a political figure and an educator. His teachings, compiled in the *Lunyu* or *Analects*, are primarily concerned with ethics, morality, and government. He described the qualities of the ideal man, how he should live his life and interact with others, and how he should contribute to society. Particularly, he emphasized self-cultivation, virtue, and harmony.

Cronbach's alpha This is an estimate of reliability, specifically the internal consistency, of a scale. Cronbach's alpha indicates how closely test items measure the same construct.

Discourse The discourse is an organized communication that aims at creating and defining relations between people and objects; a discourse is what determines a subject, meaning that in a discourse one is subjected to a place assigned by others. One's place is already there before one is born, for example, because one is first born in the discourse of one's parents, their community and society. The discourse is already written and its structure is rather rigid; it is made of statements, beliefs, and/or memories. Thus, in a discourse, all is pre-*dictable*, meaning that all is said before (foretell). There is no authentic speech in a discourse, there is no *enunciation* or speech act. The discourse is founded on identity (oneness, sameness), thus it promotes the identical (*idem et idem*, meaning over and over), and thus repetition (re-*petition*, act of saying over again). The discourse is a collection of facts and images repeating as the same; there is no telling, there is no room for something new (although a subject may really believe what s/he is saying, or what s/he is told). The discourse is closed; it can be represented as a circle.

Episteme and techne Episteme means "to know" in Greek. It refers to a form of explicit knowledge that can be shared and transmitted to others. Episteme is the theory of something. Epistemology, the study of knowledge, is derived from episteme. Conversely, techne means craftsmanship or art. It is the making or doing as opposed to the theoretical understanding or explaining. It refers to a knowledge that one can only learn by practice. Techne is the root of "technique" and "technical."

Exploratory Factor Analysis This is a technique used to explore the underlying structure (factors) of a set of observed variables (e.g. 40 items in the questionnaire are grouped into three factors). This reduced number of factors explains most of the variation in the response.

Free floating attention Also named evenly suspended or evenly hovering attention, it is described by Freud as the essential rule in psychoanalytic listening of not focusing on anything in particular and giving instead equal notice to everything one hears, no matter whether it is clear or confused.

Kurtosis A measurement used to determine whether a distribution of scores is flat (or heavy-tailedness) or peaked (how sharply curved the peak is). Kurtosis between -3 and 3 is normally accepted.

Language All Freud's work refers continuously to language: dreams, slips of the tongue, jokes, forgetfulness, symptoms, and all formations of the unconscious show how the signifier can operate. The "Interpretation of Dreams" can be read as one of the greatest texts of linguistics of all times; it shows that language is not just a tool for communicating, but we are literally spoken by the language. A famous quote from Lacan says "The unconscious is structured like a language"; *like* a language, not meaning that it is equal to a natural language (e.g. English or Italian), but indicating that it has similar logic and similar rhetorical procedures (displacement and condensation, with Freud, or metonymy and metaphor with Lacan) to language. Language is the condition of the unconscious; at the same time our speech remains partially foreign to us.

Nachträglichkeit Translated into English as "deferred action" and into French as *après-coup*, *nachträglichkeit* emphasizes the two vectors of retroactivity and after-effect. It is presented by Freud in "Sexuality in the Aetiology of the Neuroses" (1898) and in "From the History of an Infantile Neurosis" (1918) as a retroactive attribution of *meaning* to earlier events. *Nachträglichkeit* was also essential to the psychoanalytic understanding of trauma: the first scene is only understood and becomes "traumatic" when it re-emerges (or is re-created) as a memory at a second moment and is given meaning. *Nachträglichkeit* means that the meaning is an effect of speech; this implies a subversion of chronological time, indicating that memory is an active process. Also in the psychoanalytic process we may experience *nachträglichkeit* when a signifier is told and understood only later, after the session, all of a sudden.

Narcissism of minor differences This expression first appeared in "The Taboo of Virginity" (1917) and later in "Civilization and Its Discontents" (1930). Freud observed that we reserve our aggressiveness and our most resentful comments for those who are most similar to us, meaning that we feel threatened not by those with whom we have little in common but rather by those who show only small differences.

Narrative therapy A postmodern psychotherapy inspired by social constructionism. Its goal is to help clients to generate richer and/or alternative stories in order to overcome their current and problematic dominant stories, through a process of deconstruction and meaning-making. Reference authors are Michael White and David Epston.

Other The Other is the "other scene" of the dream and the unconscious. The Other indicates that things proceed by two (this AND that) and not by one (this OR that). The two is not a dichotomy or a contradiction or an opposition: the two is original, and not just a division of the one. Two: there is always Other. Two: the reference is always Other; self-reference is not possible. The place of the Other may be at times occupied by others; however, if the Other is misrecognized or neglected what remains is only one other (represented as good or bad, needy, suffering, provoking, or threatening, etc.). Without Other, there is finitude: things are represented as having an end or a limit that cannot be overcome. The Other is found in the speech act, meaning in the dissolution of one's beliefs and fantasies. Without Other, there is no speech act, but only act (and, for example, acting out). Neurosis could be thought of as a resistance to the Other, or an attempt to ignore it. But then, if the Other is misrecognized the desire cannot be recognized as being "own";

in the obsessive discourse desire is normally experienced as foreigner (like the other formations of the unconscious), and then it is perceived as excessive, harmful, or pathological. Misunderstanding indicates that there is something beyond the mirror-image of the "I." Misunderstanding is a resource, as it reveals the Other beyond our beliefs and representations. It is only the Other that can avoid an imaginary confrontation between two parties (i.e. between an "I" and a "you"), or one word against the other. There is not a subject of the Other, so the Other cannot be said to be stupid or crazy; the Other is not the place of certainty, then the Other cannot be a liar as well.

other The other person. While the Other describes a radical alterity, the absolute difference (e.g. what cannot be fully explained), the other is the similar person. The Other opens to the unknown, to the unthought, to the invention; it belongs to the mystery more than the enigma. The (small) other is inscribed in the imaginary order. It is the effect of identification, the projection of one's own image; thus, it is actually no-other. The other is easily represented through various statements; it is perceived as the familiar, as the already known; thus, the relation (which requires some distance, some difference) with the other is impossible. Since the other is one's own specular image, the two is destined to become one: either through fusion with the other or (physical) separation. The radical difference and the mystery introduced by the Other may open up the formulation of open questions; the Other opens to speech: prayer, poetry, science (thus, to open questions, not to demands or requests), which are not addressed to any small other. Conversely, the relation with the other is fantasized as possibly non-mediated by speech, as if the communication with the other would not require speech and could be unambiguous.

Person-centered therapy (or client-centered therapy) A form of non-directive psychotherapy developed by Carl Rogers in the 1940s and 1950s. It is possibly the pillar of the humanistic orientation. The therapeutic process is conceptualized as being founded mainly on the therapist's empathy and unconditional positive regard toward the client.

Play therapy It uses play to interact with and analyze and help children. It can be either directive (oriented to a cognitive and behavioral model) or non-directive (inspired by psychoanalysis and/or client-centered therapy principles).

Positive psychology Although it continues a tradition started with Maslow in the 1950s, it is known by this name only from 1998. It criticizes "traditional" psychology for focusing only on symptoms and mental illness, and urges psychologists to cultivate talent and pursuit of happiness in order to make life more rewarding and fulfilling. Reference authors are Martin E. P. Seligman and Mihaly Csikszentmihalyi.

Question/demand A demand, or request, is the articulation of a need; it is asking for something. Conversely, the question goes beyond the imagined need. A question, more than a demand, is expressed and articulated within transference, while a request comes from the ego and is addressed to the Other represented (thus, to a small other). The request originates and remains within the discourse, meaning in the circularity (i.e. taking and giving, asking and responding), and thus in the closure and the repetition of the identical (because a need can only be temporarily satisfied, a request will be repeated over and over again). Instead, the question may open to the unknown, the unexpected and unforeseen. The question arises when something cannot be fully explained and one is in a listening position (listening to the unconscious, what goes beyond the manifest meaning). The relation between questioning and listening is reciprocal: they enhance each other. On one hand, listening to the unconscious is necessary for formulating and expressing a question; on the other hand, articulating the question can refine the listening. Instead, what is represented as a need and is expressed through a demand requires only to be acknowledged by the other; it requires to be fulfilled, satisfied, meaning it requires a reply or response from the addressee, the other. A demand is asked, a request is suggested between the lines; however, it is intentional and is grounded on the manifest meaning. Articulating a question may produce a change because producing new associations it can open to the unknown or unthought. A question requires invention; conversely, a request may only provoke a reply. As the question is addressed to the Other, it may not receive an answer, but it does not go without consequences for the speaker; instead, as the demand is addressed to the other, it may remain unanswered, confirming the speaker in his/her position. A question develops along a cultural, intellectual, and artistic journey; instead, a demand or request develops in the imaginary and then is confined in the relation of dependency/control/aggressiveness with the other. Providing answers, advice, or explanations or interpretations may obstruct the psychoanalytic process, which instead should support listening and the ability to further articulate a question. When the Other is misrecognized, like in hysteria or in the obsessive discourse, recognizing or expressing a question can be particularly difficult; most likely, in these cases we can observe a high number of requests that are being addressed to the other. Roughly, we could say that hysteria originates about the fantasy of not having received enough and thus there are several complaints or blaming of the other; hysteria has many claims or demands and is continuously asking for more (shifting from one object to the next). Literally, it can be extremely demanding. Instead, the obsessive discourse is particularly active (maybe fantasizing to restore a mythical age of full realization and full enjoyment, so that in the end it is only close to perfection); the obsessive discourse has many answers. It also poses many queries. However, it finds it particularly difficult to identify and/or name his/her own question. Thus, in the obsessive discourse, it is important that the other does not stop to ask. The obsessive discourse can produce majestic philosophical systems, but finds it difficult to go the core of his/her question; it continuously goes round and round, but it can never get to the point. It raises many doubts, but doubts are different from questions; doubts reflect indecision toward one's unconscious desire, they are posed as hindrances to do anything or go anywhere; they aim at disrupting any question and giving up on it. And when one question arises, it is impersonal and normally concerning some issue that cannot be answered, like life and death. The question is more intimately linked to the unconscious desire. Thus, the formulation of the question is what counts more in analysis; reading the symptom differently, subverting each statement, analyzing signifiers, translating an obstacle into a new question and articulating this question, this is the work of analysis. The psychoanalytic process cannot proceed by accumulation of knowledge or by giving answers; in fact, a personal psychoanalysis cannot begin where others have terminated. Freud wrote that, like sculpture (and contrary to painting), psychoanalysis works by subtracting, suggesting that speech should find its lightness by abandoning old beliefs and representations and not adding new ones. This is how a question can emerge.

Signifier the Swiss linguist Ferdinand de Saussure distinguished the signified (the meaning or concept) and the signifier (the phonological element of a sign) and described their relation as arbitrary. However, it is Lacan who states that the signifier is primary and produces the signified. Signifier is not simply an equivalent of "word"; a signifier itself has no meaning but receives its meaning depending on its position in the associative chains, thus by its relation with the previous and following signifiers. Furthermore, signifiers can be portions of words combining and recombining together into new signifiers, like the case of the *famillionaire* discussed by Freud, which combined familiar and millionaire, or the case of *Signorelli*, where each segment of the word is open to an associative link. However, in other cases, entire phrases or sentences can be considered as signifiers. In this case, we can find that the same signifier can appear to organize various themes apparently unrelated to each other.

Skewness This indicates the lack of symmetry in the distribution of the sample data values. A negatively skewed distribution means that the curve is skewed to the left and positively skewed distribution means it is skewed to the right. Skewness between -1 and 1 is normally accepted.

Speech/Word (Parole) Speech is not equal to "word." Freud defines psychoanalysis as a treatment through speech, and particularly through the method of free association. The talking cure, as described by one of the first patients in the history of psychoanalysis, is not simply a treatment that "makes use" of speech: it is speech (and not just the analyst or the therapist) that operates and cures. What comes to mind is unexpected to the speaker him/herself. Talking and free associating produces the unconscious. Associative chains show the work of speech, the psychic causality (not the linear causality of logic, but the causality of the signifier). We can say that the psychoanalytic process is this shift *from the discourse to the telling*, thus *from the statement to the enunciation*, or *from repeating to associating*. Speech is original and founding the world; there is no "external" or "objective" reality that is pre-existing. Thus, direction in life is not predetermined and it cannot be simply imposed by the will; rather, it comes as an effect of our saying, in consequence of each speech act.

Standard deviation This is a measure of the spread or dispersion of a set of data. If individual observations vary greatly from the group mean, the standard deviation is large.

Task-centered therapy This is an approach that aims to help clients achieve specific goals in the short term (8–12 sessions). It originated out of the psychodynamic model in the early 1960s. It is often adopted in the social work context and is used with individuals, couples, families, and groups. Reference authors are William J. Reid and Laura Epstein.

Transference The concept of transference (and countertransference) is one of the most complex and controversial concepts in psychoanalysis, due to the various interpretations that different authors and schools have proposed over time. Nevertheless, transference is one of the cornerstones of psychoanalysis, both for the theory and the practice. Freud himself conceptualized transference differently in different stages of his research. Initially, he regarded transference mainly as a false connection and a resistance to the treatment, an obstacle that must be overcome. Gradually, however, he recognized that transference is also the driver of the cure, and "transference interpretation" became a central element of psychoanalytic process. After Freud, transference was commonly conceptualized as a distortion of reality, meaning that the patient's perception of, and attitude and feelings toward, the analyst were understood as reflecting his/her relationships with significant others in the past. Even though transference can manifest itself with very intense affective reactions, Lacan criticized an interpretation that takes into account only the imaginary. Instead, he suggested that the condition for transference is the *supposition* that the Other *knows* (for example, that the other knows something about one's own desire), and that the Other *desires*. Thus, transference is not simply the projection of feelings from the past (toward some other), but a more structural condition that reflects the analysand's peculiar position toward the Other and the questions that s/he addresses to it. Subsequently, Lacan does not mention *counter*transference, but instead he theorizes the *desire of the analyst* as one of the driving forces of the analytic process (not intended as a desire to cure, but rather as a desire to obtain absolute difference, meaning a desire of speech, a desire of analyzing and theorizing).

References

Agassi, J., & Jarvie, I. C. (1969). A study in westernization. In I. C. Jarvie (ed.), *Hong Kong, A Society in Transition: Contributions to the Study of Hong Kong Society.* (pp. 129–163) London: Routledge & Kegan Paul.

Akhtar, S. (ed.) (2007). *Listening to Others: Developmental and Clinical Aspects of Empathy and Attunement.* Lanham, MD: Jason Aronson.

Akhtar, S. (2013). *Psychoanalytic Listening, Methods, Limits, and Innovations.* London: Karnac Books.

Alperin, R. M., & Hollman, B. C. (1992). The social worker as psychoanalyst. *Clinical Social Work Journal*, 20(1), 89–98.

Ames, R. (2005). Collaterality in early Chinese cosmology: An argument for Confucian harmony (he) as *creatio in situ. Taiwan Journal of East Asian Studies*, 2(1), 43–79.

Arnold, K. (2006). Reik's theory of psychoanalytic listening. *Psychoanalytic Psychology*, 23(4), 754–765.

Au, N., Tsai, H., & Leong, K. F. (2009). Working in Macau casinos: The perceptions of Hong Kong tertiary students majoring in hospitality. *Asia Pacific Journal of Tourism Research*, 14(4), 403–417.

Bae, S. H., Joo, E., & Orlinsky, D. E. (2003). Psychotherapists in South Korea: Professional and practice characteristics. *Psychotherapy: Theory, Research, Practice, Training*, 40(4), 302–316.

Barrio Minton, C. A., & Myers, J. E. (2008). Cognitive style and theoretical orientation: Factors affecting intervention style interest and use. *Journal of Mental Health Counseling*, 30(4), 330–344.

Bates, D. G., & Flog, F. (1990). *Cultural Anthropology* (3rd edn.). New York: McGraw-Hill.

Bedford, O., & Hwang, K.-K. (2003). Guilt and shame in Chinese culture: A cross-cultural framework from the perspective of morality and identity. *Journal for the Theory of Social Behaviour* 33, 127–144.

Berger, L. K., Zane, N., & Hwang, W. C. (2014). Therapist ethnicity and treatment orientation differences in multicultural counseling competencies. *Asian American Journal of Psychology*, 5(1), 53–65.

Bergmann, M. (2004). *Understanding Dissidence and Controversy in the History of Psychoanalysis.* New York: Other Press.

Berlo, D. K. (1971). The process of communication. In W. R. Lassey (ed.), *Leadership and Social Change.* Iowa City, IA: University Associates Press.

Bettelheim, B. (1990). *Freud's Vienna and Other Essays.* New York: Knopf.

Bettini, L. G., Strepparava, G., & Rezzonico, G. (1998). L'integrazione in psicoterapia: un'indagine nel servizio pubblico. *Quaderni di Psicoterapia Cognitiva*, 52–65.
Blowers, G. H. (1997). La psychoanalyse en Chine avant 1949, Le rejet ou la distorsion. *Perspectives Chinoises*, 33–39, Centre d'Etudes Francais sur la Chine Contemporaine.
Blowers, G. H. (2003). Chine. In A. de Mijolla, B. Golse, S. de Mijolla-Mellor, & R. Perron (eds.), *Dictionnaire international de la Psychanalyse: Concepts, notions, biographies, oeuvres, evenements, institutions* (Vol.1, Rev. edn., pp. 317–319). Paris: Calmann-Levy.
Bodde, D. (1991). *Chinese Thought, Society, and Science: The Intellectual and Social Background of Science and Technology in Pre-Modern China*. Honolulu: University of Hawai'i Press.
Boey, K. W. (1999). Help-seeking preference of college students in urban China after the implementation of the "open-door" policy. *International Journal of Social Psychiatry*, 45(2), 104–116.
Bohm, T. (2002). Reflections on psychoanalytic listening. *The Scandinavian Psychoanalytic Review*, 25, 20–26.
Bollas, C. (2007). *The Freudian Moment*. London: Karnac Books.
Bollas, C. (2009). *The Infinite Question*. London: Routledge.
Bornstein, R. F. (1999). Objectivity and subjectivity in psychological science: Embracing and transcending psychology's positivist tradition. *Journal of Mind and Behavior*, 20, 1–16.
Bornstein, R. F. (2005). Reconnecting psychoanalysis to mainstream psychology: Challenges and opportunities. *Psychoanalytic Psychology*, 22(3), 323–340.
Boroditsky, L. (2001). Does language shape thought? Mandarin and English speakers' conceptions of time. *Cognitive Psychology*, 43, 1–22
Bouveresse, J. (1995). *Wittgenstein Reads Freud: The Myth of the Unconscious*. Princeton, NJ: Princeton University Press.
Brandell, J. R. (2013). Psychoanalysis in the halls of social work academe: Can this patient be saved? *Journal of Social Work Practice*, 27(3), 235–248.
Brook, T. (1993). Rethinking syncretism: The unity of the three teachings and their joint worship in late-Imperial China. *Journal of Chinese Religions*, 21, 13–44.
Brown, J. G. (2002). *Thinking in Chinese: An American's Journey into the Chinese Mind*. Philadelphia, PA: JB Linguistic Works.
Buckman, J. R. (2006). *Therapeutic Orientation Preferences in Trainee Clinical Psychologists: Personality or Training?* Unpublished dissertation, University College London. Retrieved from http://discovery.ucl.ac.uk/1444357/1/U591660.pdf.
Bushman, B. J. (2002). Does venting anger feed or extinguish the flame? Catharsis, rumination, distraction, anger, and aggressive responding. *Personality and Social Psychology Bulletin*, 28(6), 724–731.
Busiol, D. (2012a). The many names of Hong Kong: Mapping language, silence and culture in China. *Cultura: International Journal of Philosophy of Culture & Axiology*, 12, 207–226.
Busiol, D. (2012b). *Why the unconscious was not "discovered" in China*. Paper presented at the Seventh Annual Conference of the Asian Studies Association of Hong Kong.
Busiol, D. (2013). Comment on Father Valignano's letter to superior general Father Mercurian of 8 February 1574. In V. Volpi, *The Visitor: Valignano, Genius of the Renaissance Who Opened Asia to the West* (pp. 229–236). Milan: Spirali.

Busiol, D. (2015). Factors affecting the understanding and use of psychoanalysis in Hong Kong, Mainland China, and Taiwan. *Journal of the American Psychoanalytic Association*, 63(3), 411–435.
Busiol, D. (2016). Help-seeking behaviour and attitudes towards counselling: A qualitative study among Hong Kong Chinese university students. *British Journal of Guidance & Counselling*, 44(4), 382–401.
Cagape, E. W. (2007). The city that never sleeps. *Asian Correspondent*, November 3. Retrieved from http://asiancorrespondent.com/17143/the-city-that-never-sleeps.
Cesa-Bianchi, M., Rezzonico, G., Strepparava, M. G. (1997). La psicoterapia in Europa: un progetto di ricerca dell'unione European. Retrieved from http://web.tiscali.it/sipcp/Aree/2_Psico_Clinica.html.
Chan, C. K., & Young, A. (2012). *Confucian Principles of Governance: Paternalistic Order and Relational Obligations Without Legal Rules*. Retrieved from http://dx.doi.org/10.2139/ssrn.1986716.
Chan, D. W., & Lee, H. B. (1995). Practices and activities of clinical and educational psychologists in Hong Kong. *Bulletin of the Hong Kong Psychological Society*, 34/35, 57–67.
Chan, S. (1999). The Chinese learner: A matter of style, *Education & Training*, 41(6/7), 294–304. Retrieved from www.emerald-library.com.
Chan, W. (ed.) (1963). *A Source Book in Chinese Philosophy*. Princeton, NJ: Princeton University Press.
Chandler, D. (1994). *The Sapir-Whorf Hypothesis*. Retrieved from http://aber.ac.uk/media/Documents/short/whorf.html.
Chandran, S. (2011). How does psychoanalysis help in reconstructing political thought? An exercise of interpretation. *World Academy of Science, Engineering and Technology*, 5, 677–682.
Chang, C. (2001). Harmony as performance: The turbulence under Chinese interpersonal communication. *Discourse Studies*, 3(2), 155–179.
Chang, D. F., Tong, H., Shi, Q., & Zeng, Q. (2005). Letting a hundred flowers bloom: Counseling and psychotherapy in the People's Republic of China. *Journal of Mental Health Counseling*, 27(2), 104–116.
Chang, H. (2008). Help-seeking for stressful events among Chinese college students in Taiwan: Roles of gender, prior history of counseling, and help-seeking attitudes. *Journal of College Student Development*, 49(1), 41–51.
Chen, A. W., Kazanjian, A., & Wong, H. (2009). Why do Chinese Canadians not consult mental health services: Health status, language or culture? *Transcultural Psychiatry*, 46, 623–641.
Chen, M. J. (2002) Transcending paradox: The "middle way" perspective. *Asia Pacific Journal of Management*, 19, 179–199.
Chen, M. J., & Chen, H. C. (1988). Concepts of intelligence: A comparison of Chinese graduates from Chinese and English schools in Hong Kong. *International Journal of Psychology*, 23, 471–487.
Chen, X. P., & Chen, C. C. (2004). On the intricacies of the Chinese guanxi: A process model of guanxi development. *Asia Pacific Journal of Management*, 21(3), 305–324.
Cheng, C., Lo, B. C. Y., & Chio, J. H. M. (2010). The Tao (ways) of Chinese coping. In M. H. Bond (ed.), *The Oxford Handbook of Chinese Psychology* (pp. 399–419). New York: Oxford University Press.

Cheung, C. M. K., Chiu, P. Y., & Lee M. K. O. (2011). Online social networks: Why do students use Facebook? *Computers in Human Behavior*, 27, 1337–1343.

Cheung, F. (1997). The development of clinical psychology in Hong Kong. *Bulletin of the Hong Kong Psychological Society*, 38/39, 95–109.

Cheung, F. M., Cheung, S. F., Zhang, J., Leung, K., Leong, F., & Huiyeh, K. (2008). Relevance of openness as a personality dimension in Chinese culture aspects of its cultural relevance. *Journal of Cross-Cultural Psychology*, 39(1), 81–108.

Cheung, S. (2001). Problem-solving and solution focused therapy for Chinese: Recent developments. *Asian Journal of Counseling*, 8(2), 111–128.

Chia, R. (2003). From knowledge-creation to the perfecting of action: Tao, Basho and pure experience as the ultimate ground of knowing. *Human Relations*, 56(8), 953–981.

Chin, J. L., Liem, J. H., Domokos-Cheng Ham, M. A., & Hong, G. K. (1993). *Transference and Empathy in Asian American Psychotherapy: Cultural Values and Treatment Needs*. New York: Praeger.

Chodorow, N. (2003). From behind the couch: Uncertainty and indeterminacy in psychoanalytic theory and practice. *Common Knowledge*, 9, 463–487.

Choi, I., Nisbett, R. E., & Norenzayan, A. (1999). Causal attribution across cultures: variation and universality. *Psychological Bulletin*, 125, 47–63.

Chomeya, R. (2010). Quality of psychology test between Likert scale 5 and 6 points. *Journal of Social Sciences*, 6(3), 399–403.

Chomsky, N. (1978). Language and unconscious knowledge. In J. H. Smith (ed.), *Psychoanalysis and Language* (pp. 3–44). New Haven, CT: Yale University Press.

Chong, F. H. H., & Liu, H. Y. (2002). Indigenous counseling in the Chinese cultural context: Experience transformed model. *Asian Journal of Counselling*, 9(1), 49–68.

Clemens, J. (2013). *Psychoanalysis Is an Antiphilosophy*. Edinburgh: Edinburgh University Press.

Cooper, A. M. (2008). American psychoanalysis today: A plurality of orthodoxies. *Journal of the American Academy of Psychoanalysis and Dynamic Psychiatry*, 36(2), 235–253.

Coscollá, A., Caro, I., Avila, A., Alonso, M., Rodríguez, S., & Orlinsky, D. (2006). Theoretical orientations of Spanish psychotherapists: Integration and eclecticism as modern and postmodern cultural trends. *Journal of Psychotherapy Integration*, 16(4), 398–416.

Decker, H. S. (1977). *Freud in Germany: Revolution and Reaction in Science, 1893–1907*. Madison, CT: International Universities Press.

DeFrancis, J. (1984). *The Chinese Language: Fact and Fantasy*. Honolulu: University of Hawai'i Press.

Dragan, N., & Sherblom, J. (2008). The influence of cultural individualism and collectivism on US and Post-Soviet listening styles. *Human Communication*, 11(2), 177–192.

Edward, J. (2009). When social work and psychoanalysis meet. *Clinical Social Work Journal*, 37(1), 14–22.

Eizirik, C. L. (1997). Psychoanalysis and culture: Some contemporary challenges. *The International Journal of Psychoanalysis*, 78, 789–800.

Elliott, R. (2008). A linguistic phenomenology of ways of knowing and its implications for psychotherapy research and psychotherapy integration. *Journal of Psychotherapy Integration*, 18, 40–65.

Elvin, M. (2014). Scientific curiosity in China and Europe. In T. J. Liu, *Environmental History in East Asia: Interdisciplinary Perspectives* (pp. 11–39). London: Routledge.
Fan, Y. (2000). A classification of Chinese culture. *Cross Cultural Management*, 7(2), 3–10.
Fang, T. (2011). Yin Yang: A new perspective on culture. *Management and Organization Review*, 8(1), 25–50.
Fang, T., & Faure, G. O. (2010). Chinese communication characteristics: A yin yang perspective. *International Journal of Intercultural Relations*, 35(3), 329–333.
Faure, G. O., & Fang, T. (2008). Changing Chinese values: Keeping up with paradoxes. *International Business Review*, 17(2), 194–207.
Federn, E. (1992). From psychoanalysis to clinical social work: An evolutionary process. *Clinical Social Work Journal*, 20(1), 9–15.
Fine, R. (ed.) (1987). *Psychoanalysis Around the World*. New York, Haworth.
Fishkin, R. E., & Fishkin, L. P. (2014). Introducing psychoanalytic therapy into China: The CAPA experience. In D. E. Scharff & S. Varvin (eds.), *Psychoanalysis in China* (pp. 205–215). London: Karnac Books.
Foo, K. H. (2007). *Comparing Characteristics, Practices and Experiential Skills of Mental Health Practitioners in New Zealand and Singapore: Implications for Chinese Clients and Cognitive Behaviour Therapy*. PhD thesis, Massey University, Albany, New Zealand.
Freud, S. (1905). On Psychotherapy. In J. Strachey (ed. and trans.), *The Standard Edition of the Complete Psychological Works of Sigmund Freud* (Vol. 7, pp. 257–268). London: Hogarth Press.
Freud, S. (1912). Recommendations to physicians practicing psycho-analysis. In J. Strachey (ed. and trans.), *The Standard Edition of the Complete Psychological Works of Sigmund Freud* (Vol. 12, pp. 111–120). London: Hogarth Press.
Freud, S. (1913). On the beginning of treatment: Further recommendations on the technique of psychoanalysis. In J. Strachey (ed. and trans.), *The Standard Edition of the Complete Psychological Works of Sigmund Freud* (Vol. 12, pp. 122–144). London: Hogarth Press.
Freud, S. (1919). Lines of advance in psycho-analytic therapy. In J. Strachey (ed. and trans.), *The Standard Edition of the Complete Psychological Works of Sigmund Freud* (Vol. 17, pp. 157–168). London: Hogarth Press.
Freud, S. (1925a). Preface to Aichhorn's Wayward Youth. In J. Strachey (ed. and trans.), *The Standard Edition of the Complete Psychological Works of Sigmund Freud* (Vol. 19, pp. 271–275). London: Hogarth Press.
Freud, S. (1925b). An autobiographical study. In J. Strachey (ed. and trans.), *The Standard Edition of the Complete Psychological Works of Sigmund Freud* (Vol. 20, pp. 7–74). London: Hogarth Press.
Freud, S. (1925c). Negation. In J. Strachey (ed. and trans.), *The Standard Edition of the Complete Psychological Works of Sigmund Freud* (Vol. 19, pp. 235–239). London: Hogarth Press.
Freud, S. (1933). New introductory lectures on psycho-analysis. In J. Strachey (ed. and trans.), *The Standard Edition of the Complete Psychological Works of Sigmund Freud* (Vol. 22, pp. 5–182). London: Hogarth Press.
Freud, S. (1937). Analysis terminable and interminable. In J. Strachey (ed. and trans.), *The Standard Edition of the Complete Psychological Works of Sigmund Freud* (Vol. 23, pp. 209–253). London: Hogarth Press.

Freund, P. (ed.) (2012). *Trauma, Desire, Otherness*. Hong Kong: Hong Kong Society of Psychoanalysis.

Fung, Y. L. (1966). *A Short History of Chinese Philosophy*. New York: Macmillan.

Gao, G. (1996). Self and Other: A Chinese perspective on interpersonal relationships. In W. B. Gudykunst, S. Ting-Toomey, & T. Nishida (eds.), *Communication in Personal Relationships across Cultures* (pp. 81–101). Thousand Oaks, CA: Sage.

Gao, G. (1998). Don't take my word for it: Understanding Chinese speaking practices. *International Journal of Intercultural Relations*, 22(2), 163–186.

Gao, G., & Ting-Toomey, S. (1998). *Communicating Effectively with Chinese*. London: Sage.

Gao, G., Ting-Toomey, S., & Gudykunst, W. (1996). Chinese communication processes. In M. H. Bond (ed.), *The Handbook of Chinese Psychology* (pp. 280–293). New York: Oxford University Press.

Geeraerts, G., & Jing, M. (2001). International Relations Theory in China. *Global Society*, 15(3), 251–276.

Gillham, B. (2000). *Developing a Questionnaire*. London: Continuum.

Gordon, T. (1977). *Leader Effectiveness Training L.E.T., The Proven People Skills for Today's Leaders Tomorrow*. New York: Wyden.

Gorman, H. E. (2008). An intention-based definition of psychoanalytic attitude: What does it look like? How does it grow? *Psychoanalytic Revue*, 95(5), 751–776.

Graybar, S. R., & Leonard, L. M. (2005). In defense of listening. *American Journal of Psychotherapy*, 59, 1–18.

Graziani, R. (2007). Quand l'esprit demeure tout seul. *Extrême-Orient, Extrême-Occident*, 29, 5–22.

Green, A. (2005). The illusion of Common Ground and mythical pluralism. *International Journal of Psychoanalysis*, 86, 627–632.

Greenberg, J. R. (1986). The problem of analytic neutrality. *Contemporary Psychoanalysis*, 22, 76–86.

Greenson, R. R. (1960). Empathy and its vicissitudes. *International Journal of Psychoanalysis*, 41, 418–424.

Grünbaum, A. (1985). *The Foundations of Psychoanalysis: A Philosophical Critique* (Vol. 2). Berkeley, CA: University of California Press.

Gu, X.-L. (2003). *A Contrastive Analysis of Chinese and American Views About Silence and Debate*. Paper presented at Intercultural Communication Conference, California State University, Fullerton.

Gullestad, S. E. (2014). Dynamic psychotherapy: A model for teaching and supervision in China. In D. E. Scharff & S. Varvin (eds.), *Psychoanalysis in China* (pp. 231–241). London: Karnac Books.

Haag, A. (2014). Psychoanalytically oriented psychoanalysis and the Chinese self. In D. E. Scharff & S. Varvin (eds.), *Psychoanalysis in China* (pp. 21–32). London: Karnac Books.

Hall, D. L., & Ames, R. T. (1998). *Thinking from the Han: Self, Truth, and Transcendence in Chinese and Western Culture*. Albany, NY: State University of New York Press.

Hall, S. (ed.) (1997). *Representation: Cultural Representations and Signifying Practices* (Vol. 2). London: Sage.

Halliwell, M., & Mousley, A. (2003) *Critical Humanisms: Humanist/Anti-Humanist Dialogues*. Edinburgh: Edinburgh University Press.

Hansell, J. (2008). Psychoanalytic aims and attitudes. *The Psychoanalytic Quarterly*, 4, 1179–1192.

Hansen, C. (1992). *A Daoist Theory of Chinese Thought*. New York: Oxford University Press.

Hansen, J. T. (2000). Psychoanalysis and humanism: A review and critical examination of integrationist efforts with some proposed resolutions. *Journal of Counseling and Development*, 78(1), 21–28.

Hansen, J. T. (2002). Postmodern implications for theoretical integration of counseling approaches. *Journal of Counseling and Development*, 80(3), 315–321.

Haroutunian-Gordon, S. (2007). Listening and questioning. *Learning Inquiry*, 1(2), 143–152.

Heritage Foundation (2014). *Index of Economic Freedom*. Washington, DC. Retrieved from www.heritage.org/index/country/hongkong.

Ho, D. Y. F. (1996). Filial piety and its psychological consequences. In M. H. Bond (ed.), *Handbook of Chinese Psychology* (pp. 155–165). Hong Kong: Oxford University Press.

Hodges, J., & Tian, P. S. (2007). Would Confucius benefit from psychotherapy? The compatibility of cognitive behaviour therapy and Chinese values. *Behaviour Research and Therapy*, 45, 901–914.

Hoffer, A. (1985). Toward a definition of psychoanalytic neutrality. *Journal of the American Psychoanalytic Association*, 33, 771–796.

Hollanders, H., & McLeod, J. (1999). Theoretical orientation and reported practice: A survey of eclecticism among counsellors in Britain. *British Journal of Guidance and Counselling*, 27(3), 405–414.

Hong Kong Council of Social Service. (1979). *Social welfare into the 1980s*. Retrieved from www.swik.org.hk/SWIKPortal/DesktopDefault.aspx?tabIndex=0andtabid=50andItemID=55.

Hong, W., Yamamoto, J., Chang, D.S., & Lee, F. (1993). Sex in a Confucian society. *Journal of the American Academy of Psychoanalysis*, 21(3), 405–419.

Hoshino-Browne, E., Zanna, A. S., Spencer, S. J., & Zanna, M. P. (2004). Investigating attitudes cross-culturally: A case of cognitive dissonance among East Asians and North Americans. In G. Haddock & G. R. Maio (eds.), *Contemporary Perspectives On the Psychology of Attitudes* (pp. 375–397). New York: Psychology Press.

Hsu, F. L. (1949). Suppression versus repression: A limited psychological interpretation of four cultures. *Psychiatry*, 12(3), 223–242.

Hsu, F. L. K. (1971). Psychological homeostasis and jen: Conceptual tools for advancing psychological anthropology. *American Anthropologist*, 73, 23–44.

Huang, H.-Y. (2015). From psychotherapy to psycho-boom: A historical overview of psychotherapy in China. In D. Scharff (ed.), *Psychoanalysis and Psychotherapy in China* (Vol. 1, pp. 1–30). London: Karnac Books.

Huff, T. E. (1993). *The Rise of Early Modern Science: Islam, China, and the West*. Cambridge, UK: Cambridge University Press.

Hwang, K. K. (2009). The development of indigenous counseling in contemporary Confucian communities. *The Counseling Psychologist*, 37(7), 930–943.

Hwang, K. K., & Han, K. H. (2010). Face and morality in Confucian society. In M.H. Bond (ed.), *The Handbook of Chinese Psychology* (pp. 479–498). New York: Oxford University Press.

Imhof, M. (2003). The social construction of listener: Listening behavior across situations, perceived listener status, and cultures. *Communication Research Reports*, 20, 369–378.

Imhof, M., & Janusik, L. A. (2006). Development and validation of the Imhof-Janusik listening concepts inventory to measure listening conceptualization differences between cultures. *Journal of Intercultural Communication Research*, 35(2), 79–98.

Jackson, S. W. (1992). The listening healer in the history of psychological healing. *American Journal of Psychiatry*, 149(12), 1623–1632.

Jaffe, G. (2011). China's Freudian trip. *The Times* (London), January 6.

Ji, L. J., Lee, A., & Guo, T. (2010). The thinking style of Chinese people. In M. H. Bond (ed.), *The Handbook of Chinese Psychology*. New York: Oxford University Press.

Jones, G. R., & George, J. M. (1998). The experience and evolution of trust: Implications for cooperation and teamwork. *Academy of Management Review*, 23(3), 531–546.

Jullien, F. (2001). *Detour and Access: Strategies of Meaning in China and Greece*. New York: Zone Books.

Jullien, F. (2004) *Treatise on Efficacy, Between Western and Chinese Thinking*. Honolulu, University of Hawai'i Press.

Ke, R., & Zhang, W. (2003). *Trust in China, A Cross-Regional Analysis*. William Davidson Institution Working Paper No. 586. Retrieved from http://ssrn.com/abstract=57781.

Kernberg, O. F. (1993). Convergences and divergences in contemporary psychoanalytic technique. *International Journal of Psychoanalysis*, 74, 659–674.

Kiewitz, C., Weaver, J. B., Brosius, H. B., & Weimann, G. (1997). Cultural differences in listening style preferences. *International Journal of Public Opinion Research*, 9, 233–247.

Kihlstrom, J. F. (1987). The cognitive unconscious. *Science*, 237, 1445–1452.

Kihlstrom, J. F. (2008). The psychological unconscious. In O. John, R. Robins, R., & L. Pervin (eds.), *Handbook of Personality: Theory and Research* (3rd edn., pp. 583–602). New York: Guilford.

Killingmo, B. (1989). Conflict and deficits: Implications for technique. *International Journal of Psychoanalysis*, 70, 65–79.

Kim, S. (2004). *Strange Names of God, the Missionary Translation of the Divine Name and the Chinese Responses to Matteo Ricci's "Shangti" in Late Ming China, 1583–1644*. Bern: Peter Lang.

Kirsner, D., & Snyder, E. (2009). Psychoanalysis in China. In S. Akthar (ed.), *Freud and the Far East: Psychoanalytic Perspectives on the People and Culture of China, Japan, and Korea*. Lanham, MD: Jason Aronson.

Kleinman, A. (1980). *Patients and Healers in the Context of Culture: An Exploration of the Borderland Between Anthropology, Medicine, and Psychiatry*. Berkeley, CA: University of California Press.

Kleinman, A. (2011). *Deep China: The Moral Life of the Person*. Berkeley, CA: University of California Press.

Kleinman, A., & Good, B. (eds.) (1985). *Culture and Depression: Studies in the Anthropology and Cross-Cultural Psychiatry of Affect and Disorder*. Berkeley, CA: University of California Press.

Ku, A. S. (2004). Immigration policies, discourses, and the politics of local belonging in Hong Kong (1950–1980). *Modern China*, 30(3), 326–360.

Ku, Y. M., & Anderson, R. C. (2003). Development of morphological awareness in Chinese and English. *Reading and Writing*, 16(5), 399–422.

Kuhn, T. (1962). *The Structure of Scientific Revolutions*. Chicago, IL: University of Chicago Press.

Kung, W. W. (2003). Chinese Americans' help seeking for emotional distress. *Social Service Review*, 77, 110–33.
Kwan, P. Y., & Ng, P. W. (1999). Quality indicators in higher education: Comparing Hong Kong and China's students. *Managerial Auditing Journal*, 14, 20–27.
Lacan, J. (1977). On a question preliminary to any possible treatment of psychosis. In A. Sheridan (ed.), *Écrits: A Selection* (pp. 179–225). London: Tavistock.
Lacan, J. (2006). *Ecrits*. New York and London: Norton.
Lai, M. L. (2001). Hong Kong students' attitudes towards Cantonese, Putonghua and English after the change of sovereignty. *Journal of Multilingual and Multicultural Development*, 22(2), 112–133.
Lambert, M. J., Garfield, S. L., & Bergin, A. E. (2004). Overview, trends, and future issues. *Bergin and Garfield's Handbook of Psychotherapy and Behavior Change*, 5, 805–819.
Lao Tse (2008). *The Book of Tao, Tao Te Ching: The Tao and Its Characteristics*. Translated by James Legge. Maryland: Arc Manor.
Larson, W. (2009). *From Ah Q to Fei Leng*. Stanford: Stanford University Press.
Lau, S.-K., & Kuan, H.-C. (1988). *The Ethos of the Hong Kong Chinese*. Hong Kong: Chinese University Press.
Launer, J. (2005). Anna O and the "talking cure." *Quarterly Journal of Medicine*, 98, 465–466.
Laurent, E. (2006). *Guiding Principles for Any Psychoanalytic Act*. Retrieved from www.lacan.com/ericlaurent.html.
Leclaire, S. (1998). *Psychoanalyzing: On the Order of the Unconscious and the Practice of the Letter*. Stanford, CA: Stanford University Press.
Leichsenring, F. (2005). Are psychodynamic and psychoanalytic therapies effective? A review of empirical data. *The International Journal of Psychoanalysis*, 86(3), 841–868.
Lemmens, F., de Ridder, D., & van Lieshout, P. (1994). The integration of psychotherapy: Goal or utopia? *Journal of Contemporary Psychotherapy*, 24(4), 245–257.
Leong, F. T. (1986). Counseling and psychotherapy with Asian-Americans: Review of the literature. *Journal of Counseling Psychology*, 33, 196–206.
Leung, S. A. (1999). The development of counselling in Hong Kong: Searching for professional identity. *Asian Journal of Counselling*, 6(2), 77–95.
Leung, S. A., Chan, C. C., & Leahy, T. (2007). Counseling psychology in Hong Kong: A germinating discipline. *Applied Psychology, An International Review*, 56(1), 51–68.
Lewis, R. D. (1999). *When Cultures Collide*. London: Nicholas Brealey.
Li, S. (2013). China's (Painful) transition from relation-based to rule-based governance: When and how, not if and why. *Corporate Governance: An International Review*, 21(6), 567–576.
Li, Y. (2014). Research on the development of Chinese psychoanalysts and psychotherapists. In D. E. Scharff & S. Varvin (eds.), *Psychoanalysis in China* (pp. 225–230). London: Karnac Books.
Liang, B., Cherian, J., & Liu, Y. (2010). Concrete thinking or ideographic language: Which is the reason for Chinese people's higher imagery generation abilities? *International Journal of Consumer Studies*, 34(1), 52–60.
Lin, T. (2014). The encounter of psychoanalysis and Chinese culture. In D. E. Scharff & S. Varvin (eds.), *Psychoanalysis in China* (pp. 54–61). London: Karnac Books.

References

Lin, Y. (1948). *The Wisdom of Laotse*. New York: Modern Library.

Lin, Y. N. (2001). The application of cognitive-behavioral therapy to counseling Chinese. *American Journal of Psychotherapy*, 55(4), 46–58.

Liu, C. C. (2013). The Formosa model: An emerging tradition of developing psychoanalysis. In M. T. Hooke, A. Gerlach, & S. Varvin (eds.), *Psychoanalysis in Asia: China, India, Japan, South Korea, Taiwan* (pp. 225–240). London: Karnac Books.

Liu, J., & Rau, P. L. P. (2012). Effect of culture interdependency on interpersonal trust. In Y. G. Ji (ed.), *Advances in Affective and Pleasurable Design* (pp. 160–166). Beijing: CRC.

Liu, Y. (2013). Slow psychoanalysis is helpful for fast developing China. In M. T. Hooke, A. Gerlach, & S. Varvin (eds.), *Psychoanalysis in Asia: China, India, Japan, South Korea, Taiwan* (pp. 105–114). London: Karnac Books.

Liu, Z. (1984). *Society and Politics in Hong Kong*. Hong Kong: Chinese University Press.

Lo, T. W. (2005). Task-centred groupwork: Reflections on practice. *International Social Work*, 48(4), 455–465.

Loewenstein, G. (1994). The psychology of curiosity: A review and reinterpretation. *Psychological Bulletin*, 116, 75–98.

Logan, R. K. (2004). *The Alphabet Effect: A Media Ecology Understanding of the Making of Western Civilization*. New York: Hampton Press.

Lu, D. (2001). Cultural features in speech acts: A Sino-American comparison. *Language Culture and Curriculum*, 14(3), 214–223.

Ma, L. J., & Cartier, C. L. (eds.) (2003). *The Chinese Diaspora: Space, Place, Mobility, and Identity*. Boulder, CO: Rowman & Littlefield.

Ma, N. (2011). Value changes and legitimacy crisis in post-industrial Hong Kong. *Asian Survey*, 51, 683–712.

Maciocia, G. (1989). *The Foundations of Chinese Medicine: A Comprehensive Text for Acupuncturists and Herbalists*. New York: Churchill Livingstone.

McBride-Chang, C., Cho, J. R., Liu, H., Wagner, R. K., Shu, H., Zhou, A., Cheuk, C. S.-M., & Muse, A. (2005). Changing models across cultures: Associations of phonological awareness and morphological structure awareness with vocabulary and word recognition in second graders from Beijing, Hong Kong, Korea, and the United States. *Journal of Experimental Child Psychology*, 92(2), 140–160.

MacKenzie, S. B., Podsakoff, P. M., & Podsakoff, N. P. (2011). Construct measurement and validation procedures in MIS and behavior research: Integrating new and existing techniques. *MIS Quarterly*, 35, 293–334.

Makari, G. (2008). *Revolution in Mind: The Creation of Psychoanalysis*. New York: HarperCollins.

Marecek, J. (1974). *Dimensions of Feminist Therapy*. Paper presented at the 83rd Annual Meeting of the American Psychological Association (Chicago, Illinois). Retrieved from http://files.eric.ed.gov/fulltext/ED119062.pdf.

Maroda, K. J. (2009). Analytic training and the problem of infantilization and dependency. *Contemporary Psychoanalysis*, 45(3), 316–321.

Marquis, A., Hudson, D., & Tursi, M. (2010). Perceptions of counseling integration: A survey of counselor educators. *The Journal for Counselor Preparation and Supervision*, 2(1), 61–73.

Masuda, A., & Boone, M. (2011). Mental health stigma, self-concealment, and help-seeking attitudes among Asian American and European American college students with no help-seeking experience. *International Journal for the Advancement of Counseling*, 33, 266–279.

Maxwell, J. P., & Siu, O. L. (2008). The Chinese Coping Strategies Scale: Relationships with aggression, anger, and rumination in a diverse sample of Hong Kong Chinese adults. *Personality and Individual Differences*, 44(5), 1049–1059.

Mednick, S. (1962). The associative basis of the creative process. *Psychological Review*, 69(3), 220–232.

Mok, M. C. M., Kennedy, K. J., Moore, P. J., Shan, W. J. P., & Leung, S. O. (2008). The use of help-seeking by Chinese secondary school students: Challenging the myth of "the Chinese learner." *Evaluation & Research in Education*, 21(3), 188–213.

Morris, M. W., & Peng, K. (1994). Culture and cause: American and Chinese attributions for social and physical events. *Journal of Personality and Social Psychology*, 67, 949–971.

Mounin, G. (2013). *Semiotic Praxis: Studies in Pertinence and in the Means of Expression and Communication*. New York: Plenum Press.

Murdock, N. L., Banta, J., Stromseth, J., Viene, D., & Brown, T. M. (1998). Joining the club: Factors related to choice of theoretical orientation. *Counselling Psychology Quarterly*, 11(1), 63–78.

Nathan, J. (1993). The battered social work: A psychodynamic contribution to practice, supervision, and policy. *Journal of Social Work Practice*, 7(1), 73–80.

Needham, J. (1956). *Science and Civilisation in China, 2, History of Scientific Thought*. Cambridge, UK: Cambridge University Press.

Needham, J. (1969). *The Grand Titration: Science and Society in East and West*. London: Allen & Unwin.

Neimeyer, R. A. (2009). *Constructivist Psychotherapy*. New York: Routledge.

Ng, R. M., & Li, Z. (2010). East meets west: Current mental health burdens in Greater China. In C. Morgan & D. Bhugra (eds.), *Principles of Social Psychiatry* (pp. 517–530). London: Wiley-Blackwell.

Nisbett, R. E. (2003). *The Geography of Thought: How Asians and Westerners Think Differently, and Why*. New York: Free Press.

Niu, W. (2012). Confucian ideology and creativity. *Journal of Creative Behavior*, 46(4), 274–284.

Niu, W., & Sternberg, R. J. (2002). Contemporary studies on the concept of creativity: The East and the West. *Journal of Creative Behavior*, 36, 269–288.

Norcross, J. C. (1990). Comment: Eclecticism misrepresented and integration misunderstood. *Psychotherapy*, 27, 297–300.

Norcross, J. C., Karpiak, C. P., & Lister, K. M. (2005). What's an integrationist? A study of self-identified integrative and (occasionally) eclectic psychologists. *Journal of Clinical Psychology*, 61(12), 1587–1594.

Norcross, J. C., Karpiak, C. P., & Santoro, S. O. (2005). Clinical psychologists across the years: The division of clinical psychology from 1960 to 2003. *Journal of Clinical Psychology*, 61(12), 1467–1484.

Norman, J., & Rosvall, S. B. (1994). Help-seeking behavior among mental health practitioners. *Clinical Social Work Journal*, 22(4), 449–460.

Okazaki, S. (2002). Influences of culture on Asian American's sexuality. *The Journal of Sex Research*, 39(1), 34–41.

Orlinsky, D. E., Rønnestad, M. H., Willutzki, U., Wiseman, H., & Botermans, J. (2005). The prevalence and parameters of personal therapy in Europe and elsewhere.

In J. D. Geller, J. C. Norcross, & D. E. Orlinsky (eds.), *The Psychotherapist's Own Psychotherapy: Patient and Clinician Perspectives* (pp. 177–191). New York: Oxford University Press.

Osnos, E. (2010). Meet Dr. Freud: Does psychoanalysis have a future in an authoritarian state? *The New Yorker*, January 10. Retrieved from www.newyorker.com/reporting/2011/01/10/110110fa_fact_osnos.

Parker, G., Gladstone, G., & Chee, K. T. (2001). Depression in the planet's largest ethnic group: The Chinese. *American Journal of Psychiatry*, 158(6), 857–864.

Paul, G. L. (1967). Strategy of outcome research in psychotherapy. *Journal of Consulting Psychology*, 31, 109–118.

Peng, K., & Nisbett, R. E. (1999). Culture, dialectics, and reasoning about contradiction. *American Psychologist*, 54(9), 741–754.

Peng, K., Spencer-Rodgers, J., & Zhong, N. (2006). Naïve dialecticism and the Tao of Chinese thought. In U. Kim, K.-S. Yang, & K.-K. Hwang (eds.), *Indigenous and Cultural Psychology: Understanding People in Context* (pp. 247–262). New York: Springer.

Perlovsky, L., Bonniot-Cabanac, M. C., & Cabanac, M. (2010). Curiosity and pleasure. *Proceedings of Neural Networks (IJCNN), The 2010 International Joint Conference* (pp. 1–3). IEEE.

Plänkers, T. (2011). Psychic impact and outcome of the Chinese cultural revolution (1966–1976): A psychoanalytic research project at the Sigmund Freud Institut, Frankfurt (Germany). *International Journal of Applied Psychoanalytic Studies*, 8, 227–238.

Plänkers, T. (2013). When Freud headed for the East: Aspects of a Chinese translation of his works. *International Journal of Psychoanalysis*, 94, 993–1017.

Plotkin, M. B. (1997). Freud, politics, and the porteños: The reception of psychoanalysis in Buenos Aires, 1910–1943. *Hispanic American Historical Review*, 77(1), 45–74.

Poincaré, H. (1913). *The Foundations of Science: Science and Hypothesis, The Value of Science, Science and Method*. New York: The Science Press.

Popper, K. (1988). Science: Conjectures and refutations. In E. Klemke, R. Holinger, & D. Kline (eds.), *Philosophy of Science* (pp. 19–27). Buffalo, NY: Prometheus.

Powell, E. (2007). *Catharsis in psychology and beyond: A historic overview*. Primal Psychotherapy Page. Retrieved from: http://primal-page.com/cathar.html.

Price, R. B. E., & Ho, J. K. S. (2012). Mainlanders as "others" in the life and law of Hong Kong. *King's Law Journal*, 23(3), 233–255.

Public Opinion Program, the University of Hong Kong (2014). *Survey on Hong Kong People's Ethnic Identity*. Retrieved from http://hkupop.hku.hk/english/release/release1150.html.

Puig, A., Yoon, E., Callueng, C., An, S., & Lee, S. M. (2014). Burnout syndrome in psychotherapists: A comparative analysis of five nations. *Psychological Services*, 11(1), 87–96.

Purdy, M., & Borisoff, D. (1997). *Listening in Everyday Life: A Personal and Professional Approach*. Boston, MA: University Press of America.

Pye, L.W. (1992). *The Spirit of Chinese Politics*. Cambridge, MA: Harvard University Press.

Qian, M., Smith, C. W., Chen, Z., & Xia, G., (2002). Psychotherapy in China: A review of its history and contemporary directions. *International Journal of Mental Health*, 30(4), 49–68.

Randall Groves, J. (2010). *Chinese Mentality and Chinese Identity*. Retrieved from www.freewebs.com/randoc/Chinese Mentality and Chinese Identity.doc.
Rascovsky, A. (2006). Contemporary psychoanalysis in ethnic Chinese societies, new developments. *International Journal of Psychoanalysis*, 87(2), 573–576.
Redding, G. (1990). *The Spirit of Chinese Capitalism*. New York: Walter de Gruyter.
Reik, T. (1948). *Listening with the Third Ear: The Inner Experience of a Psychoanalyst*. New York: Jove Publications.
Roazen, P. (1995). *How Freud Worked: First-Hand Accounts of Patients*. Northvale, NJ: Aronson.
Robbins, S. B. (1989). Role of contemporary psychoanalysis in counseling psychology. *Journal of Counseling Psychology*, 36(3), 267–278.
Rogers, C. (1951). *Client-Centred Therapy: Its Current Practice, Implications and Theory*. London: Constable.
Roland, A. (1989). Individuation, development, and psychopathology: A cross-civilizational view. *Issues in Ego Psychology*, 12(1), 29–35.
Roy, D. (2003). *Taiwan: A Political History*. Ithaca, NY: Cornell University Press.
Rudowicz, E., & Au, E. (2001). Help-seeking experiences of Hong Kong social work students: Implications for professional training. *International Social Work*, 44(1), 75–91.
& Yue, X. D. (2000). Concepts of creativity: Similarities and differences among mainland, Hong Kong and Taiwanese Chinese. *Journal of Creative Behavior*, 34(3), 175–192.
Sandy, S. V., Boardman, S. K., & Deutsch, M. (2000). Personality and conflict. In M. Deutsch, P. T. Coleman, & E. C. Marcus (eds.), *The Handbook of Conflict Resolution: Theory and Practice* (pp. 289–315). San Francisco, CCA: John Wiley & Sons.
Saporta, J. (2011). Freud goes to China: Teaching psychoanalysis in a different culture – a dialogue. *Talking Cures* 9(1), online at www.academia.edu/1484000/Freud_goes_to_China_Teaching_psychoanalysis_in_a_different_culture_-_A_Dialogue.
Saporta, J. (2014). Psychoanalysis meets China: Transformative dialogue or monologue of the Western voice? In D. E. Scharff & S. Varvin (eds.), *Psychoanalysis in China* (pp. 73–86). London: Karnac Books.
Sass, L. A. (1989). Humanism, hermeneutics, and humanistic psychoanalysis: Differing conceptions of subjectivity. *Psychoanalysis & Contemporary Thought*, 12, 433–504.
Schachter, J., Schachter, J. S., & Kächele, H. (2012). *Traditional psychoanalytic process: A concept ready for retirement*. Retrieved from http://internationalpsychoanalysis.net/wp-content/uploads/2012/12/SchachterPsaprocessdec211.pdf.
Schafer, R. (1983). *The Analytic Attitude*. New York: Basic Books.
(2005). Listening in psychoanalysis. *Narrative*, 13(3), 271–280.
Scharff, D. (2014). Five things Western therapists need to know for working with Chinese therapists and patients. *International Journal of Applied Psychoanalytic Studies*, 11(1), 48–59.
Scheff, T. J. (2007). Catharsis and other heresies: A theory of emotion. *The Journal of Social, Evolutionary, and Cultural Psychology*, 1(3), 98–113.
Schlesinger, H. J. (2013). *The Texture of Treatment: On the Matter of Psychoanalytic Technique*. London: Routledge.

References

Schlösser, A.-M. (2009). Oedipus in China: Can we export psychoanalysis? *International Forum of Psychoanalysis*, 18, 219–224.

Scragg, P., Bor, R., & Watts, M. (1999). The influence of personality and theoretical models on applicants to a counselling psychology course: A preliminary study. *Counselling Psychology Quarterly*, 12(3), 263–270.

Scull, A. (2011).Contested jurisdictions: Psychiatry, psychoanalysis, and clinical psychology in the United States, 1940–2010. *Medical History*, 55, 401–406.

Selmer, J. (2002). Coping strategies applied by Western vs overseas Chinese business expatriates in China. *International Journal of Human Resource Management*, 13, 19–34.

Shannon, C. E. (1948). A mathematical theory of communication. *Bell System Technical Journal*, 27, 379–423.

Shea, M., & Yeh, C. J. (2008). Asian American students' cultural values, stigma, and relational selfconstrual: Correlates of attitudes toward professional help seeking. *Journal of Mental Health Counseling*, 30, 157–172.

Shedler, J. (2010). The efficacy of psychodynamic psychotherapy. *American Psychologist*, 65(2), 98–109.

Shi, Q. J., Sang, Z. Q., Li, X. Q., Zhou, J., & Wang, H. F. (2005). Current status of counseling and psychotherapy in China. In Q. J. Shi, Q. F. Zeng, X. C. Sheng, & W. Senf (eds.), *Psychotherapy: Theories and Practice* (pp. 21–34). Beijing: Chinese Medicine Pharmacy Science Publishing House.

Sing, M. (2009). The quality of life in Hong Kong. *Social Indicators Research*, 92(2), 295–335.

Sivin, N. (1973). Copernicus in China. *Studia Copernicana*, 6, 63–122.

Sivin, N. (1982). Why the scientific revolution did not take place in China–or didn't it? *East Asian Science, Technology, and Medicine*, 5, 45–66.

Sjodin, C. (2006). Interview with Jan Stensson. *International Forum of Psychoanalysis*, 15, 3–12.

Slingerland, E. (2003). *Confucius, Analects, With Selections from Traditional Commentaries*. Indianapolis, IN: Hackett.

Snyder, E. (2009). Psychoanalysis and globalization. Retrieved from http://internationalpsychoanalysis.net/wp-content/uploads/2009/09/ChinaSnyder.pdf.

Soho, T. (2010). *Tao Te Ching: Zen Teachings on the Taoist Classic*. Boston, MA: Shambhala Publications.

Soto, J. A., Perez, C. R., Kim, Y. H., Lee, E. A., & Minnick, M. R. (2011). Is expressive suppression always associated with poorer psychological functioning? A cross-cultural comparison between European Americans and Hong Kong Chinese. *Emotion*, 11(6), 1450–145.

Staples, K. C. (2002). *Reading Hong Kong Chinese Culture: Hybridity or Eclecticism, a Matter of Contemporary Configuration*. Unpublished doctoral dissertation, Edith Cowan University. Retrieved from http://ro.ecu.edu.au/theses/753/.

Stewart, J. (1983). Interpretive listening: An alternative to empathy. *Communication Education*, 32, 379–391.

Stewart, S. M., Lewinsohn, P. M., Lee, P. W., Ho, L. M., Kennard, B., Hughes, C. W., & Emslie, G. J. (2002). Symptom patterns in depression and "subthreshold" depression among adolescents in Hong Kong and the United States. *Journal of Cross-Cultural Psychology*, 33(6), 559–576.

Stoltenberg, C. D., & Delworth, U. (1987). *Supervising Counsellors and Therapists: A Developmental Approach*. San Francisco, CA: Jossey-Bass.
Sun, L. (1991). Contemporary Chinese culture: Structure and emotionality. *The Australian Journal of Chinese Affairs*, 26, 1–41.
Swartz, L., Gibson, K., Richter, L., & Gelman, T. (eds.) (2002). *Reflective Practice: Psychodynamic Ideas in the Community*. Cape Town: HSRC Press.
Tam, V. C. W., & Lam, R. S. Y. (2005). Stress and coping among migrant and local-born adolescents in Hong Kong. *Youth & Society*, 36(3), 312–332.
Tan, Z. (2007). Questioning in Chinese EL classrooms: What lies beyond it? *Regional. Language Centre Journal*, 38(1), 87–103.
Tang, T. T., Reilly, J., & Dickson, J. M. (2012). Attitudes toward seeking professional psychological help among Chinese students at a UK university. *Counselling and Psychotherapy Research*, 12(4), 287–293.
Tata, S. P., & Leong, F. T. L. (1994). Individualism-collectivism, social network orientation, and acculturation as predictors of attitudes toward seeking professional psychological help among Chinese Americans. *Journal of Counseling Psychology*, 41, 280–287.
Thomson-Salo, F. (2013). The world is looking east: Growth and development of psychoanalysis in the Asian region. *International Journal of Psychoanalysis*, 94(6), 1205–1207.
Ting, K. F., & Chiu, C. C. H. (2000). Materialistic values in Hong Kong and Guangzhou: a comparative analysis of two Chinese societies. *Sociological Spectrum*, 20, 15–40.
Toadvine, T. (2007). Culture and cultivation: Prolegomena to a Philosophy of Agriculture. In C. S. Brown & T. Toadvine (eds.), *Nature's Edge: Boundary Explanations in Ecological Theory and Practice* (pp. 207–222). Albany, NY: SUNY Press.
Tsang, S. (2004). *A Modern History of Hong Kong*. Hong Kong: Hong Kong University Press.
Tseng, W.-S. (2004). Culture and psychotherapy: Asian perspectives. *Journal of Mental Health*, 13, 151–161.
Tsoi, M. M., & Lam, D. J. (1991). The practice of behavior therapy among clinical psychologists in Hong Kong. *Journal of Behavior Therapy and Experimental Psychiatry*, 22(2), 75–82.
Varvin, S., & Gerlach, A. (2014). The development of psychodynamic psychotherapy and psychoanalysis in China. In D. E. Scharff & S. Varvin (eds.), *Psychoanalysis in China* (pp. 189–215). London: Karnac Books.
Vasco, A. B., Garcia-Marques, L., & Dryden, W. (1992). Eclectic trends among Portuguese psychotherapists. *Journal of Psychotherapy Integration*, 2(4), 321–331.
Vaughan, S. C., Spitzer, R., Davies, M., & Roose, S. P. (1997). The definition and assessment of analytic process: Can analysts agree? *International Journal of Psychoanalysis*, 78(5), 959–974.
Veenstra, C. (2004). Listening between Arabs and Americans. *Listening Professional*, 3, 5–30.
Vehviläinen, S. (2003). Preparing and delivering interpretations in psychoanalytic interaction. *Text*, 23, 573–606.
Verdiglione, A. (1986). *Processo alla parola*. Milan: Spirali.
Verdiglione, A. (1992). *La congiura degli idioti*. Milan: Spirali/Vel.

Wallerstein, R. S. (1991). *The Common Ground of Psychoanalysis*. Northvale, NJ: Aronson.

Wallerstein, R. S. (2010). The training analysis: Psychoanalysis' perennial problem. *The Psychoanalytic Review*, 97(6), 903–936.

Wang, F. (2007). "Western discourse" and contemporary Chinese culture. *Frontiers of Literary Studies in China*, 1(2), 197–212.

Watkins, D. A., & Biggs, J. B. (eds.) (2001). *Teaching the Chinese Learner: Psychological and Pedagogical Perspectives*. Hong Kong: Hong Kong University Press.

Watson, K. W., Barker, L. L., & Weaver, J. B. (1995). The listening styles profile (LSP16): Development and validation of an instrument to assess four listening styles. *International Journal of Listening*, 9, 1–13.

Watters, E. (2010). The Americanization of mental illness. *New York Times*. Retrieved from www.nytimes.com/2010/01/10/magazine/10psyche-t.html.

Wen, H. (2009). *Confucian Pragmatism as the Art of Contextualizing Personal Experience and World*. Lanham, MD: Lexington Books.

Wenzel, C. H. (2010). Isolation and involvement: Wilhelm von Humboldt, François Jullien, and More. *Philosophy East and West*, 60(4), 458–475.

White, R. S. (2001). The interpersonal and Freudian traditions: Convergences and divergences. *Journal of the American Psychoanalytic Association*, 49, 428–455.

Widlöcher, D. (2010). Distinguishing psychoanalysis from psychotherapy. *International Journal of Psychoanalysis*, 91(1), 45–50.

Wolvin, A. D., & Coakley, C. G. (1982). *Listening*. Dubuque, IA: William C. Brown Publishers.

Wong, V. T. C. (2013). Recruitment and training of psychiatrists in Hong Kong: What puts medical students off psychiatry. An international experience. *International Review of Psychiatry*, 25(4), 481–485.

World Health Organization (WHO) (2011). *Mental Health Atlas 2011*. Geneva: WHO. Retrieved from www.who.int/mental_health/evidence/atlas/profiles/en/#J.

Worthington, R., & Whittaker, T. (2006). Scale development research: A content analysis and recommendations for best practices. *Counseling Psychologist*, 34, 806–838.

Wright, A. (1953). The Chinese language and foreign ideas. In A. F. Wright (ed.), *Studies in Chinese Thought*. Chicago, IL: University of Chicago Press.

Wu, K. M. (1998). *On the "Logic" of Togetherness*. Leiden: Brill.

Wurmser, L. (2011). Metaphor as conflict, conflict as metaphor. *Psychoanalytic Inquiry*, 31(2), 107–125.

Xu, Y., Qiu, J., Chen, J., & Xiao, Z. (2014). The development of psychoanalytic psychotherapy in Shanghai mental health center. In D. E. Scharff & S. Varvin (eds.), *Psychoanalysis in China* (pp. 196–204). London: Karnac Books.

Yang, J. (2013). "Fake happiness": Counseling, potentiality, and psycho-politics in China. *Ethos*, 41, 292–312.

Yang, J., Morris, M. R., Teevan, J., Adamic, L., & Ackerman, M. (2011). *Culture Matters: A Survey Study of Social Q&A Behavior*. Barcelona, Spain: ICWSM – International Conference on Weblogs and Social Media.

Yang, W., & Ye, H. (2014). Theoretical psychology in China: Past, present, and future. *Theory & Psychology*, 24(6), 813–829.

Yang, Y. (2011). The challenge of professional identity for Chinese clinicians in the process of learning and practicing psychoanalytic psychotherapy: The discussion on the frame of Chinese culture. *International Journal of Psychoanalysis*, 92, 733–743.

Yang, Y. (2013). Psychoanalytic psychotherapy in the Chinese context: Developments and challenges. In M. T. Hooke, A. Gerlach, & S. Varvin (eds.), *Psychoanalysis in Asia: China, India, Japan, South Korea, Taiwan* (pp. 73–86). London: Karnac Books.

Ye, S., Ng, T. K., Yim, K. H., & Wang, J. (2015). Validation of the Curiosity and Exploration Inventory–II (CEI–II) Among Chinese university students in Hong Kong. *Journal of Personality Assessment*, 97(4), 403–410.

Yi, K. (1995). Psychoanalytic psychotherapy with Asian clients: Transference and therapeutic considerations. *Psychotherapy, Theory, Research, Practice, Training*, 32(2), 308–316.

Yip, K. S. (2002). Social workers' counselling role in psychiatric services in Hong Kong. *Asia Pacific Journal of Social Work and Development*, 12(2), 25–43.

Yip, K. S. (2004). Controversies in psychiatric services in Hong Kong: Social workers' superiority and inferiority complexes. *International Social Work*, 47(2), 240–258.

Young, A. (1992). A tale of two cities: Factor accumulation and technical change in Hong Kong and Singapore. In O. J. Blanchard and S. Fischer (eds.), *NBER Macroeconomics Annual 1992* (Vol. 7, pp. 13–64). Cambridge, MA: MIT Press.

Yu, C. K.-C. (2006). Defence mechanisms and suggestibility. *Contemporary Hypnosis*, 23, 167–172.

Yu, C. K. C., Fu, W., Zhao, X., & Davey, G. (2010). Public understanding of counselors and counseling in Hong Kong. *Asia Pacific Journal of Counseling and Psychotherapy*, 1(1), 47–54.

Yuen, M., Leung, S. A., & Chan, R. T. (2014). Professional counseling in Hong Kong. *Journal of Counseling & Development*, 92(1), 99–103.

Zachrisson, A. (2011). Dynamics of psychoanalytic supervision: A heuristic model. *The International Journal of Psychoanalysis*, 92(4), 943–961.

Zeal, P. (2008). Listening with many ears. *European Psychotherapy*, 8(1), 89–101.

Zerbetto, R., & Tantam, D. (2001). The Survey of European Psychotherapy Training 3: What psychotherapy is available in Europe? *European Journal of Psychotherapy, Counselling & Health*, 4(3), 397–405.

Zhang, J. (1992). *Psychoanalysis in China. Literary Transformations 1919–1949*. New York: Cornell University Press.

Zhang, J. (2003). *Psychoanalysis in the Chinese Context*. IIAS International, Institute for Asian Studies. Retrieved from www.iias.nl/iiasn/30/IIASNL30_08_Zhang.pdf.

Zhang, L. (2014). Bentuhua: Culturing psychotherapy in postsocialist China. *Culture, Medicine, and Psychiatry*, 38(2), 283–305.

Zhiping, S. (2003) Aspects of parataxis vs. hypotaxis between English and Chinese. *Journal of Northeast Normal University (Philosophy and Social Sciences)*, 2, p. 92–98.

Zhiyan, W., & Zachrisson, A. (2014). Transference and countertransference in a Chinese setting: Reflections on a psychotherapeutic process. In D. E. Scharff & S. Varvin (eds.), *Psychoanalysis in China* (pp. 166–176). London: Karnac Books.

Zhong, J. (2011). Working with Chinese patients: Are there conflicts between Chinese culture and psychoanalysis? In D. E. Scharff & S. Varvin (eds.), *Psychoanalysis in China* (pp. 150–156). London: Karnac Books.

Zhou, Y. (2008). The modern significance of Confucianism. *Asian Social Science*, 4(11). 13–16.

Zou, X., Tam, K. P., Morris, M. W., Lee, S. L., Lau, Y. M., & Chiu, C. Y. (2008). *Culture as Common Sense: Perceived Consensus vs. Personal Beliefs as Mechanisms of Cultural Influence*. Working paper, Columbia University, New York.

Zuo, B. (2001). Lines and circles, West and East. *English Today*, 67, 3–8.

Index

acculturation 136
action-orientation 22, 38, 71, 74–5, 158
active listening 63–4, 105, 134
aggressive feelings 73, 91, 168, 170
Alessandro Valignano 145
American Psychological Association 30
Analects 21, 166
analysand 47, 56–7, 166
après-coup 47
Argentina: psychoanalysis in 33
Aristotelian logic 9, 36, 38, 103, 123, 162
Aristotle 25, 161–2
Asian American 20, 117
attention: free floating or evenly hovering or evenly suspended 49, 51–6, 58, 62, 65, 99, 103–5, 112–4, 167; focused 82, 85, 104–5, 111–14, 129–131;
avoidant strategies 28

balance 36–8, 43, 69, 162
Buddhism 13, 34–5, 108, 120, 132, 156–7

catharsis 25–6, 136
causality 37, 68, 172
China American Psychoanalytic Association (CAPA) 13, 71, 143
Chinese communication 24, 112, 114–15
Chinese culture 2, 3, 8, 11, 20, 25–6, 36–7, 41–4, 69, 74, 107, 157, 159–65; and Hong Kong culture 107, 132–4
Chinese language 39, 42–3, 115, 155
Chinese thinking 37, 39, 41–2, 69, 75, 162
Christianity 19, 21, 34, 132, 154, 164

Cicero 162
cognition 156
collectivism 148–53
colony 7, 14, 139
combinatorial 41, 80, 103, 130–1
combining approaches 79–81, 94, 103, 130–1
community 19, 69, 116, 167
Concrete: solution 75, 141; thinking 69; question 71
condensation 52, 168
condominium 35, 109
Confidence interval 80, 82, 89, 111, 166
Conflicts with Hong Kong Chinese Culture scale (CHKCC) 89–90, 92–4, 96–8, 100, 103, 126–8, 134–5, 142
conformity/conformism 24, 41, 74, 152–3, 158, 160
confucianism 21–3, 34–5, 38, 40, 117, 125, 151–2, 154
Confucius 21–2, 40, 162, 166
contemplation 56
correlations among variables 87, 89, 92, 94–8, 127, 134
couch 51, 58, 60, 104
counseling 61–64; in Hong Kong 18–21, 106–10, 128–32, 139–42; and psychoanalysis 67–8, 87; among Chinese 69, 75, 112, 117, 140; scales 81, 82, 87–8
counseling approaches in Hong Kong 19–20, 78, 106–7, 108–10, 139
Counseling Attitude toward Clinical Work Scale 76, 79, 81–2, 85, 87–9, 96–8, 100–1, 111, 134
counseling professionals: in Hong Kong 77, 106, 110, 140–2; in Mainland China 139–40, 143–4;

creativity 38, 40–1, 131, 136, 165
crisis 8, 38, 139
criticalities against psychoanalysis 66–7, 68–75, 89–92
Cronbach's alpha 80, 82, 89, 167
Cultural Revolution 12, 14–15, 139
culture 72–3, 135
curiosity 56, 60, 107, 136, 160–4

Daoism 34–5, 38, 108, 117, 125, 132, 157
Darwinism 8
desire 151–2, 155–6, 168–9, 171–2; of the analysts 144–5
discourse 8, 21, 43, 45, 64, 167
displacement 52, 168
dogmatism 1–2, 29, 32, 36, 164
dualism 38–9, 41
duality 38–9, 41

eclecticism 28–33, 36, 71, 89, 108–10, 126, 129, 131, 135
effects of culture 135
empathy 54, 63, 81, 107, 124–5, 160, 169
empirical research 41, 68
episteme and techne 35, 167
Exploratory Factor Analysis 167

factor analysis 5, 80, 82, 102, 158, 167
Feuerbach 162
free will 8, 121, 153
free-association 23, 47, 55, 58–9, 62, 136, 148, 171
Freud, Sigmund 7–9, 29, 45–7, 51–3, 65

German–Chinese Academy for Psychotherapy 143
God 34, 36, 154
Greek thought 21, 25, 156–7, 160–1, 163–4, 167

harmony 23–6, 36–7, 69, 116–7, 162
help-seeking behaviors 19, 20, 24, 25, 27
high-context cultures 122–3
history of therapy 97, 100, 103–4, 127, 129–30, 140
Hong Kong 7–11, 13–14; history 14–16; culture 16–18, 23–6, 73, 74, 89, 103–5, 112, 127–8, 132–5; society 14–18, 26–8, 117;
humanism 106–8

Hume 162
hysteria 72, 170

imaginary registry 54–5, 105, 131, 157, 169–70
indifferenz 49
indigenization 7, 135–6
individualism 148–53
integration 28–32, 36–7, 39, 108–10
interdependence 152, 160
interpreting 28, 54–5, 62, 123, 142
Introspection 42, 69, 72, 117, 136
Introspection 69, 155
invention 9, 130–1, 136–7, 147–8, 150, 159, 165, 169–70

Kant 162
Kleinian 13, 53
knowledge 21, 34, 41, 157–164, 167
Kuhn, Thomas 8
Kurtosis 80, 82, 89, 167

Lacan, Jacques 57, 59, 150, 152, 155, 167–8
lapsus 52, 61, 136
Leonardo da Vinci 45
listening 4, 165, 170; in psychoanalysis 49–61, 99, 101–2, 129, 136–7, 156; in counseling 61–6, 134; in Chinese culture 27, 113–15, 161, 164; across cultures 121–3; Interpretive and empathic 53–4, 123–4, 164; in Hong Kong 110–12, 119, 136
listening cure 4, 53
listening in counseling 61, 64, 66, 101
listening oriented cultures 136, 165
listening profile 76, 112 123
listening styles 121
logos 21, 23, 36
low-context cultures 123

maieutics 159
manifest meaning 49, 52, 63, 87, 136, 158, 170
Marxism 8, 34
Matteo Ricci 145
meditation 56, 156–7
Minimum Average Partials (MAP) test 80
monotheism 34, 36
multiple regression analysis 5, 77, 93, 96, 103, 134–5
mutuality 27, 117, 149, 161

nachträglichkeit 47, 168
narcissism of minor differences 48, 168
Needham, Joseph 8, 35, 37, 39, 124
negation 52–3, 55
neutrality of the analyst 49, 70, 108, 125
Nietzsche, Friedrich 147

obsessive discourse 169–71
obsessive discourse 170–1
Opening: subscale 157–8, 161
openness 59, 158
Other 61, 104, 152–5, 168

paradoxes 9, 49, 60, 130, 162
Parallel Analysis 80
Pavlovian psychology 12
personal experience 5, 44
personal: analysis 51, 60, 71, 106, 121; therapy 78, 102–4, 140–1, 143, 150
personality 72, 153–4, 158
Plato 9, 157
pragmatism 32, 107–8
predictors 93, 96–8, 103–4
privacy 24, 107
Psyche 11, 147, 150
psychic life 59, 68
psychoanalysis 45–8, 136: origin 7–8; diffusion 9–11; indifference to 11, 136–7; in Chinese contexts 11–14, 18, 78, 106–7, 114–21, 138–9; criticalities against 66–7, 90–1, 100, 126–8, 132–5; ineffectiveness 68, 79, 89, 91, 126, 128, 134; complexity 70, 90, 100, 126, 128, 137
Psychoanalytic Attitude towards Clinical Work Scale (PACWS) 76, 79, 81–3, 87–9, 96–8, 102, 111, 134
psychoanalytic listening 4, 50–5, 57–61, 101–2, 130–1, 135, 165; components 77, 98–9, 100, 111
psychoanalytic: attitude 4, 7, 11, 48–50, 110, 135; conversation 51, 55–6, 60, 62; training 70–1, 89–90, 121, 126–9, 138–9
psychoanalytic theory 29, 47–50, 67; variable in this study 88, 94, 96–8, 100, 102, 106, 112, 127–30, 135, 142; in Hong Kong 2–3, 48, 137, 140, 165
psycho-boom in China 139–40
psychology 12–13, 30, 67–8, 143, 150; Chinese 33–4
psychotherapy 9, 29, 45–8, 58, 61, 67, 72

questioning 159

reception of psychoanalysis 7, 11, 47, 89, 121, 125–6, 134–5, 138–40, 144; across cultures and societies 33
reciprocity 27, 125, 161
Reik, Theodor 54
relations in Chinese culture 23–4, 36, 114, 117–9, 148, 154
religion 34–5, 109, 131–2, 141
representation 52, 104, 131, 163
repression 25–6, 47, 52–3, 56, 74, 142, 147
resistance 51–2, 57, 103–5, 136, 142, 144, 168, 172
rhetoric 21, 43, 124, 157, 164

Schopenhauer, Arthur 147
sectarianism 29, 36
self 46, 55, 117–20, 148–52
selfless 149
sexuality 29, 47, 107, 121, 168
shame 19, 25, 117
Signifiers 59, 62–3, 104, 121, 150–2, 171–2
silence 56, 113, 116, 157
single orientation 31–2, 110
Sino-Norway Continuous Training Program 143
Skewness 80, 82, 89, 171
slips of the tongue 52–3, 167
social network 25, 27
social sciences 68, 161, 164
solitude 47, 152, 154
somatization 25–6, 145
speaking in Chinese culture 114–15
speaking oriented cultures 136, 165
speech 9, 11, 44, 49, 171–2; in psychoanalysis 55–7, 59–60, 64, 150–3, 156–7; attitude toward 21–3, 75, 116–7, 121, 125, 132, 136; in counseling 61–3
St. Augustine 162
Standard deviation 80, 82, 89, 126, 172
subconscious 120, 147–8
subject 8, 52–3, 59, 61, 150–54, 157
superego 47, 147–8
suppression 25–6, 28
symbolic registry 131
syncretism 34–5, 132

Taiwan 13, 18–9, 143, 145
talking cure 4, 50, 53, 136–7, 171
tertium non datur 36
theoretical midpoint 111, 126–7, 158

Theorization 29–30, 34, 46, 165
therapy: narrative 20, 78, 168; client-centered or person-centered 63, 78, 106, 108–9, 169; cognitive 30, 74, 78, 106, 139; behavioral 14, 28, 61, 108; play 78, 169; positive psychology 78, 106, 139, 169; brief 78, 10, 166; task-centered 78, 106, 172
Three Teachings 34–5
transference 50–1, 57, 60, 68, 99, 138, 144, 172; scale 79, 83, 96, 104, 129–30; in Chinese context 70, 116–19, 123
trauma 49, 58, 139, 168
tripartite system 99, 138
trust 16, 19, 24, 63, 117
truth 32, 36, 49, 74–5, 114, 121, 157, 164

unconscious, in Chinese language 120–1, 156, 165
utilitarian familism 16, 148

validity 79–80, 87
void 156–7

Weltanschauung 30, 45
Western discourse 3, 9, 15, 36, 75, 136, 147, 153, 164–5
Western theories: use of 33, 40, 69
westernization 10, 164
working culture 128, 135
working units 149

yin-yang 39

Zhang, Dongsung 11
Zhuangzi 149

Helping you to choose the right eBooks for your Library

Add Routledge titles to your library's digital collection today. Taylor and Francis ebooks contains over 50,000 titles in the Humanities, Social Sciences, Behavioural Sciences, Built Environment and Law.

Choose from a range of subject packages or create your own!

Benefits for you
- Free MARC records
- COUNTER-compliant usage statistics
- Flexible purchase and pricing options
- All titles DRM-free.

Benefits for your user
- Off-site, anytime access via Athens or referring URL
- Print or copy pages or chapters
- Full content search
- Bookmark, highlight and annotate text
- Access to thousands of pages of quality research at the click of a button.

REQUEST YOUR FREE INSTITUTIONAL TRIAL TODAY

Free Trials Available
We offer free trials to qualifying academic, corporate and government customers.

eCollections – Choose from over 30 subject eCollections, including:

Archaeology	Language Learning
Architecture	Law
Asian Studies	Literature
Business & Management	Media & Communication
Classical Studies	Middle East Studies
Construction	Music
Creative & Media Arts	Philosophy
Criminology & Criminal Justice	Planning
Economics	Politics
Education	Psychology & Mental Health
Energy	Religion
Engineering	Security
English Language & Linguistics	Social Work
Environment & Sustainability	Sociology
Geography	Sport
Health Studies	Theatre & Performance
History	Tourism, Hospitality & Events

For more information, pricing enquiries or to order a free trial, please contact your local sales team:
www.tandfebooks.com/page/sales

The home of Routledge books

www.tandfebooks.com